101 WAR MOVIES

YOU MUST SEE BEFORE YOU DIE

101 WAR MOVIES
YOU MUST SEE BEFORE YOU DIE

GENERAL EDITOR
STEVEN JAY SCHNEIDER

A Quint**essence** Book

First edition for the United States and Canada
published in 2009 by Barron's Educational Series, Inc.

ISBN-13: 978-0-7641-6275-6
ISBN-10: 0-7641-6275-6
QSS.KWAR

Library of Congress Number: 2009923826

All inquiries should be addressed to:
Barron's Educational Series, Inc.
250 Wireless Boulevard
Hauppauge, NY 11788
www.barronseduc.com

This book was designed and produced by:
Quint**essence**
226 City Road
London EC1V 2TT
www.1001beforeyoudie.com

Project Editor	Chrissy Williams
Editor	James Harrison
Editorial Assistant	Helena Baser
Designer	Howard Sherwood
Editorial Director	Jane Laing
Publisher	Tristan de Lancey

Color reproduction in Singapore by Pica Digital Pte Ltd.
Printed in China
9 8 7 6 5 4 3 2 1

BORN
TO
KiLL

CONTENTS

INTRODUCTION Steven Jay Schneider, General Editor

The war movie is arguably, and ironically, the most philosophical of film genres. This is the case despite—or perhaps because of—its essential focus on something "based on true events"; true to the historical "facts"; inspired by actual people, incidents, and events. Too often for its own good, philosophy deals in abstractions, in theories, whereas the war movie typically focuses on often intense life-or-death acts, choices, and situations. That in itself changes audiences' perceptions about what is right and what is wrong and (surprisingly perhaps for what is mostly action-adventure) makes them think. War movies put philosophy—philosophies—to the test.

If horror movies provide a "bounded" experience of fear, allowing coming-of-age adolescents (in particular) to contemplate death in a hyperbolic, distanced, and ultimately safe manner, war movies offer no such buffer. They force a confrontation with, and contemplation of, the most terrifying monster of all: humankind, and its apparently inescapable need to commit atrocities against aspects of itself.

However, it is indisputable that the worst in us humans tends to bring out the best in us. And so, in the films discussed, analyzed, and celebrated herein, one finds an astonishing amount of heroism on display. At the end of the day, that may not be (sadly, almost certainly isn't) enough to outweigh all the needless death and destruction depicted in these films. But it does give one reason to hope—occasionally to marvel—at the good we humans are capable of effecting when push really does come to shove.

Steven J. Schneider

Hollywood, California

D.W.
GRIFFITH'S
· AMERICAN INSTITUTION ·
THE BIRTH OF A NATION
"THE SUPREME PICTURE OF ALL TIME"
NEW YORK MAIL
MAY 2ND 1921

THE BIRTH OF A NATION 1915 (U.S.)

Director D. W. Griffith **Producer** D. W. Griffith **Screenplay** D. W. Griffith, Frank E. Woods (based on the novel by Thomas Dixon) **Cinematography** G. W. "Billy" Bitzer **Music** Joseph Carl Breil **Cast** Ralph Lewis, Lillian Gish, Mae Marsh, Henry B. Walthall, George Siegmann, Joseph Henabery, Mary Alden, Miriam Cooper

---

D. W. Griffith's landmark *The Birth of a Nation* is technically accomplished, emotionally moving, epic in its battle sequences, and often horrifying in its depiction of race and race relations during the American Civil War and the Reconstruction era. Griffith's wildly popular epic tale, also the first feature-length film, is certainly a masterpiece, but it is often impossible to reconcile technical prowess and accomplished storytelling with a picture that helped the then-moribund Ku Klux Klan to rise from the ashes. It was controversial right from the start, when it premiered as *The Clansman*, the title of the blatantly racist Thomas Dixon novel upon which it is based.

The grand storyline follows the Northern Stoneman family—progressive statesman Austin (Lewis), daughter Elsie (Gish), and sons—and the Camerons of South Carolina—a larger brood that includes daughter Flora (Marsh) and son Ben (Walthall)—as they are plunged into Civil War. The valiant Ben is wounded, becomes smitten with Elsie, and is appalled at the changes occurring in the South during Reconstruction, particularly the rise of mulatto Northern Silas Lynch (Siegmann) to a position of political power. After Flora jumps to her death rather than face

◄

Despite its pro–Ku Klux Klan stance, *The Birth of a Nation*'s success allowed for increased running times, higher ticket prices, and a new respectability for the "flickers" among middle-class Americans.

rape at the hands of a former slave, Ben forms the Ku Klux Klan. In the film's still impressively edited climax, Ben successfully rescues Elsie from a forced marriage with Lynch, and the two lovers are shown riding triumphantly with the Klan to save the rest of the Cameron family from Lynch's militia.

There are many disturbing moments in Griffith's epic, several of them involving the depiction of the African-American male

"IF WE CONVEYED THAT WAR MAY BE HELD IN ABHORRENCE, THIS EFFORT WILL NOT HAVE BEEN IN VAIN." *INTERTITLE*

as sexual predator, most infamously so in a shot of newly installed black statesmen looking up lasciviously toward a group of white women in the gallery. Any viewer also must contend with the depiction of mixed-race characters as hypersexual and intrinsically evil, as is seen in both Silas and his conniving housekeeper. Finally, there is Griffith as puppet master, brilliantly attempting to manipulate an audience via smart shot selection and masterful editing into finding the KKK heroic. Still, Griffith deserves high praise for employing so many cinematic innovations—from cross-cutting between different planes of action to marvelous use of the iris shot—into a potent roller coaster of emotions. In its smaller moments, *Birth* can be quite touching, as when the camera follows Ben's return home, down the street and into the arms of his sister and mother, the door respectfully closing upon the trio. **JL**

► The authentic scenes depicting battlefield carnage were inspired by Matthew Brady's contemporary photographs.

SCALA  THEATRE

CHARLOTTE STREET, FITZROY SQUARE, W.

Proprietor : E. Distin Maddick.

OFFICIAL PROGRAMME

❖ ❖ ❖

Under Distinguished Patronage.

AT THE FRONT

Including

The BATTLE of the SOMME

Daily at 3 and 8.

THE BATTLE OF THE SOMME 1916 (U.K.)

Directors Geoffrey H. Malins, J. B. McDowell **Producer** William F. Jury under the auspices of the War Office Cinematograph Committee set up in 1916 under Sir Max Aitken **Cinematography** Geoffrey H. Malins, J. B. McDowell **Editors** Geoffrey H. Malins, Charles Urban **Cast** No actors; all soldiers fighting on the Front

Made during World War I, *The Battle of the Somme* was a silent propaganda film and documentary prepared by official British cinematographers Geoffrey H. Malins and J. B. McDowell. For its time, and despite being intended as patriotic propaganda, the film presented a shockingly "real" portrayal of trench warfare, showing dead and dying British and German soldiers. Some of the scenes of troops going over the tops of the trenches were staged prior to the beginning of the actual battle, but Malins and McDowell captured many iconic images from the first day of combat (July 1, 1916), when they were near the front lines.

The duo had not set out to make a feature, but once the quality and sheer volume of their footage was seen in London, the British Topical Committee for War Films made the decision to compile a feature-length film. The completed picture spanned five reels and lasted around 63 minutes. To the extent that *The Battle of the Somme* was given an official propaganda function, it came in a message from David Lloyd George, Secretary of State for War, which was read to the audience at the film's first screening on August 10, 1916: "I am convinced that when you have seen this wonderful picture, every heart will

This is an official program for the 1916 release of the documentary. Propaganda films came of age in World War I when morale boosters were commissioned.

beat in sympathy with its purpose, which is no other than that every one of us . . . shall see what our men at the Front are doing and suffering for us, and how their achievements have been made possible by the sacrifices made at home."

Two weeks later the film began showing in 34 London cinemas, opening in provincial cities the following week. It was eventually screened in 18 countries. The film was even shown

"[WITH THIS FILM] A COMPLETE IDEA OF THE SITUATION WILL BE REVEALED BEFORE THEIR EYES." *THE LONDON TIMES (1916)*

to British soldiers at rest in France, where it gave new recruits some conception of what they were about to face. The main criticism from the soldiers was that it failed to capture the sounds of battle. The title cards were remarkably forthright, however, describing in detail the graphic images of injury and death. The British public considered *The Battle of the Somme* a morale booster, and for the most part it was favorably received by critics, although some considered it immoral to broadcast scenes of violence. The Dean of Durham, for example, protested "against an entertainment which wounds the heart and violates the very sanctity of bereavement." But public response was huge, with an estimated 20 million tickets sold in only two months (that would equal about half of the U.K.'s population at the time)—a record not broken until the release of the Star Wars franchise some 60 years later. **KW**

► The British perspective was followed in 1917 by several aggressive American efforts to inspire hatred of the enemy and boost recruitment, notably *To Hell with the Kaiser.*

THE BIG PARADE 1925 (U.S.)

Director King Vidor **Producer** Irving Thalberg **Screenplay** Harry Behn (from a story by Laurence Stallings) **Cinematography** John Arnold **Music** William Axt, David Mendoza **Cast** John Gilbert, Renée Adorée, Hobart Bosworth, Claire McDowell, Claire Adams, Robert Ober, Tom O'Brien, Karl Dane, Kathleen Key

In the manner of his other masterworks, *The Crowd* (1928) and *Our Daily Bread* (1934), director King Vidor conceived *The Big Parade* as an effort to convey the experience of an ordinary man at war—in contrast to the episodic, impersonal spectacles of the typical war movies of the time. It is not, however, an explicitly anti-war picture (in the manner of the later *All Quiet on the Western Front* [1930]), though at the time the sheer novelty of its dramatic realism made it seem that way. Vidor explained, "I do not wish to appear to be taking any stand about war. I certainly do not favor it, but I would not set up a preachment against it." At the box office, it proved the most financially successful of all silent films.

In précis the narrative sounds trite: John Gilbert plays a society wastrel who joins up, falls in love with a French farm girl, sees his friends killed, and loses a leg in the fighting. However, the film itself boasts a powerful realism, not only in the vivid, still shocking glimpses of trench warfare and hand-to-hand combat, but also in the early comic scenes, contrasting the romantic propaganda version of army life with the often crude realities. The whole of the film's first hour, in fact, alternates

◄

Vidor's silent movie account of the fighting in World War I mixed the terrors of trench warfare with a clichéd romance (as audiences in peacetime were looking for more escapism).

roughhouse army comedy and pastoral romance, and it is only in the second half that the horrors of war intrude fully. By this time our emotional investment in the characters is such that the random injustice of their fates carries real dramatic impact.

The superbly rhythmic editing and constant sense of movement (both physical and dramatic) ensure the film is never boring, despite its considerable length. In his book *On*

"ALL THE WAR PICTURES HAD BEEN GLAMOROUS . . . THERE HAD NEVER BEEN ONE ABOUT THE ORDINARY GUY." *VIDOR*

Film-Making, Vidor recalled that "each one of the several thousand scenes [was] trimmed to start as late as possible and end the moment the climax was reached." This care in post-production pays off in the film's many set piece highlights, among them the visually impressive "big parade" of troops and tank reinforcements making its perilous and seemingly endless journey down a long, dusty road; the incredibly tense scene in which the soldiers progress slowly through an eerie, sun-dappled wood infested with concealed snipers; and the powerful sequence in which Gilbert proves incapable of killing a wounded German soldier he has followed into a shell-hole, instead offering him a final cigarette.

There is undeniable power in Vidor's vision of a doughboy's episodic odyssey through the vast landscape of war, and one is never left in any doubt that he was a major talent. **MC**

► Early filmmakers were reluctant to make war movies because the set pieces, such as the eponymous big parade shown here, were very expensive to recreate, requiring hundreds of extras in authentic outfits.

THE GENERAL 1927 (U.S.)

Directors Clyde Bruckman, Buster Keaton **Producers** Buster Keaton, Joseph M. Schenk **Screenplay** Buster Keaton, Clyde Bruckman, Al Boasberg, Charles Henry Smith (based on the book by William Pittenger) **Cinematography** Bert Haines, Dev Jennings **Cast** Buster Keaton, Marion Mack, Glen Cavender, Jim Farley, Frank Barnes

Hollywood history is full of great films that for one reason or another failed to click with the paying public at the time of their original release. Either they were ahead of their time or simply, through no fault of their own, out of fashion. But *The General* appeared in a climate warmly disposed both to Keaton himself and to silent comedy generally, yet somehow it proved a failure and was more or less ignored until the Keaton revival got underway in the 1960s. It is now routinely cited as Keaton's masterpiece and quite possibly the greatest silent comedy of them all, and though he luckily lived to see the picture's rehabilitation, it effectively marked the end of his great years as a filmmaker.

Fascinatingly, *The General* was actually inspired by a true story (which was later retold by Disney in 1956 as *The Great Locomotive Chase*) in which a gang of Union spies stole a Confederate locomotive in April of 1862. Keaton uses this true event as a springboard for a relentless chase comedy in which his Southern engine driver has to chase and retrieve his beloved locomotive (the titular General) and save his girl (Mack) who happens to be aboard at the time.

◄

The poster tries to exploit Keaton's comic trademark— his "stone face" expression.

Few other comedies are so tightly controlled, so carefully structured and so perfectly balanced in their maintenance of dramatic momentum while at the same time keeping up a seemingly unbroken stream of unflaggingly inventive gags. Indeed the film's most certain claim to greatness lies in the seamless integration of its gags within the narrative; not a one feels grafted on or fails to pay off in terms of plot. And because

"RAILROADS ARE A GREAT PROP. YOU CAN DO SOME AWFUL WILD THINGS WITH RAILROADS." BUSTER KEATON

the audience is genuinely concerned that Keaton's mission should prove successful, his comic inventiveness is not merely hilarious but also dramatically exciting. His persona, too, seems better suited to our age than those of many of his contemporaries: he is essentially a minimalist, he neither strains for effect nor attempts to generate emotion, maintaining instead an attitude of unyielding stoicism, however maliciously the fates seem to conspire against him, that is both funny and oddly inspiring.

One of the film's more surprising incidental merits is its highly convincing sense of period, with every detail of props, costumes, engines, and weapons meticulously researched and accurately recreated. Like a book of old sepia photographs brought magically to life, it evokes the atmosphere of the Civil War better than many a straight drama. **MC**

► Undoubtedly his finest film, Buster Keaton's fast-paced comedy-adventure saw him pitted against a gang of Confederate train-nappers.

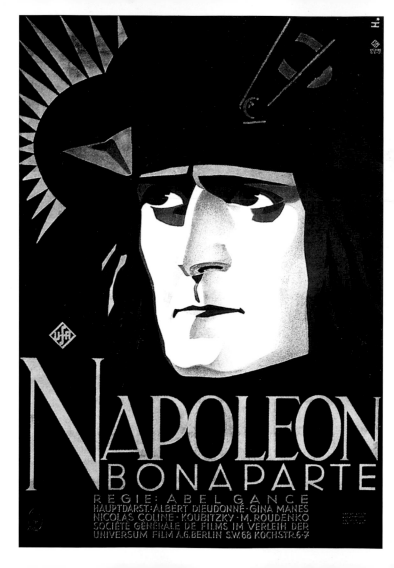

NAPOLEON 1927 (FRANCE)

Director Abel Gance **Screenplay** Abel Gance **Cinematography** Léonce-Henri Burel, Jules Kruger, Joseph-Louis Mundwiller, Nikolai Toporkoff **Music** Arthur Honegger **Cast** Albert Dieudonné, Vladimir Roudenko, Edmond Van Daële, Alexandre Koubitzky, Antonin Artaud, Abel Gance, Gina Manès, Suzanne Bianchetti

One of the most ambitious productions in motion picture history, Abel Gance's *Napoleon* is a six-hour silent epic that tells the story of the rise of Napoleon I of France. It begins with Napoleon's youth, where he managed a schoolyard snowball fight like a military campaign, and ends with his victorious invasion of Italy in 1797. Despite the fact that Gance was unable to complete his plan to tell Napoleon's entire life story over the course of six movies, audiences are nevertheless carried away by the beautiful construction and the lyrical quality of its images. The pace is breathless, the result of new techniques that Gance invented specifically for this picture, including cameras on horseback or on swings, and the superimposition of images. As for Arthur Honegger's score, it remains as powerfully seductive as when it was first composed. And the fact that the final reel of *Napoleon* was intended to be screened as a triptych via triple project (or Polyvision) was a great publicity coup upon the film's initial release in 1927.

Nowadays, however, critics focus more on Gance's historical rigor than on his stylistic innovations; and it is true that nothing in this production was left to chance. In terms of historical

◄
This epic masterpiece was produced in Polyvision, which allowed it to be screened at three times the standard size.

accuracy, it is a masterpiece. And Gance loved *Napoleon* so much that he released later versions, notably one with sound, a feature the director had planned for when he made the actors articulate the words of the dialogue for the soundtrack that was to come (with Antonin Artaud giving the most dramatic performance of Marat in the history of the cinema). *Napoleon* was first screened in a gala premiere at the Paris Opéra in April

"FEW FILMS HAVE TRUMPETED THE TECHNICAL INNOVATIONS OF THE ART FORM IN . . . THE SAME WAY." *MATT BARRY*

1927. It had only been shown in eight European cities before Metro-Goldwyn-Mayer bought out the rights; after it was screened intact in London, it was cut dramatically in length, with only the central panel of the widescreen sequences retained before being put on limited release in the United States. Sadly, it was only indifferently received there, at a time when talkies were just starting to appear.

The film was restored and has been re-released a number of times, most successfully in the 1990s by Kevin Brownlow, with a live orchestra conducted by Carl Davis, running to five hours. There is also a four-hour version by Francis Ford Coppola, with music by his father Carmine. Largely as a result of these restorations, *Napoleon* is today regarded as the definitive film of the life of the French general, and one of the unrivalled masterpieces of early French cinema. **KW**

▶
Albert Dieudonné is the perfect embodiment of Bonaparte.

WINGS 1927 (U.S.)

Director William Wellman **Producer** Lucien Hubbard **Screenplay** John
Monk Saunders (story), Hope Loring, Louis D. Lighton, Julian Johnson (titles)
Cinematography Harry Perry **Music** J. S. Zamecnik **Cast** Clara Bow, Charles
Rogers, Richard Arlen, Jobyna Ralston, El Brendel, Richard Tucker, Gary Cooper

Paramount's *Wings* was the studio's premiere release for 1927, a
then incredibly expensive two million dollar production that
would do for the air corps what *The Big Parade* (1925) had done
for the army. As in many a big-budget studio film, the
spectacular stunts and set pieces are far more enthralling than
the melodramatic, sometimes sluggish storyline, which finds
neighbors Jack Powell (Rogers) and David Armstrong (Arlen) in
love with the same woman, Sylvia Lewis (Ralston), who only has
eyes for wealthy David. Top-billed Clara Bow is the neglected
Mary Preston, who pines away for middle-class Jack. When Jack
and David train to become fighter pilots, they put class
differences aside, becoming best friends. Indeed, the story
works best when the two men develop what we might now
term a "bromance." Friendship ends in tragedy, however, when
Jack mistakes the valiant David for a German pilot and shoots
his plane down. Jack returns to small-town America, keeping
David's heroism alive and settling down with Mary.

Though the creative reins of what would eventually become
Wings passed through several celebrated hands, including
D. W. Griffith and Victor Fleming, the project ended up under

◀
**The first and only
silent movie to
win an Oscar for
Best Picture, *Wings*
focused on the
air force.**

the command of relative novice William "Wild Bill" Wellman, the only Hollywood director who had actually flown World War I combat missions. The demanding Wellman, with the aid of the War Department, shot most of the picture over a period of six months in San Antonio, Texas, employing more than 3,500 infantry men and 72 planes to capture the climactic Battle of Saint Michel. Pilots often functioned as cameramen, and

> ## "THEY GAVE ME WINGS BECAUSE I WAS THE ONLY DIRECTOR WHO HAD BEEN A FLYER, IN ACTION." WILLIAM WELLMAN

cameras were even strapped onto planes, thrilling audiences with a realism heretofore not encountered in a war movie. But even the smaller scenes manage to impress, for example when the camera travels through a smoky Parisian nightclub filled with bubbles to rest on the very inebriated Jack.

Wings, the first film to win the Academy Award for what is now considered Best Picture, continues to influence filmmaking in many aspects. Tony Scott studied *Wings'* magnificent aerial sequences when making *Top Gun* (1986), hoping to capture the same heart-pounding spectacle. And while many remember a young Gary Cooper in the small, poignant role of a doomed pilot, they've forgotten the focus on Cooper's cache of Hershey's chocolate bars, one of early cinema's most prominent instances of product placement. Or maybe everyone would just like to forget and instead concentrate on the thrills? **JL**

▶
The flying sequences were shot in an early widescreen process called Magnascope, which used two projectors to fill the screen.

ALL QUIET
ON THE
WESTERN FRONT

Directed by **LEWIS MILESTONE** • *a* **CARL LAEMMLE** Jr. Production • *Story by* **ERICH MARIA REMARQUE**
Adaptation and Dialogue by **MAXWELL ANDERSON** *and* **GEORGE ABBOTT**

A UNIVERSAL PICTURE

ALL QUIET ON THE WESTERN FRONT 1930 (U.S.)

Director Lewis Milestone **Producer** Carl Laemmle Jr. **Screenplay** Lewis Milestone, Maxwell Anderson, George Abbott, Del Andrews **Cinematography** Arthur Edeson, Karl Freund **Music** Sam Perry, Heinz Roemheld **Cast** Lew Ayres, Louis Wolheim, Slim Summerville, John Wray, Raymond Griffith, Russell Gleason, Beryl Mercer

Though it returned only a modest profit on its then-massive production budget, *All Quiet on the Western Front* was instantly recognized as the first complete masterpiece of the all-talking cinema, giving the relatively second-string Universal Studios a huge critical and popular success, and their first Best Picture Oscar winner (and their last until 1973).

Shot simultaneously as a talkie and a silent (the latter a reel longer in running time), it is the talkie that made the impact, with the added dimension of terrifyingly vivid sound effects making the scenes of trench warfare even more harrowing and convincing than those of *The Big Parade* (1925), which the picture closely resembles in several key respects. The big difference, of course, is that while Vidor's film was cynical about war it was not a pacifist tract, taking care to provide its hero with a happy future at the fade-out. Milestone's film, by contrast, is unerring in its commitment to the view that the futility of war contaminates, degrades, and ultimately destroys all it touches. As the opening caption makes clear, it is the story

◄
Based on the classic anti-war novel by Erich Maria Remarque, the movie took Academy Awards for Best Picture and Best Director.

of "a generation of men who, even though they may have escaped its shells, were destroyed by the war." The film's most famous sequence remains its ending, in which Lew Ayres carelessly reaches for a butterfly that has landed near the loophole of his trench and is gunned down by a French sniper. Throughout, however, the pre–Hays Code detail remains startling. A scene in which Ayres first stabs in the throat and

> "OUR BODIES ARE EARTH AND OUR THOUGHTS ARE CLAY, AND WE SLEEP AND EAT WITH DEATH." PAUL BÄUMER

then pathetically tends to a French soldier until he dies, though reminiscent of a similar scene in *The Big Parade*, is vastly more disturbing in its realism, as is a shock moment in which a soldier grappling with barbed wire is hit by a shell, leaving only his severed hands still clinging to the wire when the smoke clears.

Superbly directed by Milestone, with massive, swooping crane shots, pans, and sweeps emphasizing the sheer inhuman scale of the war, *All Quiet on the Western Front* is also notable for the art direction of Charles D. Hall, whose German village set is now instantly familiar from its incessant reuse in later Universal horror movies. The convincingly boyish Lew Ayres stands out amongst the uniformly excellent cast: ironically, considering the universal praise the film received for its unequivocal pacifism, when Ayres declared himself a conscientious objector during World War II, it virtually ended his career. **MC**

▶

Lew Ayres (left) was anti-war himself on moral grounds, which did him no favors with the Hollywood establishment.

THE CHARGE OF
THE LIGHT BRIGADE 1936 (U.S.)

Director Michael Curtiz **Producers** Hal B. Wallis, Jack L. Warner **Screenplay** Michael Jacoby, Rowland Leigh, Alfred Lord Tennyson (poem) **Cinematography** Sol Polito **Music** Max Steiner **Cast** Errol Flynn, Olivia de Havilland, Patric Knowles, Henry Stephenson, Nigel Bruce, Donald Crisp, David Niven, C. Henry Gordon, Robert Barrat

Loosely drawn from Alfred Lord Tennyson's poem about the infamous military blunder that took place during the Crimean War in 1854, this highly fictionalized film adaptation saves the incident for the climax. It focuses instead on brothers Geoffrey and Perry Vickers (Flynn and Knowles, respectively) who have a falling out over a woman, Elsa Campbell (de Havilland), while soldiering in Imperial India, then meet again in 1856 when Geoffrey—now a Major—leads some 600 lancers in the eponymous "charge" against an artillery encampment in the treacherous Balaklava valley.

According to the film, this suicide charge against the combined forces of the Russian army and the Indian ruler Surat Khan (Gordon) wasn't a mistake at all, but a calculated act of revenge on the part of Vickers' regiment—known as the 27th Lancers—for an earlier massacre perpetrated by Khan at a British outpost where women and children were slaughtered. It seems these brave soldiers were more than willing to lay down their lives to achieve vindication, and that they created enough

◄

Errol Flynn was the swaggering action hero in the early era of sound—the true heir of Douglas Fairbanks.

of a diversion to help the British win the war. (Well, not really, but that's the movies for you.) Flynn was only 27 years old when he made *The Charge of the Light Brigade*, and was at the very top of his game after *Captain Blood* the year before, which was also directed by Michael Curtiz, had made him one of Hollywood's biggest stars. Funny and cunning here, his one blind spot is his love of Elsa; while he's been out fighting with his men and

"I HAVE A COWARDLY AVERSION TO MEETING REPTILES SOCIALLY 'TIL I'VE HAD ONE SHERRY." *SIR C. MACEFIELD*

making friends with the enemy in India, she has unintentionally fallen for Perry. The film's light, adventure-heavy first half ends with Geoffrey shooting a leopard and thereby saving Khan's life, only to return home unaware of the drama that had unfolded without him.

It is actually a little disconcerting to see Flynn on the losing end of the battle for de Havilland, given his leading man status and the fact that their best-known work together is as Robin Hood and Maid Marian in Curtiz's wonderful *The Adventures of Robin Hood* (1938). Fortunately, however, Curtiz downplays the sudsy romance in favor of military action, vividly re-creating the Light Brigade's charge in a sweeping ten-minute set piece of men and horses dashing across a battle-marred landscape. The result is stirring entertainment with some noble sentiments thrown in, albeit very little regard for history. **KW**

▶
The infamous charge recreated with Curtiz's well-honed skills for action-adventure sequences. A 1968 movie with the same name produced a more horrific charge.

JEAN GABIN
PIERRE FRESNAY
et
ERIC VON STROHEIM
dans

LA GRANDE ILLUSION

Adaptation et dialogues de
JEAN RENOIR et **CHARLES SPAAK**

Musique de **KOSMA**

avec **DALIO**

Un film de
JEAN RENOIR

LA GRANDE ILLUSION 1937 (FRANCE)

Director Jean Renoir **Producers** Albert Pinkovitch (uncredited), Frank Rollmer (uncredited) **Screenplay** Charles Spaak, Jean Renoir **Cinematography** Christian Matras **Music** Joseph Kosma **Cast** Jean Gabin, Marcel Dalio, Dita Parlo, Pierre Fresnay, Erich von Stroheim, Julien Carette, Georges Péclet, Werner Florian, Jean Dasté

Directed by Jean Renoir, son of the Impressionist painter Pierre-Auguste Renoir, *La Grande Illusion* (a.k.a *The Grand Illusion*) debuted during a period of extreme economic and political turmoil in Europe. The scars from World War I had not yet healed, and the threat of renewed violence was palpable. Consequently, it is tempting to read Renoir's depiction of French prisoners and their sympathetic German captors during the First World War as merely a pacifist film against a rising tide of nationalist fervor and fascist politics in Germany, Italy, and Spain. However, this overlooks the film's expansive scope—*La Grande Illusion* is a profound critique of the imaginary edifices human beings erect to support absolute difference. These "grand illusions" perpetuate discrimination based on race, class, and ethnicity, that prevent people from recognizing their shared humanity.

When, following the film's initial release, Joseph Goebbels condemned *La Grande Illusion*, it was obvious that Renoir's work had far exceeded the boundaries of a simple call for peace or condemnation of violence. In its depiction of the friendship forged between the working class soldier, Lt. Maréchal (Gabin), and the wealthy, altruistic Lt. Rosenthal (Dalio), Renoir exploded

◄ Renoir's complex story became the first foreign language film (and is still one of only a few) to be nominated for an Oscar for Best Picture.

stereotypes informing anti-Semitic propaganda. Additionally, their friendship revealed the potential for a new perception of solidarity among people of various ethnicities and social classes that, as aristocratic characters like Capt. de Boeldieu (Fresnay) and Capt. Von Rauffestein (von Stroheim) grudgingly acknowledge, threatened to topple antiquated cultural hierarchies based on familial and racial privilege. In a time of

"YOU CAN'T SEE BORDERS, THEY'RE MAN-MADE. NATURE COULDN'T CARE LESS." LT. ROSENTHAL

escalating tensions between capitalist nations with long-standing traditions, such ideas proved too dangerous to foster, and the film was quickly banned throughout Europe.

By eliding battle sequences, Renoir's film focuses instead upon on the human toll that armed international conflict exacts upon people irrespective of race, class, sex, and religion. In war, every combatant is susceptible to the destructive properties of bullets and disease. Renoir's film acknowledges that the suffering does not end there. During *La Grande Illusion*'s final reels, Maréchal and Rosenthal find sanctuary in the home of Elsa (Parlo), a German farmer who has lost her husband and brothers to the war and is now caring for her farm and daughter on her own. In her budding romance with Maréchal and tenderness toward an ailing Rosenthal, Renoir counters the "illusion" with the possibility of the creation of a transcendent human family. **JM**

► Fresnay as a French officer is unsure whether to follow his patriotic duty to escape, or his personal code of honor not to disgrace the camp commandant (von Stroheim) in such an attempt.

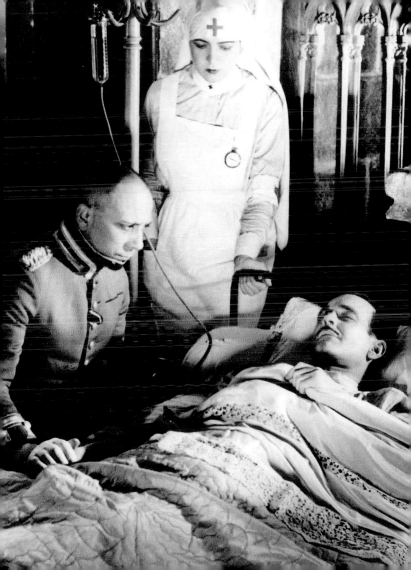

Charlie Chaplin

in **THE** *Great*

Produced, Written and Directed by CHARLES CHAPLIN

DICTATOR

with Paulette Goddard

JACK OAKIE · HENRY DANIELL · REGINALD GARDINER
BILLY GILBERT · MAURICE MOSCOVICH
RELEASED THRU UNITED ARTISTS

THE GREAT DICTATOR 1940 (U.S.)

Director Charles Chaplin **Producer** Charles Chaplin **Screenplay** Charles Chaplin
Cinematography Karl Struss, Roland Totheroh **Music** Charles Chaplin, Meredith
Willson **Cast** Charles Chaplin, Paulette Goddard, Jack Oakie, Henry Daniell,
Reginald Gardiner, Billy Gilbert, Grace Hayle, Carter Del laven, Maurice Moscovitch

Arriving five years after Charlie Chaplin's previous film (*Modern Times* [1935]) to intense speculation and not a little controversy, *The Great Dictator* was Chaplin's first all talking film. It was also the last appearance of his traditional tramp characterization, here recast as a timid Jewish barber who just happens to be the exact double of fascist dictator Adenoid Hynkel.

The idea that Chaplin should play Hitler had been suggested many times, but the real impetus to make the film emerged after Chaplin's first hand experience of the craven atmosphere of appeasement, justification, and even outright support that Hitler's fascists received in certain sections of the Hollywood community. With America neutral and most U.S. citizens keen to stay that way, the idea of lampooning so volatile a world leader seemed to many an unconscionable act of provocation, and much effort was put into trying to close the production. But unconditional support from President Roosevelt ensured the project would go ahead, and Chaplin responded by abandoning all caution, playing Hynkel as a homicidal megalomaniac, ranting in pidgin German, dancing with an inflatable globe, and in one extraordinary moment ending a frenzied oration by

◄
**Chaplin's satirical
assault on Hitler
and Mussolini
alerted Americans
to the facist threat
from Germany
and Italy.**

pouring iced water down the front of his trousers, presumably to cool his erection. Supporting his lead performance, Chaplin cast portly comic actor Billy Gilbert as Herring (Goering), taciturn character actor Henry Daniell as Garbitsch (Goebbels) and, most cleverly of all, Jack Oakie as Napaloni, a brilliant takeoff of Mussolini. It was a difficult shoot: Chaplin's notorious creative indecision resulted in scores of reshoots and last-minute

"I'M SORRY, BUT I DON'T WANT TO BE AN EMPEROR. THAT'S NOT MY BUSINESS."

CHARLIE CHAPLIN IN THE GREAT DICTATOR

changes, some of them requiring the complete rebuilding of torn-down sets. Meanwhile the events of the war, worsening daily as they shot, threatened to overwhelm the production.

What finally emerged is an often strange and schizophrenic mix of impassioned polemic and broad clowning. This is even more disquieting when the two streams merge, such as when Chaplin and Paulette Goddard dodge murderous storm troopers on the ghetto streets with beautifully choreographed slapstick maneuvers, and in the famous finale in which Chaplin steps out of both characters to deliver an impassioned pacifist monologue. Though he later claimed that he would have been entirely unable to make the film had he known the full extent and horror of "the homicidal insanity of the Nazis," it proved a valued and successful gesture of comic defiance, provoking cheers and standing ovations when shown in Blitz-torn Britain. **MC**

► Chaplin's portrayal of maniacal dictator Adenoid Hynkel is a hilarious and effective satire of Adolf Hitler.

BUCK PRIVATES 1941 (U.S.)

Director Arthur Lubin **Producer** Alex Gottlieb **Screenplay** Arthur T. Horman, with special material by John Grant **Cinematography** Jerry Ash, Milton Krasner
Cast Bud Abbott, Lou Costello, the Andrews Sisters, Lee Bowman, Alan Curtis, Jane Frazee, Nat Pendleton, Samuel S. Hinds, Harry Strang, Nella Walker, Leonard Elliott

Historians of the future, seeking an accurate representation of the exact social climate of America as it headed toward engagement in World War II, could do worse than take a look at this propaganda masterpiece disguised as a throwaway knockabout comedy.

It was the first starring vehicle for the former vaudeville and radio double-act of Bud Abbott and Lou Costello, following their successful guest star spot in the previous year's *One Night In the Tropics*. Combining the slick wisecracking of Bob Hope and the harsh physical slapstick of the Three Stooges (and sharing with both these acts the complete absence of sentimentality or depth of characterization) they caught exactly the mood of the times, ushering in the slicker, brasher American comedy of the war years. (Among the many who found themselves being ushered out as a result were Laurel & Hardy, whose decline began with a rushed-together slavish imitation called *Great Guns* the following year.)

Though the team is now top-billed, this is still basically a variety show in which their self-contained routines (such as the hilarious "crap game"—a rare example of Lou outsmarting Bud)

◄
Bud Abbott's impatient foil to Lou Costello's accident-prone antics served the duo well in over 30 comedies from 1940 to 1956.

are spaced out between scenes of romantic subplot and the era-defining songs of the Andrews Sisters. Later films would integrate them more fully—their best writer, John Grant, is here credited only with "special material" for the duo—but little of their later work was quite as sparkling or energetic. The surrounding sequences have a semi-documentary feel, beginning with actual newsreel footage of President Roosevelt

"BUCK PRIVATES *IS AN EIGHTY-FOUR MINUTE SLICE OF AMERICAN HISTORY.*"

STEPHEN COX

signing the draft bill and the drawing of the first number, and proceeding to realistic scenes of enlistment, basic training and maneuvers. It seems clear that the chief purpose of the movie was to prepare a population for war—there are several long and earnest speeches about the serious importance of it all, and a massive parade for the climax—with Bud and Lou and the Andrews Sisters (singing "The Boogie-Woogie Bugle Boy" and "You're a Lucky Fellow, Mr. Smith") serving as recruitment tools.

It certainly worked—both stars and film became smash hits, and Universal rushed them straight into navy and air force follow-ups. However, the official peacetime sequel, *Buck Privates Come Home* (1947), was not a success, perhaps indicating that the times had moved on once again, and the post-war world was no longer as optimistic or as innocent as the one that welcomed them so fulsomely in *Buck Privates*. **MC**

▶

The Andrews Sisters singing "The Boogie-Woogie Bugle Boy" were classy bait for the recruitment drive that underlay this movie.

SERGEANT YORK 1941 (U.S.)

Director Howard Hawks **Producers** Howard Hawks, Jesse L. Lasky, Hal
B. Wallis **Screenplay** Abem Finkel, Harry Chandlee, Howard Koch, John Huston
Cinematography Sol Polito **Music** Max Steiner **Cast** Gary Cooper, Walter Brennan,
Joan Leslie, George Tobias, Stanley Ridges, Margaret Wycherly, June Lockhart

Sergeant York portrays the life story of the American World
War I hero, Alvin C. York, who distinguished himself during the
Meuse-Argonne offensive in 1918 as a sharpshooter. Based
on York's own diary, and made with his stipulation that Gary
Cooper play him, the film was produced during the period
of World War II before America's entry into the war when it
maintained an isolationist position. The film begins with the
national anthem playing while the opening credits roll, and
ends with York returning home a war hero who is rewarded
socially, financially, and romantically for his patriotic service.

    Sergeant York is an all-American film for many reasons beyond
the patriotic propagandist message it presents. It weaves
together many traditional American narrative forms to tell
York's story. Because of this, Alvin York, a Tennessee hillbilly, is
transformed into a figure who symbolically represents
American history and the quintessential American man, and, in
turn, reaffirms a particular construction of American citizenry.
The conflict that York feels between the church and the law
reflects the very tensions that characterized the Puritan
communities during the colonial period; the process York goes

◄
The movie has
often been
discussed as
an attempt to
dismiss U.S.
ambivalence and
prompt American
involvement in
World War II.

through as he sobers up and works to buy better land so that he can build a farm of his own and start a family mirrors the settling of America and the myth of the self-made American man. York's acceptance of his role as a soldier represents the United States' emergence as global policeman, and his sharpshooting heroics prefigure American global dominance in the 20th century; while York's assertion that he killed in order

> # "SOME AS DONE IT, DIDN'T COME BACK, AND THAT KIND OF THING AIN'T FOR BUYING AND SELLING." YORK

to save lives echoes the rationale behind the atomic bomb. There are actually two moments of conversion in the film. The first is when York becomes a born-again Christian, and the second is when he decides to fight in the war rather than continue being a conscientious objector. It is significant that the second conversion is prompted by education of national history and a speech inviting him to relate to the figure of Daniel Boone, as well as reminding him that the traditions of self-reliance and self-determination are American heritages worth preserving at the cost of life.

► **Gary Cooper scooped an Oscar for Best Actor with his portrayal of hillbilly war hero Alvin York.**

Thus, the film's trajectory follows American history and privileges citizenship and the nation by reconciling religion with national interests and capitalist structures. York himself personifies the representative American, and the film is a quintessential all-American narrative. **KB**

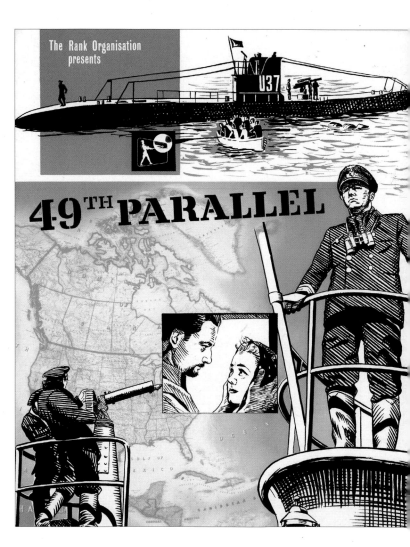

49TH PARALLEL 1941 (U.K.)

Director Michael Powell **Producer** Michael Powell **Screenplay** Emeric Pressburger, Rodney Ackland (scenario) **Cinematography** Freddie Young **Music** Ralph Vaughan Williams **Cast** Richard George, Eric Portman, Raymond Lovell, Laurence Olivier, Niall MacGinnis, Peter Moore, John Chandos, Basil Appleby, Leslie Howard, Raymond Massey

Powell's British World War II thriller *49th Parallel* (a.k.a. *The Invaders*) is expertly crafted, emotionally compelling, was politically influential on release, and pivotal for the British film industry.

Shot in 1941 shortly after the fall of France, *49th Parallel* was written as a propaganda piece with the express objective of persuading the U.S. to enter the war. Toward this effort, the film imagines the Nazi menace hovering on America's doorstep, as a marauding German U-boat is intercepted by the Canadian Air Force and sunk in Hudson Bay. Six Nazis survive the attack and flee across Canada toward the still-neutral United States.

The film follows the Nazis' flight across thousands of miles of Canadian territory, through an episodic series of confrontations with patriotic Canadians and free-thinking citizens of the world. *49th Parallel* carefully contrasts the Nazis' murderous determination with the warmth, humanity and rich diversity of the people they encounter. In a character-driven film, the acting is paramount—and here the performances are delivered by a top international cast, including Laurence Olivier, Anton Walbrook, Leslie Howard, Raymond Massey, Eric Portman, and Niall MacGinnis—who almost steals the movie as the Nazi

◄
The movie won the Academy Award for Best Writing—Original Story.

soldier who begins to self-doubt and have second thoughts. The British film industry was on the brink of collapse in 1941, and in no mood to finance such an ambitious feature. Director/producer Michael Powell and screenwriter Emeric Pressburger nonetheless recruited the all-star cast and crew, insisting that the picture would be important in the fight against Hitler. Impassioned, the actors signed on, agreeing to work for half

"THE 49TH PARALLEL: THE ONLY UNDEFENDED FRONTIER IN THE WORLD." *PROLOGUE*

their normal rates, and the financing soon followed. Similarly inspired by the project's political engagement, legendary composer Ralph Vaughan Williams wrote the effective musical score; marking his first foray into writing music for film at the age of 69. On the technical side, the movie had the benefit of talented cinematographer Freddie Young, along with accomplished young editor David Lean, still a year away from directing his first feature.

49th Parallel was successful on many levels, winning an Academy Award for Best Original Story. It was a major box-office success in America and inspired J. Arthur Rank, head of Britain's General Film Distributors, to establish independent production companies The Archers, Cineguild, and Two Cities, which went on to revitalize the industry, and produce some of the most important British films in the history of cinema. **RG**

► Eric Portman plays Lieutenant Hirth—marauding in his U-boat close to the Eastern seaboard.

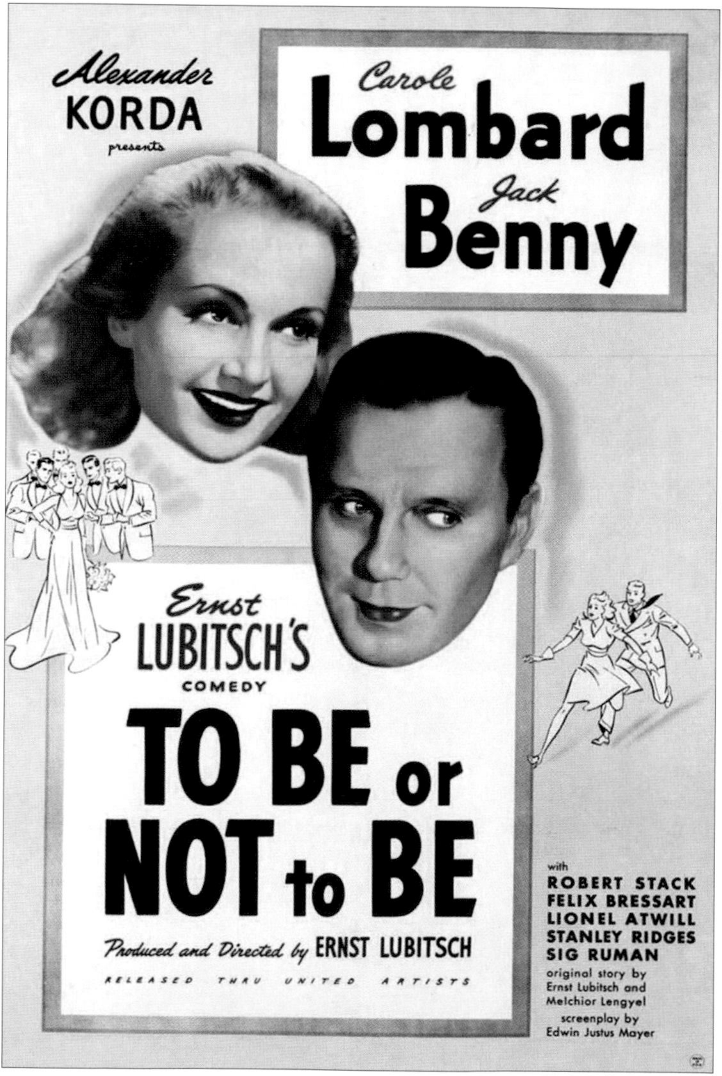

Alexander
KORDA
presents
Carole
Lombard
Jack
Benny
Ernst
LUBITSCH'S
COMEDY
TO BE or
NOT to BE
Produced and Directed by ERNST LUBITSCH
RELEASED THRU UNITED ARTISTS
with
ROBERT STACK
FELIX BRESSART
LIONEL ATWILL
STANLEY RIDGES
SIG RUMAN
original story by
Ernst Lubitsch and
Melchior Lengyel
screenplay by
Edwin Justus Mayer

TO BE OR NOT TO BE 1942 (U.S.)

Director Ernst Lubitsch **Producer** Ernst Lubitsch **Screenplay** Edwin Justus Mayer, Melchior Lengyel (story) **Cinematography** Rudolph Maté **Music** Miklós Rózsa, Werner Heymann **Cast** Jack Benny, Carole Lombard, Robert Stack, Felix Bressart, Stanley Ridges, Sig Ruman, Lionel Atwil, Tom Dugan, Charles Halton, George Lynn

At the beginning of America's involvement in World War II, while most of the studios were producing patriotic combat movies, United Artists distributed Ernst Lubitsch's screwball satire showing up Hitler as simply "a man with a little moustache." Perhaps it was the death of star Carole Lombard in a plane crash before the picture's release, or perhaps it was reviewers who simply didn't "get" what Lubitsch was trying to do here, but upon its initial release *To Be or Not to Be* bombed at the domestic box office. Today, however, it is recognized as one of American cinema's greatest satires, and alongside Charlie Chaplin's *The Great Dictator* (1940) as a contemporary indictment through comedy of the Hitler war machine.

The film's plot is a complicated one: discovering that the voice of the Polish exiled government, Professor Siletsky (Ridges), is in fact a Gestapo spy, a young Polish airman (Stack) based in England, parachutes back into occupied Warsaw to warn the underground of the professor's duplicity. He is too late, though, and the traitor has already arrived. He enlists the help of a group of actors, led by that "great, *great* Polish actor" Joseph Tura (Benny) and his wife Maria (Lombard), to intercept

◄
Mel Brooks and Ann Bancroft revived the roles of Jack Benny and Carole Lombard in a 1983 remake.

Siletsky before he can meet with the Gestapo's man in Warsaw, Col. Ehrhardt (Ruman). The actors proceed to devise a series of ruses and disguises in order to subvert the Nazi war effort in Poland. But simply to describe the plot is insufficient to capture the comedy's "Lubitsch touch"; in fact, at the level of plot description, *To Be or Not To Be* appears to be yet another espionage picture Hollywood was used to producing. The film's dialogue is

"WELL, COLONEL, ALL I CAN SAY IS . . . YOU CAN'T HAVE YOUR CAKE AND SHOOT IT, TOO." *JOSEPH TURA*

rife with double entendres of sexual innuendo: "Shall we drink to a blitzkrieg?" "I prefer a slow encirclement." The main comedic purpose of the movie is to deflate the ominous Nazi threat in Europe. When Siletsky asks Maria, "Do I look like a monster?" her reply, "of course not," is sincere: Siletsky isn't a monster, just a sad little letch. Lubitsch includes little background details, like German soldiers buying postcards at the bookshop that is the front for the Underground's headquarters, to deflate the image of the Aryan supermen. The greatest deflation, however, is reserved for "Concentration Camp" Ehrhardt; as portrayed by Ruman, Ehrhardt is a bumbling fool rather than a bloodthirsty monster. Lubitsch's satire is primarily aimed at deflating pomposity in all its forms, whether vain actors like Tura or Gestapo commanders like Ehrhardt. Unfortunately, in 1942, America wasn't ready to get the joke. **MK**

▶
A photo opportunity with the Hitler war machine for Jack Benny, Carole Lombard, and Robert Stack.

MRS. MINIVER 1942 (U.S.)

Director William Wyler **Producer** Sidney Franklin **Screenplay** Arthur Wimperis, George Froeschel, James Hilton, Claudine West **Music** Herbert Stothart **Cinematography** Joseph Ruttenberg **Cast** Greer Garson, Walter Pidgeon, Teresa Wright, Richard Ney, Dame May Whitty, Henry Travers, Henry Wilcoxon

A huge wartime success with both critics and public on both sides of the Atlantic, *Mrs. Miniver* swept the Academy Awards in 1942 and was the year's top box-office hit. How unfortunate that William Wyler's sincere plea to put aside class differences and selflessly unite to ensure Britain's survival is often overlooked today, and merely seen as a well-made Hollywood release. While *Mrs. Miniver* is indeed lushly made, it is also one of World War II's most stirring examples of the conversion narrative, the wartime tale in which characters learn to make sacrifices for the good of the nation.

Adapted from Jan Struther's popular novel, a book that both Roosevelt and Churchill praised for boosting wartime morale, *Mrs. Miniver* tells the story of the Miniver family—architect husband Clem (Pidgeon), wife Kay (Garson), Oxford student and older son Vin (Ney), and two younger children—and the sacrifices faced by the Minivers and their quaint village once war has broken out. Vin joins the R.A.F. and falls in love with the pragmatic yet idealistic Carol Beldon (Wright), granddaughter of Lady Beldon (Whitty), the aristocrat who lives next door and likes things the old way, and people in their place.

◄

Among the technical Oscars, *Mrs. Miniver* scooped Best Cinematography, Best Editing, Best Special Effects, and Best Sound.

The film also recalls the Dunkirk evacuation and the Blitz. Heroics ensue. Clem rescues troops stranded in Dunkirk, and Mrs. Miniver captures a wounded German pilot in the backyard. But when Carol is killed during an air raid, the horror of war is brought home to the Minivers, to Lady Beldon, and to everyone in the village. The final scene unites all villagers in the church, the camera panning past empty seats of those lost to the war

"THIS IS NOT ONLY A WAR OF SOLDIERS IN UNIFORM. IT IS A WAR OF ALL OF THE PEOPLE!" MRS. MINIVER

as the vicar reminds his parishioners that every Brit is fighting this battle, and that class differences must be put aside if this great nation is to survive.

Wyler may have had doubts as to whether he hadn't overblown the whole home front experience, but the death of Carol remains *Mrs. Miniver*'s most memorable moment, still startling to today's audiences. Kay and Carol are returning home through a wooded area when a stray bullet hits the car. Director Wyler has created an eerie nighttime scene here, with the car pulling to the side of the road as Mrs. Miniver slowly realizes that Carol has been wounded. Kay takes Carol home, leaving the room for a minute as the young woman dies. The look of a sad but stiff upper lip after Carol's death would win Garson the Oscar. It was also a stern warning for American audiences: unless you're willing to help, these sad fates might soon be yours. **JL**

► Henry Wilcoxon as the Vicar delivers a rousing sermon to the village parishioners in the (literally) war-torn church. The sermon was broadcast on Voice of America radio under Roosevelt's prompting.

THE GREATEST MOTION PICTURE
OF OUR TIME!
TWO CITIES PRODUCTIONS presents
Noel COWARD'S
"IN WHICH WE SERVE"
starring NOEL COWARD
Directed by NOEL COWARD and DAVID LEAN
Released Thru UNITED ARTISTS

IN WHICH WE SERVE 1942 (U.K.)

Directors Noël Coward, David Lean **Producer** Noël Coward **Screenplay** Noël Coward **Cinematography** Ronald Neame **Music** Noël Coward **Cast** Noël Coward, Bernard Miles, John Mills, Celia Johnson, Michael Wilding, Ballard Berkeley, Hubert Gregg, James Donald, Michael Whittaker, Kenneth Carten, Derek Elphinstone

In more ways than one, 1942 was an extraordinary year for World War II propaganda films. Following the attack on Pearl Harbor and America's resulting involvement in the conflict in the preceding year, 1942 saw Hollywood embracing full-scale propaganda, with the release of instant classics like *Casablanca*. Meanwhile the Disney and Warner Bros. animation studios were appropriated wholesale by the government to churn out war related entertainment and instructional films.

Since the most celebrated European directors had fled to exile in the United States, where many of them made pictures that rallied public support for American involvement (for example, Alfred Hitchcock's *Foreign Correspondent* [1940]), the British film industry felt pressured to produce a full-blown war epic of its own.

The unlikely person that was chosen to take on this prestigious project was actor-writer-director Noël Coward, whose play *Blithe Spirit* had been only the most recent in a string of massive West End stage successes. Given his "dressing gown and cigarette holder" celebrity persona, there were some concerns about his credibility as a captain in a realistic war film,

◄

An unlikely combination of clipped Coward theatrics and David Lean's sweeping action shots ensured that box office takings doubled.

when Coward said he would only agree to write, produce, and direct the film if he was also allowed to play the lead role. He also demanded complete authority over every aspect of the production. Such was Coward's fame at the time that all of his demands were immediately met, and he started to develop his script on the basis of the recent sinking of the H.M.S. *Kelly* during the Battle of Crete. Spending time with the naval fleet

"HERE ENDS THE STORY OF A SHIP, BUT THERE WILL ALWAYS BE OTHER SHIPS; WE ARE AN ISLAND RACE." *CLOSING VOICEOVER*

in numerous harbors and expeditions, he finalized a first draft that would have run eight to nine hours. However Coward managed to trim down his ambitious screenplay to scenes only of the ship and its crew.

As shooting drew near, Coward realized that his experience as a stage director left him unprepared to face the technical challenges of filmmaking, so he approached his friend David Lean to handle the action scenes. As the shoot progressed, Coward soon found himself bored by the daily technicalities, and only came to the set for scenes in which he appeared. Despite his dubious directing credit, as writer, producer, co-director, and even scoring the final picture, Coward's fingerprints remain all over this celebration of stiff-upper-lip commanding officers—a theme David Lean gave more nuanced examination in *The Bridge on the River Kwai* (1957). **DH**

► Noël Coward won an Honorary Academy Award for Outstanding Production Achievement for this dated but still potent epic.

WENT THE DAY WELL? 1942 (U.K.)

Director Alberto Cavalcanti **Producer** Michael Balcon **Screenplay** John Dighton, Angus MacPhail, Diana Morgan (from a short story by Graham Greene) **Cinematography** Wilkie Cooper **Music** William Walton **Cast** Leslie Banks, C V France, Valerie Taylor, Marie Lohr, Basil Sydney, David Farrar, Mervyn Johns

Made for Ealing Studios by Alberto Cavalcanti (a significant talent who also directed the most famous sequences of Ealing's 1945 horror classic *Dead of Night*), *Went the Day Well?* (a k a *48 Hours*) begins with a sequence set after the war in which the church-warden of a picture-perfect English village (Mervyn Johns, speaking direct to camera) offers to explain why there is a memorial to dead German soldiers in the churchyard. ("They wanted England, those Jerries did—and this is the only bit they got.") Cleverly, the film then affects to flashback to the year it was actually made, and becomes a brilliant suspense drama, as well as a superbly designed piece of propaganda.

An army platoon, supposedly on maneuvers, arrives in the town and is at first welcomed by the villagers. But they are in fact an undercover Nazi regiment, preparing the way for a full-scale invasion under the knowing jurisdiction of the quisling local squire (Banks, superb as always). When eventually they are exposed and forced to take the whole village hostage, some of the villagers attempt a desperate resistance. At this point, the doom-laden tension so carefully maintained throughout the film gives way to some quite unexpectedly

◄
The main theme of this Ealing drama was that English calm would win the day against German cunning. The film also served to warn others to be on their guard against enemy agents.

explicit violence—including a shocking killing with an axe and a scene in which a woman allows herself to be blown up by a hand grenade so as to save a room full of children—that seems all the more brutal in so idyllically English a setting. As a result it made a lasting impression on wartime audiences combining compelling realism with entertainment. As in real life, characters are killed more or less at random as circumstances

"PEOPLE OF THE KINDEST CHARACTER... AS SOON AS THE WAR TOUCHES THEM, BECOME ABSOLUTE MONSTERS." CAVALCANTI

dictate, in ways both heroic and banal, regardless of their likability or centrality to the plot. This, quite obviously, was the whole point of the enterprise.

Ironically, the release of the film was delayed by a year over concerns that such factors might prove counterproductively harrowing, inducing panic rather than any preparedness. (It certainly belied Ealing's habitual reputation for gentility.) Now, without such imperatives to consider, the picture can be seen more clearly as the exceptional piece of work it always was, while its durability and power may be indicated by the fact that its central idea reappears in both *The Eagle Has Landed* (1976) and the film version of U.K. television show *Dad's Army* (1971). The film's title, incidentally, comes from an anonymous World War I poem: "Went the day well? We died and never knew. But, well or ill, Freedom, we died for you." **MC**

► A Nazi paratrooper poses as a British soldier as he and his fellow platoon infiltrators capture a quintessential English village.

Aldo
FABRIZI
in:
ROMA città aperta
Anna MAGNANI
Regia R. ROSSELLINI
Prod. EXCELSA FILM

ROME, OPEN CITY 1945 (ITALY)

Director Roberto Rossellini **Producers** Giuseppe Amato (uncredited), Roberto Rossellini (uncredited) **Screenplay** Sergio Amedei, Federico Fellini, Roberto Rossellini (uncredited) **Cinematography** Ubaldo Arata **Editor** Eraldo Da Roma **Music** Renzo Rossellini **Cast** Aldo Fabrizi, Anna Magnani, Marcello Pagliero, Maria Michi, Harry Feist

Set in Rome during the very last days of the Nazi occupation, *Rome, Open City* (a.k.a. *Roma, Città Aperta*) follows the story of resistance leader Giorgio Manfredi (Pagliero), who is being hunted by the Gestapo. Once denounced, he goes into hiding while priest Don Pietro Pellegrini (Fabrizi) and friend Francesco organize his escape. Meanwhile, Pina (Magnani), Francesco's pregnant fiancée, awaits their wedding. The Germans turn to Manfredi's lover Marina Mari (Michi) for information, and she eventually breaks. When the Germans come for Francesco, Pina runs after him and as the truck pulls away she is shot dead in the street. For collaborating with the resistance, Don Pietro is executed in a field with the neighborhood children watching from behind a fence. The final scene of *Rome, Open City* immortalizes these children as the image of Italy's future as they move across the hill solemnly toward the city.

◄

The priest Don Pellegrini (Aldo Fabrizi) stands up to the brutal Nazis in this Italian neorealist masterpiece, shot on the streets of Rome because the Cinecittà studios had been damaged in the war.

Conceived initially as a documentary, *Rome, Open City* is widely considered one of the earliest films of the Italian neorealist moment. As the highest-grossing domestic release of 1945, it was also one of the most commercially successful. Characteristic of this body of Italian post-war cinema is the gritty realism of Rossellini's newsreel aesthetic, achieved partly through the use of inconsistent film stocks due to shortages. Shot on location with non-professional actors in supporting roles and post-synchronized sound, the film's aura of authenticity had a particularly potent resonance for the war-torn nation. Catholic priest Don Pietro's collaboration with the resistance paints a portrait of Italy as a nation unified against

> # "THE TRAGEDY OF WAR . . . WE WERE ALL ITS VICTIMS. I SOUGHT ONLY TO PICTURE THE ESSENCE OF THINGS." *ROSSELLINI*

the evil of Nazi Germany, and the image of Pina's body in the street with her skirt raised, revealing the top of her stockings, became a metaphor for Italy's courage and loss.

It is clear now to critics that the film uses techniques rooted firmly in the classical narrative cinema from which the Italian neorealist movement supposedly broke, rather than neorealism itself. Most explicit is the extreme portrayal of the Germans, who are led by a snake-like and effeminate commander with a lesbian assistant who fixes upon Marina like a vampire. Belying the movement's commitment to authenticity and realism, this problematic typecasting is more typical of conventional cinema rather than the edgy newsreel and raw power that neorealism sought to convey. Nevertheless, *Rome, Open City*'s expert blend of documentary, violence, and melodrama cements it as a watershed film. **AKa**

► The pregnant Pina (Magnani) is murdered by Nazi soldiers. Her death is emblematic of Rome's courage under fire.

A MATTER OF LIFE AND DEATH

1946 (U.K.)

Directors Michael Powell, Emeric Pressburger **Producers** Michael Powell, Emeric Pressburger, George R. Busby **Screenplay** Michael Powell, Emeric Pressburger **Cinematography** Jack Cardiff **Music** Allan Gray **Cast** David Niven, Kim Hunter, Roger Livesey, Raymond Massey, Marius Goring, Robert Coote, Richard Attenborough

---

A Matter of Life and Death (a.k.a. *Stairway to Heaven*) is recognized as not only one of Powell and Pressburger's best films, but also one of the best British films of all time. It is a heady recommendation; and for once, a recommendation in which the film lives up to its hype. For those who come to *A Matter of Life and Death* cold are certain to be amazed and enraptured by this truly-ahead-of-its-time motion picture.

The film's plot is surprisingly complex: a young R.A.F. pilot, Peter Carter (Niven), falls in love with a W.A.A.C. named June (Hunter), when the Heavenly Conductor (Goring) assigned to escort him to the afterlife misses his target in the English fog. Although Carter is allowed an appeals hearing in order to grant him a life sufficiently long to love June, he must first defend his existence in a celestial court of law. The prosecution advocate is a Brit-hating American, the first Colonial to have been killed in the American Revolution, Abraham Farlan (Massey), who does not like it that a Brit wants extended life in order to have a romance with an American woman. What makes *A Matter of Life and Death* so remarkable cinematically, however, is not its plot,

◄
British surrealism meets British stiff upper lip as a dying pilot (Niven) appeals to a heavenly court of historical characters to let surgeons save his life so he can woo his love (Hunter).

but its complex visual style. The earth-bound sequences are filmed in color, but the heavenly sequences are all in monochrome. While this is not so astonishing in itself, it does reverse the template set up by *The Wizard of Oz* (1939), wherein the "real" world is in monochrome and the fantasy realm is colored. In addition to the remarkable use of color and black-and-white cinematography, the various cinematographic tricks

"YES JUNE, I'M BAILING OUT. I'M BAILING OUT BUT THERE'S A CATCH, I'VE GOT NO PARACHUTE." *PETER*

used by Powell and Pressburger are also outstanding. For example, the freeze-frame during the table-tennis match and the remarkable set design of the heavenly realm are both stunning. None of the techniques used are wholly innovative in themselves—some have been around at least since Georges Méliès—but one certainly doesn't expect this level of cinematographic fantasy in a war picture.

▶
David Niven prepares to meet his maker—or so he thinks. Some 60 years later this intelligent and sensitive war movie remains a cult classic.

Powell and Pressburger had already had an extraordinary run with three prior war movies—*49th Parallel* (1941), *One of Our Aircraft Is Missing* (1942), and *The Life and Death of Colonel Blimp* (1943)—but while at the basic story level *A Matter of Life and Death* is a typical, wartime melodrama, its filmic qualities are nothing short of breathtaking. The duo became the most exciting creative partnership in British cinema, inspiring the likes of Coppola, Spielberg, and Scorsese. **MK**

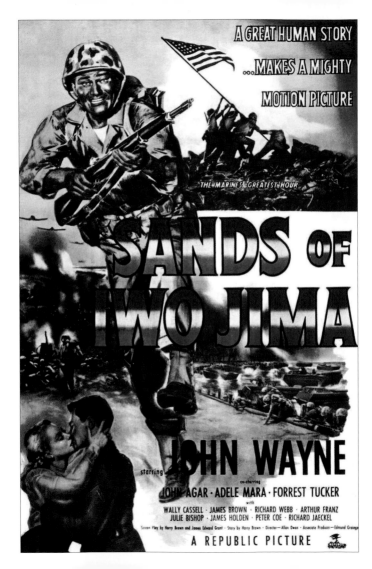

SANDS OF IWO JIMA 1949 (U.S.)

Director Allan Dwan **Producer** Edmund Grainger **Screenplay** Harry Brown, James Edward Grant **Cinematography** Reggie Lanning **Music** Victor Young
Cast John Wayne, John Agar, Adele Mara, Forrest Tucker, Wally Cassell, James Brown, Richard Webb, Arthur Frantz, Julie Bishop, James Holden, Richard Jaeckel

Straight shooters, that's what they are. A platoon of Marines, riflemen trained to kill. They fight where there's a need for a fight: the Guadalcanal, the Tarawa Atoll, a small Pacific island called Iwo Jima. It's not a question of politics for the Marines in *Sands of Iwo Jima*. This is a combat film. Why do they fight? Guys are shown engaging in combat just for the guy next to them. No honor, no homeland, no haughtiness.

The Marines are led by feared Sergeant John M. Stryker (Wayne): a man who is weak in his strength and gets strong in his weakness. Being a failure in civil life, he lives only for war. More precisely: for his subordinate soldiers, to whom he is caring and compassionate although stern and stringent. He trains them to survive. They are shown in their military instruction as well as their cabin fevers, their comradely quarrels as well as their love affairs, and their combat experiences. The movie doesn't distinguish between these activities but weaves a panorama of parallels; that's how it gets its vibrant rhythm between contraction and expansion. But the point is made clear: you have to behave like a soldier, no matter if you're dancing with a girl or using a bayonet. War fuses everything

◄

A great flag-waver metaphorically and filmically for U.S. involvement in World War II, the theme was revisited by Clint Eastwood in his *Flags of Our Fathers* and *Letters from Iwo Jima* (both made in 2006).

together in civilian matters, civilian matters converge to war. Director Allan Dwan was born about ten years before the birth of cinema. He started his work with jobs for D. W. Griffith and shot about 400 movies between 1911 and 1961, westerns and melodramas, comedies, and action adventures. "He didn't dwell on things," Howard Hawks remarked about his fellow filmmaker. "He just hit 'em and went on." In this way, Dwan's

"LIKE MICKEY MANTLE AND THE NEW YORK YANKEES, JOHN WAYNE BECAME ONE OF MY HEROES." *VIETNAM VET RON KOVIC*

cinema is characterized by expressiveness without adornment, significance without instructiveness. For him, shooting *Sands of Iwo Jima* was especially a matter of directing John Wayne.

Wayne brings his mythic Western persona to the movie while simultaneously subverting it. Playing Sgt. Stryker he knows what a man has to do, but he is also a drunk and an embittered divorcee, making him a truly tragic hero. In the end, just after we see the Marines running up the American flag at Mount Surabaachi—a small hill by the sands of Iwo Jima—he gets killed entirely out of nowhere, and it is an absolute accident. He dies in the manner in which he used to live, as a professional. Dwan stages the film fluidly, evidently aiming for compositions that capture the essence of physical presence. *Sands of Iwo Jima* is a war movie that's shot completely straight, dealing with logical conduct and logical consequence. **IR**

► Sgt. Stryker (Wayne) instructs his Marines to raise the flag, including three men who actually did this in real life and were captured by Joe Rosenthal's iconic photograph.

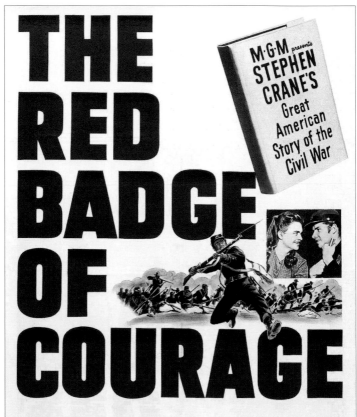

THE RED BADGE OF COURAGE
1951 (U.S.)

Director John Huston **Producers** Gottfried Reinhardt, Dore Schary
Screenplay John Huston, Albert Band (from the eponymous novel by Stephen
Crane) **Cinematography** Harold Rosson **Music** Bronislau Kaper **Cast** Audie
Murphy, Bill Mauldin, Douglas Dick, Royal Dano, John Dierkes, Arthur Hunnicutt

Based on the classic novel by Stephen Crane, *The Red Badge of
Courage* tells the story of Henry Fleming (Murphy), who went to
war a scared boy and came out of it a brave man. Although at
first he talks tough on the outside, boasting at training camp of
becoming a hero in battle, Henry is frightened on the inside
and finds during his first actual conflict that the explosions of
both friendly and enemy fire cause him to panic and run away.
He sees his comrades wounded and regards them with envy,
wishing that he too had a red badge of courage. Eventually,
Henry manages to collect his nerve and leads the men on an
aggressive attack carrying the colors. He is later recognized by
the general for leading this charge

    How this movie got made to begin with has become a well-
known battle all its own. As detailed by Lillian Ross in her book
of collected *New Yorker* articles concerning the production,
legendary director John Huston found himself stuck in the
middle of a hostile takeover of Louis B. Mayer's MGM by studio
executive Dore Schary. While Huston admired what Crane's
1893 novel had to say about the futility of war and the coming

◄

The movie had to
rely on a voiceover
commentary,
drawn from Stephen
Crane's account
of the Civil War,
to help make sense
of all the re-editing.

of age through crisis, the two executive combatants saw it only as a reason to fight over valuable turf, with Mayer hating the new trend in films that was leaning toward realism—including Huston's own 1950 heist thriller, *The Asphalt Jungle*—and Schary ultimately giving the go-ahead to this relatively small but suddenly important (for political reasons) picture. Despite having to deal with a multitude of distractions during the

"A CLASSIC WAR STORY ABOUT A FRIGHTENED YOUNG SOLDIER OVERCOMING FEAR . . ." DENNIS SCHWARTZ

production, both from the studio side and also of a personal nature (he got married, had a child, and unexpectedly lost his father), Huston still felt that this may have been his best work . . . at least until Schary, wanting to control the filmmaking process, went ahead and made severe cuts to the picture after Huston was pulled away to do post-production on *The African Queen* (1951).

▶
Audie Murphy as "The Youth" and Douglas Dick as "The Lieutenant" shot in the dustily faded textures of Matthew Brady's Civil War photographs.

Even after adding James Whitmore as a narrator for the sake of "clarity" and shortening the movie to a mere sixty-nine minutes, *The Red Badge of Courage* remains a minor classic in the war genre, notable for its sensitive depiction of a young man's struggle to come to terms with his own identity. Sadly, Huston's original cut has been lost, which made the director insist in all subsequent contracts that he be given a copy of the very first cut of any film he made. **KW**

WORLD PREMIERE

IN THE PRESENCE OF H.R.H. THE DUKE OF EDINBURGH

IN AID OF KING GEORGE'S FUND FOR SAILORS

The Cruel Sea

BY NICHOLAS MONSARRAT

EALING STUDIOS PRESENT A MICHAEL BALCON PRODUCTION starring

JACK HAWKINS
DONALD SINDEN
DENHOLM ELLIOTT
VIRGINIA McKENNA

DIRECTED BY CHARLES FREND   PRODUCED BY LESLIE NORMAN   SCREENPLAY BY ERIC AMBLER

THURSDAY, MARCH 26

LEICESTER SQUARE THEATRE

TICKETS FROM: 1 CHESHAM STREET SW1 (SLOANE 0331)

Printed in England by GRAPHIC REPRODUCTIONS LTD

THE CRUEL SEA 1953 (U.K.)

Director Charles Frend **Producer** Leslie Norman **Screenplay** Eric Ambler (based on the novel by Nicholas Monsarrat) **Cinematography** Gordon Dines **Music** Alan Rawsthorne **Cast** Jack Hawkins, Donald Sinden, Denholm Elliott, Virginia McKenna, Moira Lister, June Thorburn, Megs Jenkins, Meredith Edwards, Glyn Houston

The Cruel Sea was adapted by Ealing Studios from Nicholas Monsarrat's bestselling novel. Monsarrat had seen active service on convoy protection during World War II, and his story reflected the grim reality of his personal experiences. This quality was successfully carried over into a film that proved remarkably bleak, especially when compared with other more gung-ho 1950s British war movies such as *The Dambusters* (1955) and *The Colditz Story* (1955). *The Cruel Sea* centers on the war careers of two officers, Captain Ericson (Hawkins) and his second-in-command Lockhart (Sinden), from their first encounter on the ship *Compass Rose* in 1940, through the traumatic sinking of that ship, onto their service on board the *Saltash Castle* at the end of the war. Around them are arrayed a range of colorful characters from all ranks, many of whom die over the course of the story.

The Cruel Sea's most famous scene involves Ericson ordering depth charges to be dropped on some survivors of a U-boat attack in order to get at the U-boat that sank their ship. Even today this is a powerful moment. In the context of 1950s British cinema, the aftermath is even more shocking for, as Lockhart

◄

The movie was an authentic, bleak, and grueling saga of Allied shipping making the Atlantic "run" against the dreaded German U-boats.

looks on, we see Ericson—in a career-best performance by Hawkins—weeping over his actions. When reviewing the movie as a whole it is striking how early this scene comes, less than halfway through a narrative in which it functions as just one incident among many in a gradual accumulation of exhaustion, despair, and stoicism. Ericson's assertion in *The Cruel Sea*'s opening voiceover that "the men are the heroes, the

"THE ONLY VILLAIN IS THE SEA, THE CRUEL SEA THAT MAN HAS MADE MORE CRUEL." *OPENING VOICEOVER*

heroines are the ships" is endorsed by a narrative in which wives and girls occasionally feature, but where the real emotional attachments occur on board male-only ships out at sea. Lockhart in particular has a more intense relationship with Ericson than he does with his bland girlfriend, who seems to have been wheeled in simply to assure the audience of Lockhart's "normality." By contrast, Ericson's wife is mentioned but never seen and seems to play no significant part in his life. Not all men are the same, however, and it is one of the film's limitations that the sole working-class character who does not know his place—Stanley Baker's pushy ex-car salesman First Lieutenant—is quickly removed by a convenient duodenal ulcer.

The Cruel Sea takes the 1950s British war film into uncharted emotional territory, but it is not entirely free of the middle-class bias that characterizes this type of picture. **PH**

► The British Admiralty gave its full support to the project, helping director Charles Frend who had a background in documentaries.

STALAG 17 1953 (U.S.)

Director Billy Wilder **Producers** Billy Wilder, William Schorr **Screenplay** Billy Wilder, Edwin Blum (based on the play by Donald Bevan and Edmund Trzcinski) **Cinematography** Ernest Laslo **Music** Leonid Raab **Cast** William Holden, Otto Preminger, Sig Ruman, Harvey Lembeck, Don Taylor, Robert Strauss, Richard Erdman

Besides Charlie Chaplin's *The Great Dictator* (1940), very few comedies have been made about German prisoner camps; the images that emerged out of the Holocaust were presumably not funny even for the crassest Hollywood tastes. *Stalag 17* is a deservedly acclaimed exception to that rule, a film whose slapstick comedy is brilliantly juxtaposed with the grim reality of the men's camp. It was also the inspiration for the popular TV series, *Hogan's Heroes*.

Based on the stage play by Donald Bevan and Edmund Trzcinski, and in turn based on Trzcinski's own wartime experiences, *Stalag 17* depicts the devious means by which captive GIs try to subvert the authoritarian rule of their camp's commandant, Col. von Scherbach (Preminger) and his not-so-intelligent sergeant Schultz (the great Sig Ruman). The central plot that runs as a vein throughout the picture is the search for a spy inside Bunker 4; one of the American servicemen in there is somehow leaking vital information to their German captors, including escape plans, which results in the deaths of two soldiers. Suspicion falls on the sardonic Sgt. Sefton (Holden), who pretty much keeps to himself and seems to be honing his

◄
The lower portion of the film's poster was deliberately obscured, having been deemed too risqué.

business skills as he acquires greater and greater amounts of contraband, often in plain sight of the Germans. Part of the darkness of the film comes from the strong influx of Jewish humor throughout. The casting of Jewish actors Sig Ruman and Otto Preminger as Nazis certainly adds an ironic dash of flavor to the production, but the character of Private Shapiro (Lembeck) in particular adds a bitter aftertaste to the laughs, as

> ## "THERE ARE TWO PEOPLE IN THIS BARRACKS WHO KNOW I DIDN'T DO IT. ME AND THE GUY THAT DID DO IT." SEFTON

he keeps pondering what the worst thing the Germans could do to him would be; less than ten years after the liberation of the death camps, the world knew all too well what the worst that could happen to someone named "Shapiro" could be in these circumstances.

Another way of reading the film, and one which permeates so many pictures in the early 1950s, is to see the shadow of McCarthyism throughout the narrative. As the men in Bunker 4 are searching for the traitor in their midst, they inevitably all turn on one another. An element of film noir now pervades this P.O.W. drama which heightens the references to "blacklisting" people who don't conform. It is only the sobering voice of Sefton who points how Americans "squealing on other Americans" in these circumstances will result in all their deaths. That line must have had particular resonance in 1953. **MK**

► Sgt. Sefton seeks any way he can to con his fellow P.O.W.s and make a fast buck.

FROM HERE TO ETERNITY 1953 (U.S.)

Director Fred Zinnemann **Producer** Buddy Adler **Screenplay** Daniel Taradash (from the novel by James Jones) **Cinematography** Burnett Guffey **Music** George Duning **Cast** Burt Lancaster, Montgomery Clift, Deborah Kerr, Donna Reed, Frank Sinatra, Philip Ober, Mickey Shaughnessy, Ernest Borgnine, Harry Bellaver, Jack Warden

Though frequently classified as a war film, *From Here to Eternity* is predominantly a picture about the tumultuous bonds of love and friendship, despite being cast against a backdrop of pre-war tension in the events immediately preceding the Japanese attack on the American army base at Pearl Harbor. The thematic prominence of love is encapsulated in a famous and much-parodied scene on a Hawaii beach, in which Burt Lancaster and Deborah Kerr embrace on the sand with waves washing over one another, symbolically depicting their indifference to the elements, and their ability to see only each other in that moment.

Notable for its realism and at times pessimism with regard to love and human relationships, *From Here to Eternity* is a film very much ahead of its time, especially insofar as it gives center stage to the feelings of women. In many ways, the two central female characters experience contrary love stories whereby each woman craves that which the other has. Alma "Lorene" Burke (Reed) is the struggling club girl who craves a "proper" life of financial stability and status, but struggles to reconcile this with her love for Robert Prewitt (Clift), a lowly private in the

◀

Frank Sinatra and Donna Reed won Best Supporting Actor and Actress respectively in this movie.

U.S. Army; whereas Karen Holmes (Kerr), on the other hand, has a proper life in a loveless marriage as the wife of an army captain, but desires true love and is willing to give up the security of her marriage in pursuit of it.

Yet intertwined with these fraught relationships, much consideration is also given to the complexities of male friendship. Private Prewitt is a former star boxer who will not

> ## "WHEN A MAN LOVES A THING, THAT DON'T MEAN IT'S GOT TO LOVE HIM BACK." PREWITT

fight for his new regiment because he once blinded a man in the ring. Despite enduring punishing "treatment" from his peers and superiors, Prewitt exhibits a determination, strength of character, and single-mindedness that earns him the deep respect of many, including fellow Private Angelo Maggio (Sinatra), who provides many of the film's lighter moments, and senior officer Sergeant Milton Warden (Lancaster), a brooding but nevertheless honest and decent man.

This respect is so deeply felt in the latter case that during a poignant scene with Karen toward the end of the film, Sergeant Warden is distracted from her heartfelt words because he thinks that he has managed to locate the missing Prewitt in a crowd of people. This is the moment that ultimately reveals much about his otherwise steely character, and not least his feelings for both Prewitt and Karen. **SR**

▶
The final reel gets into full war mode with the attack on Pearl Harbor and the protagonists' U.S. Army base. The stunning black-and-white cinematography was also rewarded with an Oscar.

THE DAM BUSTERS 1955 (U.K.)

Director Michael Anderson **Producer** Robert Clark **Screenplay** R. C. Sherriff (from the book by Paul Brickhill and Guy Gibson) **Cinematography** Erwin Hillier **Music** Leighton Lewis, "Dam Busters March" by Eric Coates **Cast** Michael Redgrave, Richard Todd, Basil Sydney, Derek Farr, Patrick Barr, Ursula Jeans

The Dam Busters remains among the most popular as well as the most famous of British war films, in part because of the manner in which it manages to celebrate both sides of the British war effort. One side is invention, represented by Michael Redgrave's eccentric inventor Barnes Wallis, who devised the revolutionary bouncing bomb. The other side is bravery, represented by Richard Todd's Wing Commander Gibson who, together with the men of 617 Squadron, was entrusted with the task of using it to flood the Ruhr dams and destroy the adjoining Nazi military-industrial complexes.

The film is structured in two parts of differing style and mood, the first showing the progress of Wallace's bomb from an idea developed on a ping-pong table, to tests in miniature tanks, to full-scale trials; the second documenting the application of his ideas in the mission itself. The climactic, almost documentary-like scenes in the war room are nail-bitingly tense, and the sequences depicting the bomb trials and the raid itself are augmented with actual documentary footage, creating a vivid, highly convincing atmosphere only partially dissipated by some sadly unconvincing model and special effects shots of the

◄

While the special effects were not that realistic, they earned an Oscar nomination for George Blackwell and Gilbert Taylor, although most fans remember the stirring music by Eric Coates.

dam-busting itself. The film ably conveys the fear and difficulties of piloting a hazardous mission, the difficulties of communicating and coordinating with the other planes, and the incredible precision required to ensure the bombs land exactly on target. But its particular distinction lies in the decision to portray Wallace as, in his own way, equally heroic, refusing to give up on his invention despite a number of failed trials, seemingly endless

"THERE'S SUCH A VERY THIN DIVIDING LINE BETWEEN INSPIRATION AND OBSESSION . . ." BARNES WALLIS

red tape and bureaucratic obstruction, and the cost to his health in working day and night to perfect it. Ultimately, the success or failure of the mission rests on his shoulders, but once the planes take off, he can only watch and wait as impotently as everyone else as reports of the bombers' progress come through with agonizing slowness and imprecision.

This is reinforced in the final scene, which shows Wallace reflecting that, had he known of the human cost of his theories he may never have been able to continue, and Gibson reassuring him that none of the pilots would have chosen otherwise. The picture thus ends on an unexpected note of quiet poignancy that is surprising and highly effective. For most viewers, however, the most abiding feature of the movie remains Eric Coates's stirring "Dam Busters March," one of the most famous compositions in the history of the genre. **MC**

▶

Wing Commander Guy Gibson (Todd) is the stereotypical stiff-upper-lipped R.A.F. pilot in charge of the bold bombing mission.

A THRILLING
LOVE STORY
THAT DEFIES ALL
CONVENTION!

A man's stormy love...
a woman's passion
for freedom.

"HILL 24
DOESN'T
ANSWER!"

*The First Major Motion Picture
to be produced entirely in English
in the Holy Land!*

Starring

MICHAEL WAGER • HAYA HARARIT • EDWARD MULHARE

(Winner of Best Actress
Award Cannes Festival)

and

SHOSHANA DAMARI

A SIKOR FILMS Presentation   A Continental Distributing Inc. Release

HILL 24 DOESN'T ANSWER 1955 (ISRAEL)

Director Thorold Dickinson **Producers** Thorold Dickinson, Peter Frye
Screenplay Peter Frye, Zvi Kolitz **Cinematography** Gerald Gibbs **Music** Paul
Ben Haim **Cast** Edward Mulhare, Michael Wager, Margalit Oved, Arik Lavie, Michael
Shilo, Haya Harareet, Eric Greene, Stanley Preston, Haim Eynav, Zalman Lebiush

At 5:45 A.M. on July 18, 1948, the U.N. established the original
borders that established the State of Israel after the War of
Independence. Any territory held by the Israeli Defense Forces
(I.D.F.) at that time became Israeli by U.N. decree. *Hill 24 Doesn't
Answer* (a.k.a. *Giv'a 24 Eina Ona*) is a portmanteau film that tells
three stories about those who fought for the establishment of
Israel, using this deadline as a structuring device.

Four Israeli soldiers—James Finnegan (Mulhare), Allan
Goodman (Wager), Esther Hadassi (Oved) and David Airam
(Lavie)—are sent to hold Hill 24, just outside of Jerusalem,
before that fateful deadline. On their way up to the hill, the
three men each tell their story about why they are fighting this
war (significantly, the one woman's story is subsumed within
Goodman's story, thereby denying her a voice of her own).
Finnegan is ex-British police, part of the Mandate's policy of
blockading the shores preventing illegal Jewish refugees from
escaping the ashes of the Holocaust. Through falling in love
with a Palestinian Jew, Finnegan is won over to the Israeli cause.
Goodman, a New York Jew vacationing in Israel, bought a ticket
for a tour of the Old City of Jerusalem, but due to increased

◄
**This was the first
movie produced
in Israel. Its Hebrew
title was *Giv'a 24
Eina Ona*, although
the film is shot
mostly in English.**

attacks on Jewish tourists by Arab partisans, his paid-for tour is cancelled; he joins the I.D.F. because he objects to being prevented from his tourist activities. During the siege of Jerusalem, Goodman is injured and is caught in the Old City along with the other Israeli soldiers (Hadassi helped nurse him back to heath—that's the extent of her story). Finally, Airam, a Sabra, on maneuvers against the Egyptian army

> ## "THE COURAGE AND DEDICATION DISPLAYED . . . IS NOT ONLY PLAUSIBLE BUT OFTEN MOVING." *NEW YORK TIMES*

captures who he thinks is an Egyptian but turns out to be an injured ex-Nazi. Airam treats the enemy's wounds, even after he finds the SS tattoo on the soldier's chest.

There is a distinctly didactic aspect to *Hill 24 Doesn't Answer*: Finnegan is motivated by love for a woman, Goodman for love of Jerusalem and historic Judaism, and finally Airam, in confronting a Nazi, is motivated by love even for his worst enemy. The film is almost entirely in English, which suggests that the British-born Dickinson intended it for export, specifically to American audiences, to propagandize the West in support of Israel. Therefore, one may conclude that the picture is trying to appeal to a wide variety of Jewish and non-Jewish views, and thus insists that the forging of Israel was not out of hate (of Nazis, of Arabs, of the West), but Christ-like, out of various forms of love. **MK**

► **The film ends not with "The End" written across the screen, but with "The Beginning" referring to the newly established Israeli state.**

THRONE OF BLOOD 1957 (JAPAN)

Director Akira Kurosawa **Producers** Akira Kurosawa, Sojiro Motoki
Screenplay Shinobu Hashimoto, Ryuzo Kikushima, Akira Kurosawa,
Hideo Oguni **Cinematography** Asakazu Nakai **Music** Masaru Sato
Cast Toshirô Mifune, Isuzu Yamada, Minoru Chiaki, Takashi Shimura

Akira Kurosawa remains Japan's most well known director in
the West. He directed two Shakespeare adaptations: the first,
Throne of Blood (a.k.a. *Kumonosu jô*), is based upon *Macbeth*;
while the second, *Ran* (1985), is based upon *King Lear*. While the
main themes of *Macbeth* remain in the former —an ambitious
man is encouraged by his domineering wife to kill his superior
in order to take power, only to be haunted by the ghosts of the
dead and eventually die—its haunting, lyrical style owes much
to traditional Japanese cinematic aesthetics along with the
stylized format of Noh theater.

Instead of 11th century Scotland, the film is set in 16th-
century Japan, a turbulent time in Japanese history marked by
civil unrest during which warlords known as *daimyo* competed
for control over land, property, and ultimately the country itself.
The three witches from *Macbeth* are condensed into a forest
spirit that Taketori Washizu (Mifune) and his General Miki
(Chiaki) come across one day in the aptly named Cobweb
Forest. The spirit tells him that he will become the leader of
Cobweb Castle (also known as the North Castle), Miki will be
promoted, and his son will be Washizu's successor.

◀
**While adaptations
of Shakespeare can
feel "stagey," here
the use of Japanese
Noh theater
enhances rather
than detracts from
the overall impact.**

While Macbeth holds on to the idea of free will, Washizu cannot escape his fate and neither can Miki or his son. The use of Cobweb as a prefix for both the forest and castle emphasizes the centrality of fate in *Throne of Blood*. The belief in fate was common to many Samurai at the time the play is set. As in *Macbeth*, Washizu is encouraged by his scheming wife, Lady Asaji Washizu (Yamada), to kill Lord Tsuzuki so that he can

"POSSIBLY THE FINEST SHAKESPEAREAN ADAPTATION EVER COMMITTED TO THE SCREEN." DEREK MALCOLM

become Lord of the Castle. Soon after the murder, Lady Asaji tells Washizu that she is pregnant, suggesting that the prophecy may not come true. When Washizu returns to the forest, he is told that he will remain Lord until the Cobweb Forest moves. However the child is stillborn and the Cobweb Forest does in fact move toward the castle, although by natural and not supernatural forces. The stunning and protracted end sequences in which Washizu is killed as his men turn upon him is a cinematic tour de force.

► **Filmed in black and white, *Throne of Blood* is beautifully shot as seen here with a misty, ethereal boat scene.**

Most of the action takes place either in the forest or in the castle—imprisonment and entrapment signified by the spider imagery. There are few close-ups, keeping the viewer at a distance until the final scenes in which Washizu is shot multiple times by his subjects' arrows. The use of close-ups here enhances Washizu's desperation as he attempts to escape his fate. **CB**

FILM PRODUKCJI POLSKIE
REŻYSERIA: ANDRZEJ WAJDA
WYKONAWCY: TERESA IŻEWSKA
TADEUSZ JANCZAR
WIENCZYSTAW GLIŃSKI
EMIL KAREWICZ I INNI

Kanał

NAGRODA:
SPECIALNA JURY
SREBRNA PALMA
NA MFF W CANNES – 1957R
ZŁOTY MEDAL
NA FESTIWALU MŁODZIEŻY
W MOSKWIE

KANAŁ 1957 (POLAND)

Director Andrzej Wajda **Screenplay** Jerzy Stefan Stawiński (screenplay and story) **Cinematography** Jerzy Lipman **Music** Jan Krenz **Cast** Teresa Berezowska, Wieńczysław Glinski, Tadeusz Gwiazdowski, Teresa Izewska, Tadeusz Janczar, Emil Karewicz, Stanisław Mikulski, Vladek Sheybal, Zofia Lindorf, Janina Jablonowska

Kanał (a.k.a. *Canal*) is one of the most bitterly ironic and fatalistic war films ever. One minute into the movie a voice-over tells us to "watch closely" the men whose story we are about to see, "for these are the last hours of their lives." From the very start, then, there is no hope of survival.

Kanał chronicles a Polish militia company's adventures during the 1944 uprising in Warsaw. A magisterial four-minute opening shot introduces us to several of them: their leader Lieutenant Zadra (Glinski), second-in-command Wise (Karewicz), messenger girl Halinka (Berezowska), and officer-cadet Korab (Janczar). As they snake and crawl through the ruins of Warsaw they are joined by good-time girl Daisy (Izewska). Each time this group of hopeless heroes appears to find some relief, an abrupt explosion or gunfire disrupts the peace. The only way out seems by climbing into the sewers. But that is exactly where true hell starts.

The last ten minutes give *Kanał* its real irony and fatalism. The company splits up into three groups, but none of the groups makes it out of the sewers alive. Daisy escorts the injured Korab to one exit, but finds it blocked by iron bars. She

◀
The black-and-white cinematography enhances the morbid psychology of the doomed characters while the sewers of Warsaw stand as a metaphor for the utter debasement of war.

can see the light and smell the green grass, but cannot get to it. A second group, led by Wise, finds an open exit. But as they climb out, German soldiers stand waiting. They are robbed of their possessions (personal belongings that had kept many of them going) and executed. War is reduced to its (literally) filthy reality in the sewers of Warsaw. ("Kanał" is "sewer" in Polish.) Only a duo led by Zarda seems to reach freedom. But not really.

> ## "THESE ARE THE TRAGIC HEROES: WATCH THEM CLOSELY IN THE REMAINING HOURS OF THEIR LIVES." NARRATOR

When Zarda asks Kula (Gwiazdowski), the company's record-keeper, where the rest are, Kula admits they got lost a long time ago. Unable to comprehend that he did not lead his company to safety, Zarda shoots Kula dead. With a despairing look on his face he descends into the sewers again. As he disappears underground, the records scatter into the wind—lives lost forever.

▶ The grim irony that in order to carry on the war against the Nazis, the Polish fighters, such as Zarda (Glinski), have to live and die in excrement, is never far away.

The initial reception of *Kanał* was one of critical acclaim and at least a moderate commercial success. The film was released widely in Western Europe, and then found its way to North American campuses and art house theaters. Over the decades, *Kanał*'s reputation has grown consistently to consolidate its place in the cinematic pantheon as one of the greatest Polish films of all time—one that captured the ethos of a people's history continually altered by war. **EM**

THE BRIDGE ON THE RIVER KWAI

1957 (U.K. • U.S.)

Director David Lean **Producer** Sam Spiegel **Screenplay** Michael Wilson,
Carl Foreman (from the novel by Pierre Boulle) **Cinematography** Jack Hildyard
Music Malcolm Arnold **Cast** William Holden, Alec Guinness, Jack Hawkins,
Sessue Hayakawa, James Donald, Geoffrey Horne, André Morell, Peter Williams

Described variously as a rousing World War II adventure yarn,
a metaphorical portrait of cultural conflict, and an
autobiographical deconstruction of director David Lean's
legendary status as an on-set tyrant and control freak, *The
Bridge on the River Kwai* is perhaps most fascinating for the
multiple readings it offers and encourages. This richness in
meaning and appeal appears to derive precisely from all the
problems and conflicts producer Sam Spiegel saw this project
go through before it finally reached completion.

Spiegel had conceived of it from the start as a large-scale
prestige picture that would combine the Cinemascope
spectacle of its exotic locale with the highbrow appeal derived
from the literary source material and a top-notch cast and crew.
But finding his key personnel for this morally complex adventure
story proved to be far more difficult than expected: Alec
Guinness first turned down the role of Colonel Nicholson,
objecting to the screenplay as "too anti-British," the part was
subsequently turned down by Charles Laughton, Laurence
Olivier, Noël Coward, Ray Milland, and James Mason, while the

◄
A hugely popular
success and
multiple Oscar
winner upon its
release, the film's
reputation as
a classic today
continues to
overshadow
its troublesome
production history.

role of Shears, originally envisioned for Humphrey Bogart, was rejected by an equal number of leading actors. Similar problems plagued Spiegel's choice of director: John Ford, Howard Hawks, and Nicholas Ray were all considered and approached, while full-scale construction of the eponymous bridge on location in Ceylon was already underway as production costs continued to skyrocket. Meanwhile, a succession of screenwriters labored

"DO NOT SPEAK TO ME OF RULES. THIS IS WAR! THIS IS NOT A GAME OF CRICKET!" *COL. SAITO*

on Pierre Boulle's novel, the final version written primarily by the blacklisted Carl Foreman and Michael Wilson, denied both screen credit and the resulting Oscar until 1984, when they were posthumously awarded.

Given these tremendous difficulties and the unremitting hardship of location work on the picture's remote jungle set, the film's artistic success seems to confirm the hypothesis that troubled productions often result in richer, more challenging works than those produced in environments of harmony and consensus. The strife and dissent that plagued the production from the start also seems to have fed into the movie's uncompromising portrayal of the moral and ethical boundaries it explores and lays bare with such skill. Perhaps in this case a warlike environment was required to create such a convincing portrayal of a wartime dilemma. **DH**

▶
Col. Saito (Hayakawa) and Colonel Nicholson (Guiness) stand in front of the eponymous and still intact bridge.

НОВЫЙ ХУДОЖЕСТВЕННЫЙ ФИЛЬМ
В. РОЗОВА
МИХАИЛА КАЛАТОЗОВА
ЛЕТЯТ ЖУРАВЛИ

THE CRANES ARE FLYING 1957 (U.S.S.R.)

Director Mikhail Kalatozov **Producer** Mikhail Kalatozov **Screenplay** Viktor Rozov
(based on his play) **Cinematography** Sergei Urusevsky **Music** Moisey Vaynberg
Cast Tatyana Samojlova, Aleksey Batalov, Vasili Merkuryev, Aleksandr Shvorin,
Svetlana Kharitonova, Konstantin Nikitin, Valentin Zubkov, Antonina Bogdanova

One of the most critically acclaimed films produced during the
Soviet Union's cultural and artistic "thaw" following Stalin's
death, Mikhail Kalatozov's *The Cranes Are Flying* (a.k.a. *Miprinaven
tseroebi*) is a powerful portrait of the losses suffered in World
War II. Memorable depictions of brutal land battles, as well as
re-creations of the devastating German air strikes on Moscow,
punctuate this landmark of Soviet cinema—but it is the war's
impact upon the lives of Boris Ivanovich (Batalov) and his
beautiful girlfriend, Veronika (Tatyana Samojlova in an amazing
performance) that constitutes Kalatozov's primary focus.

While this may initially seem fodder for a clichéd melodrama,
The Cranes Are Flying successfully grounds its narrative in
psychological realism that exposes the emotional desolation
that separation and loss can inflict. When war erupts and Boris,
having volunteered to serve, departs for the front, Veronika
struggles to come to terms with her true love's sudden absence.
This proves more difficult than she anticipates when her family
perishes during a German air strike and Boris's cowardly cousin
Mark (Shvorin) rapes her. Forced into a loveless marriage and
faced with the possibility that Boris may have died in action,

◄

**On its release
in the U.S.S.R.
the movie caused
a stir because it
ducked away from
the propagandist
line that insisted
every war film
had to celebrate
Lenin's and Stalin's
leadership.**

Veronika's world soon totters on the verge of total collapse. Perhaps the most impressive component of *The Cranes Are Flying* is Sergei Urusevsky's amazingly fluid cinematography. Urusevsky's ever-mobile camera virtually becomes a character in its own right. In one astounding continuous take, Urusevsky's camera bobs and weaves its way through a teeming crowd as Veronika races desperately toward the train of departing

"CRANES LIKE SHIPS SAILING IN THE SKY; WHITE ONES AND GREY ONES, WITH LONG BEAKS THEY FLY." VERONIKA

soldiers in the hopes of saying farewell to her beloved Boris. When she reaches the front of the crowd, the camera, still without cutting away, soars upward to capture the swarming masses and departing train in an extreme long shot that at once captures the chaos of the moment and emphasizes Veronika's heartbreak. In such sequences, Urusevsky, a frequent collaborator of Kalatozov, proves himself one of the world's most talented cinematographers, joining an elite group comprised of visionaries like Gregg Toland, Sven Nykvist, Vittorio Storaro, and Kazuo Miyagawa.

► **Veronika (Samojlova) feels only isolation as her loved one departs for the Russian front.**

Kalatozov and Urusevsky would go on to break even more ground cinematically with 1964's *I Am Cuba*, but it is their remarkable contributions to *The Cranes Are Flying* that earned the film top prize at the 1958 Cannes Film Festival and captured the attention of filmgoers around the globe. **JM**

PATHS OF GLORY 1957 (U.S.)

Director Stanley Kubrick **Producer** James B. Harris **Screenplay** Stanley Kubrick, Calder Willingham, James Thompson (based on the novel by Humphrey Cobb)
Cinematography Georg Krause **Music** Gerald Fried **Cast** Kirk Douglas, Ralph Meeker, Adolphe Menjou, George Macready, Wayne Morris, Richard Anderson

Seldom have the absurdities of "running a war" (as one general calls it) been exposed so effectively as in Kubrick's *Paths of Glory*, the story of French Army regiment 701 in the trenches during the stalemate of the World War I. The regiment is ordered to take the heavily fortified Ant Hill from the Germans. The regiment's commander, Colonel Dax (Douglas), tries to convince the General Staff that the attack is suicide, but he is told to advance regardless. The attack fails. None of the troops come even near the Ant Hill. Infuriated, the general in command of the offensive orders the artillery to fire on its own men. When that order is refused, he has a hastily installed court martial try three random soldiers for cowardice and mutiny. Colonel Dax defends his men, but they are found guilty and shot by a firing squad.

Paths of Glory pitches the upright dutifulness of Dax and the defendants (who sit straight and talk straight) against the sinister and power-hungry General Mireau (Macready), who cynically observes that the "men died beautifully," and the manipulative Chief of Staff General Broulard (Menjou). The film hammers home the point that, just as in times of peace, the powerful play games and the poor still die in their wars.

◄

Paths of Glory's brave message has secured its place in the pantheon of cinema.

The soldiers are naive, sad characters. The officers are their real enemy. We never even see the German soldiers. *Paths of Glory* delivers this message bluntly. At the same time, the picture is full of magisterial stylistics, be it the long traveling shots through the trenches, the creepiness of a tense nighttime reconnaissance, during which a suddenly lit flare reveals a bump in the terrain to be a corpse, the stupendous crane shots

"A BITTER AND BITING TALE, TOLD WITH STUNNING POINT AND NERVE-WRACKING INTENSITY." *JUDITH CRIST*

of the meticulously choreographed mass attack scene, the backlights in the barracks that give the convicted soldiers a saint-like aura during their "last meal," or the tight geometrical procedures of the execution.

In a touching epilogue, Kubrick shows a terrified German girl (Susanne Christian—the later Mrs. Kubrick) being dragged onto a barn stage and ordered to sing for the rowdy and boisterous soldiers of the 701st. As she sings her sad song, they fall silent, and a series of sharply carved close-ups reveals to us how these men are suddenly reminded of their humanity and reduced to silent tears.

▶
Kirk Douglas not only played the lead, but also financed the movie through his production company.

Kubrick's uncompromising rendition of the subject matter in *Paths of Glory* did not make it easy for audiences and critics to warm to the film. Indeed in a few countries, such as France, it was even withheld from distribution. **EM**

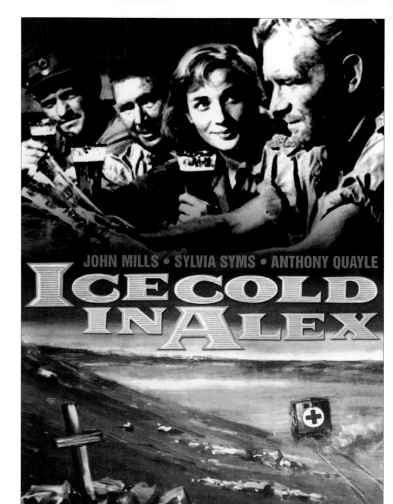

JOHN MILLS • SYLVIA SYMS • ANTHONY QUAYLE

ICECOLD IN ALEX

ICE COLD IN ALEX 1958 (U.K.)

Director J. Lee Thompson **Producer** W. A. Whittaker **Screenplay** Christopher Landon (based on his novel), T. J. Morrison **Cinematography** Gilbert Taylor **Music** Leighton Lucas **Cast** John Mills, Sylvia Syms, Anthony Quayle, Harry Andrews, Diane Clare, Richard Leech, Liam Redmond, Allan Cuthbertson

In the 1950s, World War II was still a frequently used backdrop for British dramas. Films such as *The Cruel Sea* (1953), *The Dam Busters* (1955), and *The Bridge on the River Kwai* (1957) were based in part on real-life accounts, and increasingly explored the psychological trauma of the war. This reached its apogee perhaps with *Ice Cold in Alex* (a.k.a. *Desert Attack*).

The story starts after the fall of Tobruk in North Africa in 1942: An alcoholic, battle-fatigued Eighth Army captain (Mills), a sergeant-major (Andrews) and two nurses set off in an ambulance to Alexandria. They soon pick up a stranded South African officer in the desert, Van der Poel (Quayle), but after negotiating a minefield they are spotted by German tanks that open fire. Anson allows alcohol to impede his judgment, resulting in one of the nurses being killed, and he vows that the next drink he has will be an ice-cold lager in Alexandria.

Over the course of the journey, Van der Poel's behavior becomes increasingly suspicious to the others—he is twice able to persuade the Germans to let them go and always carries a large pack with him in his very punctual toilet breaks. By the time they confirm that he is a spy, he has become a valuable

◄

The poster shows part of the film's most famous scene—the group enjoying that long-yearned-for beer in Alexandria, their collective struggle finally over.

member of the team, so that when he falls into a salt marsh they work hard to save him. Nurse Diana (Syms) is a plucky independent woman, but the sudden romance between her and Captain Anson seems to be rather incongruous and, with all the sweaty male flesh on display, their love scene at times seems to have been almost bolted on as an afterthought, purely to dampen down any suspicion of homoeroticism.

"WORTH WAITING FOR."
CAPTAIN ANSON (MILLS) AFTER DRAINING HIS GLASS OF BEER.

J. Lee Thompson's skilled direction keeps the tension taut throughout—the audience faces each new obstacle with the crew, sharing their fear, fatigue, and occasional despair. Some critics have argued that the picture explores a British sense of inferiority and uncertainty in the post-war, post-imperial world—comparing the strong, calm colonial Van der Poel with the neurotic, worn-out Captain Anson. Indeed, Mills here subtly subverts a history of playing dashing patriotic chaps in films made during World War II and it is tempting to see his character as representing a nation in decline. However, there is still plenty of plucky British decency and resourcefulness being celebrated, and *Ice Cold in Alex* is perhaps more accurately seen as a call to "keep calm and carry on" regardless. In this, the figure of the tireless, unflappable working-class sergeant-major represents the yeomanly bedrock of traditional British grit. **KM**

► **Captain Anson (Mills) and Nurse Diana Murdoch (Syms) provide an unlikely romance against all the pervasive sweaty male bonding.**

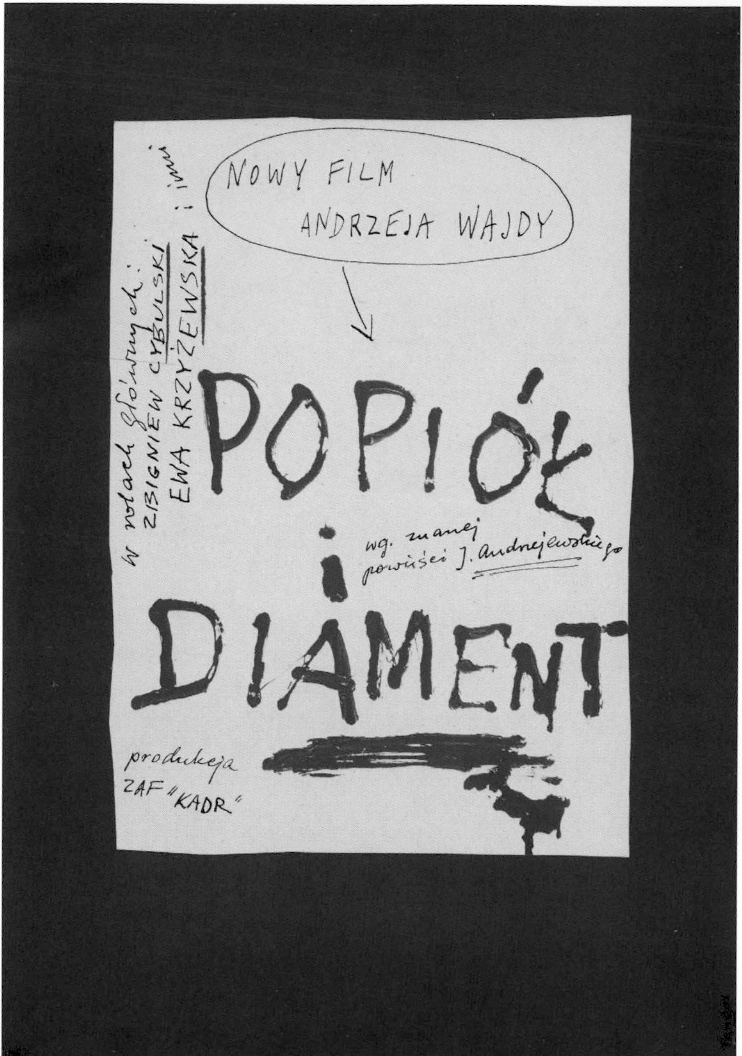
NOWY FILM
ANDRZEJA WAJDY
w rolach głównych:
ZBIGNIEW CYBULSKI
EWA KRZYŻEWSKA
i inni
POPIÓŁ
i
DIAMENT
wg. znanej
powieści J. Andrzejewskiego
produkcja
ZAF "KADR"

ASHES AND DIAMONDS 1958 (POLAND)

Director Andrzej Wajda **Screenplay** Andrzej Wajda, Jerzy Andrzejewski
(from his novel) **Cinematography** Jerzy Wójcik **Music** Filip Nowak, Jan Krenz
Cast Zbigniew Cybulski, Ewa Krzyzewska, Waclaw Zastrzezynski, Adam
Pawlikowski, Bogumił Kobiela, Jan Ciecierski, Stanisław Milski, Artur Młodnicki

For a few years at the end of the 1950s, after Italian neorealism
waned and before the French New Wave rolled in, Polish cinema
was *the* art cinema. With their complex, often ambiguous tales of
wartime solidarity, sacrifice, and commitment, the Poles offered
the most cogent example yet of socialism with a human face.
Films by Aleksandr Ford, Andrzej Munk, Jerzy Kawalerowicz and
others won a slew of festival prizes and attracted international
audiences. But perhaps the finest of all the Polish films of this
era—the one that came to stand for an emerging generation
of East European artists and intellectuals—was Andrzej Wajda's
Ashes and Diamonds (a.k.a. *Popiół i diament*).

Based on the controversial novel by Jerzy Andrzejewski,
Wajda's masterpiece unspools on the last day of World War II.
With Poland decimated and Warsaw in ruins, the country is
effectively a blank slate. The enemy may have surrendered, but
the winners aren't sure what they've won: both Communists
and Nationalists can already sense that their fragile wartime
alliance is unraveling. Enter Maciek (Cybulski), a young hothead
attached to the Nationalist underground in a provincial town.
He is assigned to kill the recently arrived Communist district

◄

**Part of an
unplanned
trilogy along with
Generation (1954)
and *Kanal* (1957),
Wajda's *Ashes
and Diamonds*
continues the
theme of World
War II and
the younger
generation.**

leader and holes up for the night in a run-down hotel. But this is just about the first night of peace that Maciek has known in his adult life, and he's eager to see what else this world might offer. He meets and falls for a pretty young barmaid (Krzyzewska), and his attention to her threatens to get in the way of his mission.

Throughout *Ashes and Diamonds*, Wajda employs a looming deep focus, so that disparate characters, as well as opposing

"REVEALS A . . . TROUBLED AND NUANCED PERSPECTIVE ON POLAND'S CHANGING POLITICAL TIDES." *SCOTT TOBIAS*

political agendas, take on equal weight in the frame. Yet the real show is Wajda's revelation of Cybulski as Maciek. With his eyes perpetually hidden behind shades and his slightly gawky but endearing manner, Cybulski was hailed as the "James Dean of the East," the symbol for a generation that wanted to look past political labels and wartime angst to focus on an individual's human qualities. (The actor's reputation as the Polish James Dean was cemented with his tragic death in a 1967 train accident.) Within the space of a few shots, Cybulski is able to go from dementia to helplessness to anger; his final "death dance," with his chilling laughter as he staggers through a field after being shot, is surely one of the most powerful—and often quoted— endings in film history. And while it can't really be called a thriller, there are aspects of film noir in *Ashes and Diamonds'* tale of a fatalistic, violent hero plunging toward his doom. **RP**

►
Zbigniew Cybulski as Maciek with the looks, shades, and demeanor of a Polish James Dean.

BALLAD OF A SOLDIER 1959 (U.S.S.R.)

Director Grigori Chukhrai **Producer** M. Chernova **Screenplay** Grigori Chukhrai, Valentin Ezhov **Cinematography** Vladimir Nikolayev, Era Savelyeva **Music** Mikhail Ziv **Cast** Vladimir Ivashov, Zhanna Prokhorenko, Antonina Maksimova, Nikolai Kryuchkov, Yevgeni Urbansky, Elza Lezhdev, Aleksandr Kuznetsov, Yevjeni Teterin

Nineteen-year-old Pvt. Alyosha Skvortsov (Ivashov) manages to destroy two German tanks; instead of a medal, he asks for a leave to see his mother and fix the roof of his house. The train ride home through war-ravaged Russia is more complicated than planned, however, and becomes an "Odyssey" full of dangers, temptations, and disappointments, but also romance. Alyosha's endeavors are all the more tragic because narration at the beginning of the film warns us that he is one of those who never came back from the war. The short leave we witness is his last journey home, and the few minutes he gets to have with his mother are all the more poignant for that.

Ballad of a Soldier (a.k.a. *Ballada o Soldate*) has a deceptively simple structure, but its episodes and ingenious attention to detail inform the film with a profound humanity and an insight into not only the "Russian soul" but the human condition in general. A minor event from World War I thus becomes an epic, and Alyosha—brave, innocent, open-hearted, ready to help— is the archetypal Russian hero. His true heroism is not in his almost accidental destruction of the German tanks; it is evident in his humanity throughout the delay-ridden journey.

◄

This well-received, lyrical tear-jerker showed the softer domestic underbelly of wartime Russia away from the frontline.

He misses his train trying to help an invalid soldier who is reluctant to go back to his wife because of his injuries; he falls in love with a girl who is hitch-hiking on the military train, but misses it (and her) when he goes for some water; already late, he still goes to deliver the gift to a fellow-soldier's wife, who turns out to be an adulteress so he takes it to the soldier's father instead; at a bombed bridge he heroically rescues

"HE WAS, AND IN OUR MEMORY WILL FOREVER REMAIN, A SOLDIER . . . A RUSSIAN SOLDIER." *NARRATION*

women and children from the burning train. Successfully passing all these trials he barely has time to say his last good-byes to his mother and his village. Grigori Chukhrai captures the greatness of Russian landscapes and the complexities of the Russian soul without overt idealization or ideology. Together with touching examples of love, faith, stubbornness, and the will to live, Alyosha also encounters bribery, betrayal, and ungratefulness (almost causing the film to be censored in Russia). The stunning black-and-white images, impeccably photographed, are iconic and perfectly accentuate this archetypal story told from the perspective of common soldiers and civilians. As the narration sums up: "He could have become a remarkable man. He could have become a builder or beautified the land with gardens. But he was, and in our memory will forever remain, a soldier . . . a Russian soldier." **DO**

▶
Granted four days' home leave before having to return to the front, Pvt. Alyosha Skvortsov (Ivashov) embarks on a sort of pilgrim's progress through war-torn Russia.

Titanus
ARLO PONTI *presenta* UN FILM DI VITTORIO DE SICA

SOPHIA LOREN *in*
LA CIOCIARA

JEAN PAUL BELMONDO · ELEONORA BROWN · RAF VALLONE
ALBERTO MORAVIA · CESARE ZAVATTINI

TWO WOMEN 1960 (ITALY · FRANCE)

Director Vittorio De Sica **Producers** Carlo Ponti, Joseph E. Levine
Screenplay Cesare Zavattini, Vittorio De Sica (from the novel by Alberto Moravia)
Cinematography Gábor Pogány **Music** Armando Trovajoli **Cast** Sophia Loren,
Jean-Paul Belmondo, Eleonora Brown, Carlo Ninchi, Andrea Checchi

For her role in *Two Women* (a.k.a. *La Ciociara*), Sophia Loren
(then just 26 years old) deservedly won the Academy Award for
Best Actress, the first time a non-American actress in a foreign-
language film received this honor. Adapted from a novel by
Alberto Moravia, this may not be the greatest of all the Vittorio
De Sica–Cesare Zavattini collaborations (one need only
consider 1948's *The Bicycle Thief*)—some of the movie suffers
from poor pacing and a general sense of listlessness—but
Loren is a marvel to behold nonetheless.

She plays Cesira, a thirty-something widow in 1943 Italy who
leaves her grocery store in San Lorenzo in the hands of her
sometime lover Giovanni (Vallone), fleeing the daily bombings
by the Allied forces with her angelic teenage daughter Rosetta
(Brown) in tow. Cesira's plan is to return to the rural Southern
village of her youth, Sant Eufemia, where she believes they will
be safer. Arriving after a difficult journey by train, she meets
Michele Di Libero (Belmondo), the sensitive, intelligent son of a
local farmer with whom Rosetta falls in love, though he in
return finds himself falling for her lovely mother. As the town
grows increasingly besieged by bombings and shortages, the

◄
De Sica and
Zavattini's previous
collaborations
included *Shoeshine*
(1946) and
Umberto D.
(1952)—both
arguably better
neorealism classics
than this Loren
tour de force.

anti-fascist Michele—too proper and shy to do anything about his affection for Cesira—is forced to guide some fleeing Germans on an escape route, while Cesira and Rosetta unwisely decide to head back to Rome before the anticipated arrival of the Americans to clear the roads. Along the way, mother and daughter suffer a tragedy that changes both of their lives forever. The two women are captured by a retreating platoon

> "I WENT WITH THE FIRST ONE THAT SAID 'I WILL BRING YOU TO ROME.' I MARRIED ROME, NOT HIM." CESIRA

of Moroccan troops and brutally raped on the grounds of a bombed-out church, despite Cesira's best efforts to protect her child from the ravages of war.

Loren also won the Best Actress Award at the Cannes Film Festival, and the same honor from the British Film Academy; more importantly, however, she demonstrated in *Two Women* that she was a mature actress with talent that matched her looks. Despite being deglamorized here, she was still magnificent. And although the plot may at times feel predictable, Loren rises to the occasion by exhibiting a primal maternal force almost as old as time itself.

▶

Cesira (Loren) faces a terrible tragedy as she and her daughter get caught up with retreating Axis soldiers at the end of Italy's war against the Allies.

Although *Two Women* doesn't quite match the brilliant simplicity of De Sica–Zavattini's earlier neorealist masterpieces, it remains a remarkably moving, humane vision of individual struggle in an inhumane, war-torn world. **KW**

The Greatest High Adventure Ever Filmed!

COLUMBIA PICTURES presents

GREGORY PECK | DAVID NIVEN | ANTHONY QUINN

in CARL FOREMAN'S

THE GUNS OF NAVARONE

co starring

STANLEY BAKER · ANTHONY QUAYLE · IRENE PAPAS · GIA SCALA and JAMES DARREN

Written & Produced by | Based on the novel by | Music Composed & Conducted | Directed by | A HIGHROAD | COLOR and
CARL FOREMAN | ALISTAIR MacLEAN | by DIMITRI TIOMKIN | J. LEE THOMPSON | PRESENTATION | CINEMASCOPE

THE GUNS OF NAVARONE 1961 (U.K. • U.S.)

Director J. Lee Thompson **Producer** Carl Foreman **Screenplay** Carl Foreman
(based on the novel by Alistair MacLean) **Cinematography** Oswald Morris
Music Dimitri Tiomkin **Cast** Gregory Peck, Anthony Quinn, David Niven,
Stanley Baker, Irene Pappas, Gia Scala, James Robertson Justice, Richard Harris

The Guns of Navarone is usually seen as a classic action-
adventure yarn, so it might be surprising to learn that many of
the people involved in its production thought that they were
making an anti-war film. In an eventful narrative interspersed
with fight scenes, betrayals, and explosions, the more serious
elements are easily overlooked, but nevertheless they remain
an important part of a picture that is more complex and
challenging than its popular reputation might suggest.

The story of *The Guns of Navarone* involves what at first
glance looks like a straightforward "men on a mission" endeavor,
with a disparate group of individuals sent behind enemy lines
in the Aegean to destroy two powerful guns that are threatening
British forces. Each team member has his own idiosyncrasies—
David Niven's explosives expert is posh but anti-authority,
Stanley Baker's trained killer is traumatized by the deaths that
he has caused, Anthony Quinn's project leader is naively
enthusiastic, and so on—but we confidently expect them to
bond as the mission proceeds. However, this process turns out
to be both more fraught and more verbose than is usually the
case in films of this type. Examples include the team debating

◄
The movie
was a big color
spectacular and
won an Oscar
for Best Special
Effects—the
eponymous guns
being no larger
than an ordinary
table top.

whether they should leave behind or kill one of their number who has been injured or, in one of the movie's big dramatic scenes, whether they should execute a young woman who has betrayed them to the Nazis. The pragmatic, and sometimes ruthless, perspective in these debates is provided by Mallory, Gregory Peck's character, who has become the group leader. From today's perspective, Mallory resembles a proto-Jack

"THE ONLY WAY TO WIN THE WAR IS TO BE JUST AS NASTY AS THE ENEMY."

KEITH MALLORY

Bauer-24 figure who achieves his ends by any means necessary and who, as the film amply demonstrates, is capable of killing in cold blood and, when he judges it necessary, lying to his companions as well. However, *The Guns of Navarone* constantly pulls back from the more extreme and disturbing potentialities in this character.

It is striking in this respect that in the scene with the female traitor, Mallory is saved from shooting her by the intervention of a female Greek resistance fighter who kills her instead. The explosive action that brings the story to a spectacular end—with Peck and Niven successfully blowing the big guns to kingdom come—obviously provides a welcome relief from these dark moments. However, by that stage most of the team are either dead or captured, and the film's final moments are appropriately mournful. **PH**

▶
Mexican actor Anthony Quinn's swarthy, craggy looks graced over 100 films. *The Guns of Navarone* was one of his most successful roles.

ХУДОЖЕСТВЕННЫЙ ФИЛЬМ

Оператор ВАДИМ ЮСОВ

В главных ролях: Коля БУРЛЯЕВ, В. ЗУБКОВ, Е. ЖАРИКОВ, С. КРЫЛОВ и др.

Режиссёр-постановщик Андрей ТАРКОВСКИЙ

Авторы сценария: Владимир БОГОМОЛОВ, Михаил ПАПАВА

ИВАНОВО ДЕТСТВО

ПРОИЗВОДСТВО КИНОСТУДИИ МОСФИЛЬМ   Первое творческое объединение

IVAN'S CHILDHOOD 1962 (U.S.S.R.)

Director Andrey Tarkovsky **Screenplay** Vladimir Bogomolov, Mikhail Papava
Cinematography Vadim Yusov **Music** Vyacheslav Ovchinnikov **Cast** Nicolay
Burlyaev, Valentin Zubkov, Valentina Malyavina, Yevgeni Zharikov, Nikolai Grinko,
Stepan Krylov, Dmitri Milyutenko, Irma Rausch, Ivan Savkin, Vladimir Marenkov

As the quote overleaf suggests, this is a film about youth
obliterated by the horrors of war—an elegant if chilling portrait
of a boy's innocence vanquished by human cruelty and sudden
death. It is also the debut film that introduced viewers to the
articulations of a unique visual language that would come to
define the style of one of the great masters of 20th-century
cinema—Andrey Tarkovsky.

From the film's memorable opening shot of a bright-eyed
Ivan (Burlyaev) glimpsed through the strands of a spider's web,
Tarkovsky's poetic vision gradually ensnares his audience. These
ethereal and frequently nightmarish dreamscapes punctuate
this tragic narrative of a child who, orphaned during the
German invasion of the Soviet Union during World War II,
volunteers as a scout for a military unit. The unit is stationed
along the war's front line, and the child uses his diminutive
stature and aptitude for stealth as a means of determining
enemy positions. Emaciated and temperamental, Ivan's feral
stare and flailing limbs reveal a lust for vengeance eased only
through sleep, and the all-too-brief access to pleasant memories
that this altered state of consciousness provides. It is young

◄
**Andrey
Tarkovsky's
debut feature
(a.k.a.** *My Name
Is Ivan* **and** *Ivanovo
Detstvo*) **won the
Golden Lion at
the 1962 Venice
Film Festival.**

Ivan's inability to sate his rage, or even to imagine German soldiers as human beings capable of possessing a rich cultural history, that constitute the truly heartbreaking component of *Ivan's Childhood*. Unlike Masha (Malyavina), the film's delicate and naive Russian nurse whose eventual transfer allows her to escape the increasingly deadly encampment, Ivan is literally and figuratively trapped, destined to trudge through a

"ALL ATTRIBUTES OF CHILDHOOD . . . HAD GONE IRRETRIEVABLY OUT OF HIS LIFE." *ANDREY TARKOVSKY*

►

Ivan's fate is sealed in the domain of dreams as we see him waving happily at his smiling mother and chasing his laughing sister along the shore before running headlong into a sudden darkness.

darkened landscape from which there is no exit save death. *Ivan's Childhood* is likewise remarkable for its formal structure, especially its use of narrative ellipses, elaborate tracking shots, and Tarkovsky's uncanny ability to reveal the haunting beauty contained in even the most desolate of landscapes. Eschewing conventional battle sequences, the picture favors quieter, though by no means serene, exchanges that allow audiences to engage with the characters' emotional realms without being inundated by trite sentiment and tired clichés. Lt. Col. Gryaznov (Grinko), Lt. Galtsev (Zharikov), and Col. Katasonov (Krylov) function as a surrogate family for Ivan, but never do we succumb to the illusion that these three flawed soldiers could ever begin to replace what Ivan has lost. They can't even provide adequate role models upon which the boy might copy and overcome the all-consuming rage that inevitably seals his fate. **JM**

42 INTERNATIONAL STARS!

DARRYL F. ZANUCK'S

THE LONGEST DAY

FROM THE BOOK BY
CORNELIUS RYAN
RELEASED BY

20.
Century-Fox

THE LONGEST DAY 1962 (U.S.)

Directors Ken Annakin, Andrew Marton, Bernhard Wicki, Darryl F. Zanuck
Producer Darryl F. Zanuck **Screenplay** Cornelius Ryan, Romain Gary, James Jones, David Pursall, Jack Seddon **Cinematography** Jean Bourgoin, Walter Wottiz
Music Maurice Jarre **Cast** Paul Anka, Richard Burton, Sean Connery, Henry Fonda

The Longest Day is an epic blow-by-blow account of the Normandy invasion as told from the perspective of everyone from the lowliest of privates to the highest-ranking of officers. The film was groundbreaking in shooting from three different national perspectives and, unheard of at the time, using subtitles so that actors spoke in their own native language.

To help realize these varying national perspectives of D-Day, three directors were employed (supplemented at times by Zanuck himself) and—unusually—all three shot in different locations at exactly the same time. Recreating an attack that involved 3,000,000 men, 11,000 planes and 4,000 ships (still the largest armada the world has ever seen) was never going to be an easy task. But the dogged commitment of legendary Hollywood producer Darryl F. Zanuck, himself a veteran of two world wars, ensured that Warner Bros. provided a sizeable ten million dollar budget for the film.

Nominated for five Oscars, the film's bravura cinematography and numerous special effects were rewarded with two Academy Awards. The picture was nearly shut down on several occasions as Warners sought to cash in on what footage they

◄

As the poster boasts, never had so many heavyweight celluloid action heroes been assembled in one movie—Wayne, Connery, Mitchum, Burton, Buttons, Fonda, to name a few of the forty-two.

had in the wake of the financially crippling overrun of its other epic, *Cleopatra* (1963). For Zanuck, the film became something of a personal obsession. The studio's spectacular mismanagement of the latter picture meant that he was able to wrestle back control of the studio he founded (after several years as an independent producer) and was able to give *The Longest Day* the platform its scale and grandeur deserved.

"HE'S DEAD. I'M CRIPPLED. YOU'RE LOST. DO YOU SUPPOSE IT'S ALWAYS LIKE THAT? I MEAN WAR." CAMPBELL

Shooting in an impressive 31 separate external European locations, *The Longest Day* is arguably the first true World War II epic. Boasting possibly one of the biggest all-star casts of all time, the roster of stars was a fantasy regiment of players that included, among others, Henry Fonda, Robert Mitchum, Sal Mineo, Rod Steiger, George Segal, Red Buttons, Sean Connery, and John Wayne. If the sheer weight of the film's star power sometimes feels a little gimmicky, *The Longest Day*'s complex weave of a narrative necessitated a large cast. Comparisons with more recent war movies are inevitable. Contemporary films, such as *Saving Private Ryan* (1998), have offered a level of blood-and-guts realism that make *The Longest Day* now look a little tame. But it would be unfair to judge the earlier picture in this respect. *The Longest Day* remains a complex, spectacular, and urgent look at D-Day. **RH**

► Robert Mitchum gave a gritty performance to add to the spectacular filmmaking that still has considerable impact today.

From the creators of "The Bridge On The River Kwai."
Columbia Pictures presents The SAM SPIEGEL · DAVID LEAN Production of

LAWRENCE OF ARABIA

❝I deem him one of the greatest beings alive in our time.
...we shall never see his like again. His name will live in history.
It will live in the annals of war...It will live in the legends of Arabia!❞
—WINSTON CHURCHILL

Featuring
ALEC GUINNESS · ANTHONY QUINN
JACK HAWKINS · JOSE FERRER
ANTHONY QUAYLE · CLAUDE RAINS · ARTHUR KENNEDY
PETER O'TOOLE as 'LAWRENCE' · OMAR SHARIF as 'ALI'
ROBERT BOLT · SAM SPIEGEL · DAVID LEAN · TECHNICOLOR®

SUPER PANAVISION 70®

LAWRENCE OF ARABIA 1962 (U.K.)

Director David Lean **Producer** Sam Spiegel **Screenplay** Robert Bolt, Michael Wilson **Cinematography** Freddie Young **Music** Maurice Jarre **Cast** Peter O'Toole, Omar Sharif, Arthur Kennedy, Jack Hawkins, Alec Guinness, Anthony Quinn, Donald Wolfit, Anthony Quayle, José Ferrer, Claude Rains, I. S. Johar, Gamil Ratib, Michel Ray

Generally regarded as the best and most intelligent of David Lean's post-war blockbusters, *Lawrence of Arabia* fully lives up to its reputation as the war epic that even those who hate war epics admire, distinguished especially by its near-mystic visual sense and by its lush and romantic score by Maurice Jarre.

The subject of the film is T. E. Lawrence, an English aesthete and academic who, despite shortness of stature, an eccentric nature, and no military experience, managed to lead an Arab regiment to significant victories against the Turkish army. While in no way skimping on the grandeur, vast canvases, and vividly staged action sequences characteristic of Lean's other epic movies (such as *Bridge on the River Kwai* and *Doctor Zhivago*), the film is unusual in placing equal weight on psychological drama.

As played by Peter O'Toole in his first major starring role (after scores of other, vastly less suitable stars had been considered and either rejected or refused), Lawrence is alternately unassuming and forceful, retiring and pretentious, given to fits of indecision and self-loathing and yet capable of rousing himself to acts of incredible stamina and shocking (not least to himself) ferocity. The screenplay (by Robert Bolt,

◄
The movie scooped Oscars in most of the non-acting categories, including Freddie Young's haunting desert cinematography, and the seamless editing by Anne Coates.

author of *A Man for All Seasons*, and an originally uncredited, blacklisted Michael Wilson) is as much concerned with penetrating the mind of its central character as in depicting his achievements; the result is a film as divided and (in a sense) contradictory as Lawrence himself, and thus the perfect marriage of content and form. The cast mixes scene-stealing newcomers like O'Toole and Omar Sharif (as his Arab companion

"I PRAY THAT I MAY NEVER SEE THE DESERT AGAIN. HEAR ME, GOD."

LAWRENCE

Sherif Ali) with a fine supporting roster of British reliables, but the real star is ultimately the desert itself. Photographed with an almost hallucinatory intensity by Freddie Young, the landscape of the film is its essential defining feature. Logistical problems were considerable. Shooting miles away from the nearest facilities in intense heat, the cast and crew came under frequent barrage from heavy sandstorms and a variety of insects, and production was slowed by the need for teams of men to smooth over the vast expanses of sand after each take. The results, however, entirely justified the efforts of all concerned. The film was considerably re-edited after the initial preview showings, but in 1989 Lean supervised a masterful restoration that returned it to its original length of 222 minutes, replacing several lost sequences and having required some new over-dubbing by O'Toole and Sharif. **MC**

► Lawrence (O'Toole) riding camelback as he leads the Arabs to another victory against the Turks. "I've always been fascinated by these English nuts," said director David Lean.

1:06 AM

WHAT WENT INTO THESE FEW SECONDS...

1:07 AM

THE HELL...THE HEROISM...THE HIGH ADVENTURE...

1:08 AM

MAKE FOR THE SCREEN'S GREAT ENTERTAINMENT!

1:09 AM

THE GREAT ESCAPE

THE GREAT ESCAPE 1963 (U.S.)

Director John Sturges **Producer** John Sturges **Screenplay** James Clavell, W. R. Burnett (from the book by Paul Brickhill) **Cinematography** Daniel L. Fapp **Music** Elmer Bernstein **Cast** Steve McQueen, James Garner, Richard Attenborough, James Donald, Charles Bronson, Donald Pleasence, James Coburn, David McCallum

For many, *The Great Escape* is the archetypal war film. Never dull despite a methodical 173-minute running time, the whole movie (until the great escape itself) is set claustrophobically within the wires of Stalag Luft III, the Nazi P.O.W. camp built expressly for the containment of the most troublesome and escape-prone Allied soldiers ("We have in effect put all our rotten eggs in one basket," says the camp commandant, "and we intend to watch this basket carefully.") The film goes on to show the slow formulation of the escape plan, the ingenuity of its design and accomplishment, the toil and bravery of those who construct it, and then, after a number of false starts and interceptions, the escape bid itself and its largely tragic aftermath. Each section is given its own due weight and attention, and the whole is masterfully marshaled by director John Sturges.

The film is full of effective acting cameos and eternally memorable moments: Steve McQueen as the "cooler king," monotonously throwing his baseball against the wall of his solitary confinement cell; James Garner as "the scrounger," bribing gullible camp guards to obtain cameras, documents,

◄ No Oscars, but plenty of box office appeal was provided by this American production, sprinkled with well-cast British actors and underpinned by a highly catchy hum-along score.

and other essential items; Gordon Jackson caught out at the station by unthinkingly responding in English to the injunction "Good luck" from a German policeman; escape controller Richard Attenborough and the other captured men being told to stretch their legs by the German guards and instead being ruthlessly gunned down; Donald Pleasence (a real-life P.O.W. though more commonly a Nazi on screen) as the short-sighted

"YOU'RE CRAZY . . . TWO HUNDRED AND FIFTY GUYS JUST WALKIN' DOWN THE ROAD, JUST LIKE THAT?" *CAPT. HILTS*

forger who tries to fake the eye test that will decide whether he is included among the escapees or left behind. ("Thank you for getting me out," he says to Garner as he dies.)

Technically, the film is pretty much flawless, distinguished especially by Fapp's beautiful photography of authentic locations, and Elmer Bernstein's score, one of the most memorable ever recorded and impossible to stop humming. Despite a few excesses (notably McQueen's motorcycle chase), the film stays commendably close to the historical facts and makes no effort to dodge the reality that, though unquestionably heroic and ingenious, the escape was not in itself a success. Intercepted when it was barely underway, the majority of men never escaped at all, while of those who did only two made it to safety; others were recaptured and 50 (to whom the picture is dedicated) were killed. **MC**

▶

Steve McQueen was the epitome of celluloid cool in the 1960s.

DWARFING THE MIGHTIEST ! TOWERING OVER THE GREATEST !
The supreme spectacle that had to come thundering out of the most thrilling continent!

Joseph E. Levine presents

A Stanley Baker - Cy Endfield Production

TECHNICOLOR® TECHNIRAMA®

The Massacre of Isandhlwana ! The Mating Song of the Zulu Maidens ! The Incredible Siege of Ishiwane ! Night of the 40,000 Spears ! Day That Saved A Continent ! Mass Wedding of the 2,000 Warriors and 2,000 Virgins ! Amid the Battle's Heat...the Flash of Passion !

Starring
Stanley Baker · Jack Hawkins · Ulla Jacobsson · James Booth · Michael Caine
Screenplay by John Prebble and Cy Endfield · Suggested by an Article Written by John Prebble · Directed by Cy Endfield · A Diamond Films Ltd. Production
A Paramount Pictures Release ● Foreword Spoken by Richard Burton

ZULU 1964 (U.K.)

Director Cy Endfield **Producers** Stanley Baker, Cy Endfield **Screenplay** John Prebble, Cy Endfield **Cinematography** Stephen Dade **Music** John Barry
Cast Stanley Baker, Michael Caine, Nigel Green, Jack Hawkins, James Booth, Ulla Jacobsson, Ivor Emmanuel, Paul Daneman, Glynn Edwards, Neil McCarthy

In January 1879, a small band of British soldiers engaged in battle with a numerically superior force of Zulu warriors and won a famous, if strategically unimportant, victory. With eleven Victoria Crosses awarded, it remains one of the most medal-laden battles in British history. *Zulu* is the glorious myth-making rendition of that encounter. It was the first film from Stanley Baker's production company and, as directed by Cy Endfield, was richly detailed, boasted high production values, and offered some impressive performances.

Starring alongside Baker was Michael Caine in his first major screen role, and the picture generally was populated by character actors doing some of their best work, most notably Nigel Green providing a marvelous portrayal of the unflappable professional soldier Colour Sergeant Bourne. In many ways, *Zulu* is the quintessential British war film, with the British facing impossible odds with emotional understatement and resolution. It is also a film that exudes a deep nostalgia for the long-gone glory days of the British Empire, with the bright red uniforms of the British soldiers enacting a kind of pageantry against the arid backdrop provided by the Natal landscape.

◄

An epic all-color paean to war and heroism, *Zulu* is also a wistful acknowledgment of the end of the British bulldog spirit, not to mention the Empire itself.

To modern eyes, *Zulu*'s treatment of the Zulu people is more problematic. From the beginning onward—in a scene in which bare-breasted women dance toward their husbands-to-be—they tend to be presented in terms of spectacle and from a distance, and their motivation for attacking the British is never clearly explained. To its credit, *Zulu* does suggest the obvious motivation—that the British do not belong in the Zulu

"ONE THOUSAND BRITISH SOLDIERS HAVE BEEN MASSACRED."

OTTO WITT

homeland—when a Boer asks one of the soldiers what they are doing in Natal. The question remains unanswered, however, and the movie, unburdened by any postcolonial awareness, ends up presenting the conflict in more primal terms, as a battle for survival and a test of fortitude and manliness, with this culminating in a conclusion in which the Zulu warriors salute the courage of their opponents.

For all the political issues it raises, the spectacle, the rhythm, and the general swagger of *Zulu* can still stir and excite an audience. The Zulu chants, the hearty chorus of "Men of Harlech" sung in response by the mainly Welsh soldiers, the repeated shouts of "Fire" from Baker and Caine as wave after wave of Zulus throw themselves against the British forces—it all builds up to an expertly choreographed crescendo before lapsing into a more pensive mood. **PH**

► Lieutenant John Chard (Baker) stands stunned on the battlefield strewn with the corpses of Zulu warriors.

DR. STRANGELOVE OR: HOW I LEARNED TO STOP WORRYING AND LOVE THE BOMB 1964 (U.K.)

Director Stanley Kubrick **Producer** Stanley Kubrick **Screenplay** Stanley Kubrick, Terry Southern, Peter George (from the novel *Red Alert, a.k.a. Two Hours to Doom* by Peter George) **Cinematography** Gilbert Taylor **Music** Laurie Johnson **Cast** Peter Sellers, George C. Scott, Sterling Hayden, Slim Pickens, Peter Bull, James Earl Jones

While director Stanley Kubrick is not particularly known for his sense of humor, at least in his movies, he is responsible for perhaps the funniest film ever made about the Cold War. Peter George's novel, *Red Alert, a.k.a. Two Hours to Doom*, upon which the film is based, was played straight, but the absurdity of the situation struck Kubrick as demanding a satirical approach and, quite literally, cinema history was born.

When an air force general goes insane and issues the code for his wing command to attack the Soviet Union with nuclear weapons, President Merkin Muffley (Sellers) and the Joint-Chiefs of Staff convene to try and figure out how to rescind the order. The satire of the film is reflected in the obscene understatement and double-talk reflected in Cold War rhetoric. "Peace is our Profession" reads out the signs all over Burpelson Air Force Base, while Burpelson's commander, Brig. Gen. Jack D. Ripper (Hayden) rants on about "Communist infiltration,

◄
Many cinemagoers know the movie as just *Dr. Strangelove*. Other titles that were considered early on included *The Edge of Doom* and *The Delicate Balance of Terror*.

Communist indoctrination, and Communist subversion of our precious bodily fluids" due to water fluoridation and oversteps his remit by starting a nuclear war.

The sequences in the War Room are filled with pseudo-diplomatic double-speak, particularly when President Muffley talks to the Soviet premier Kissoff. Irony abounds as Muffley reprimands both his general "Buck" Turgidson (Scott) and the

"HOW MANY TIMES HAVE I TOLD YOU GUYS THAT I DON'T WANT NO HORSING AROUND ON THE AIRPLANE?" KONG

Soviet Ambassador de Sadesky (Bull) by saying: "Gentlemen, you can't fight in here. This is the War Room!" Kubrick's detached and sophisticated style of filmmaking is perfectly suited to this kind of satire. The lighting throughout the picture is cold and often backlights the action, giving a documentary feel to the scenes while also successfully alienating the characters from any attempts by the audience to identify with them. This visual style enables Kubrick to have it both ways: Making the action feel absurdist and surreal while also enhancing the all-too-real truth of the absurdity of nuclear Armageddon. The image of Major "King" Kong (Pickens) riding the bomb down to its target while giving out a rebel yell is, likewise, both absurd and frightening. The film ultimately belongs to Sellers though, playing three roles: President Muffley, Gen. Ripper's assistant Mandrake, and the eponymous Dr. Strangelove. **MK**

▶
Peter Sellers is both comic and creepy as Dr. Strangelove, a former Nazi scientist with a hand that just will not obey orders. Sellers was nominated for an Oscar for this role.

SCÉNÁŘ L. GROSMAN, J. KADÁR, E. KLOS
REŽIE JÁN KADÁR, ELMAR KLOS
KAMERA VLADIMÍR NOVOTNÝ
HUDBA ZDENĚK LIŠKA
V HLAVNÍCH ROLÍCH
IDA KAMIŃSKÁ, JOZEF KRONER

OBCHOD
na
KORZE

filmová tragikomedie
podle novely
L. Grosmana

THE SHOP ON MAIN STREET
1965 (CZECHOSLOVAKIA)

Directors Ján Kadár, Elmar Klos **Producers** Jordan Balurov, Milos Broz, Jaromír Lukás
Screenplay Ladislav Grosman, Jan Kadar, Elmar Klos **Cinematography** Vladimír
Novotný **Music** Zdenek Liska **Cast** Ida Kaminska, Jozef Króner, I lana Slivková,
Frantisek Zvarík, Martin Hollý, Adám Matejka, Mikulas Ladizinsky, Martin Greqor

The Shop on Main Street (a.k.a. *Obchod na Korze*) is a quiet little
film that received much fanfare in the mid-1960s, when it was
first released, but is much less well-known today than it should
be. As a Holocaust-themed picture, it adds much to the
arguments some commentators have made against the actual
re-creation of scenes in the death camps. Even without the big
emotional scenes of terror and death that Hollywood seems to
feel the need to include in everything it releases, this subtle
and quiet film is warm, funny, sad, and quite beautiful.

   During the Nazi occupation of Czechoslovakia, Tono
(Króner) is a local carpenter in a small village with little
ambition, much to the frustration of his wife, Evelyna (Slivková).
Her brother, Marcus (Zvarík), is the local Fascist commander to
whom Tono flatly refuses to salute, thereby making it
impossible for the hapless carpenter to receive any kind of
promotion. Marcus "gives" Tono some assistance in the form of
a small button shop repossessed under the Fascist Aryanization
scheme from an elderly Jewish widow, Mrs. Lautmann
(Kaminska). The glitch is that Mrs. Lautmann is both deaf and

◄

**Also known as *The
Shop on the High
Street*, this little
gem was part of
the Czech film
miracle of the mid-
1960s that, along
with *Daisies* and
*Closely Observed
Trains* (both 1966)
poked fun at the
Communist code
of socialist realism.**

senile, and completely unaware that her shop has been Aryanized and its goods already well-looted by the Nazis. She is quite unaware of the war raging around them, and has no idea about Adolf Hitler.

The local Jewish community has taken Mrs. Lautmann under its care, levying a tax among themselves to help her out—stocking her store and supplying her with customers

"I'M YOUR ARYAN AND YOU'RE MY JEWESS . . . UNDERSTAND?"

TONO BRTKO

who "buy" her buttons, only to return them back into her stock. Tono steps into this world of community deception and tries to help old Mrs. Lautmann run her shop. The Jewish community even manage to raise a small salary to help Tono out in his role as go-between between their ersatz ghetto and the Aryan world outside.

As the film is a gentle and warm-hearted comedy, all the anti-Jewish brutality of the era is kept largely off-camera, Mrs. Lautmann's deafness and senility acting as a metaphor of sorts for Jewish denial about what was going on under the Nazis. At the center of *The Shop on Main Street* is Kaminska's remarkable performance as Mrs. Lautmann. Kaminska only did a few screen performances; she was most noted as a stage actress in the pre-war Yiddish theater companies that toured Poland, America, and the Pale of Settlement. **MK**

► **Jozef Króner plays Tono the local carpenter in Ján Kadár and Elmar Klos's New Wave movie, which won an Oscar for Best Foreign Language Film.**

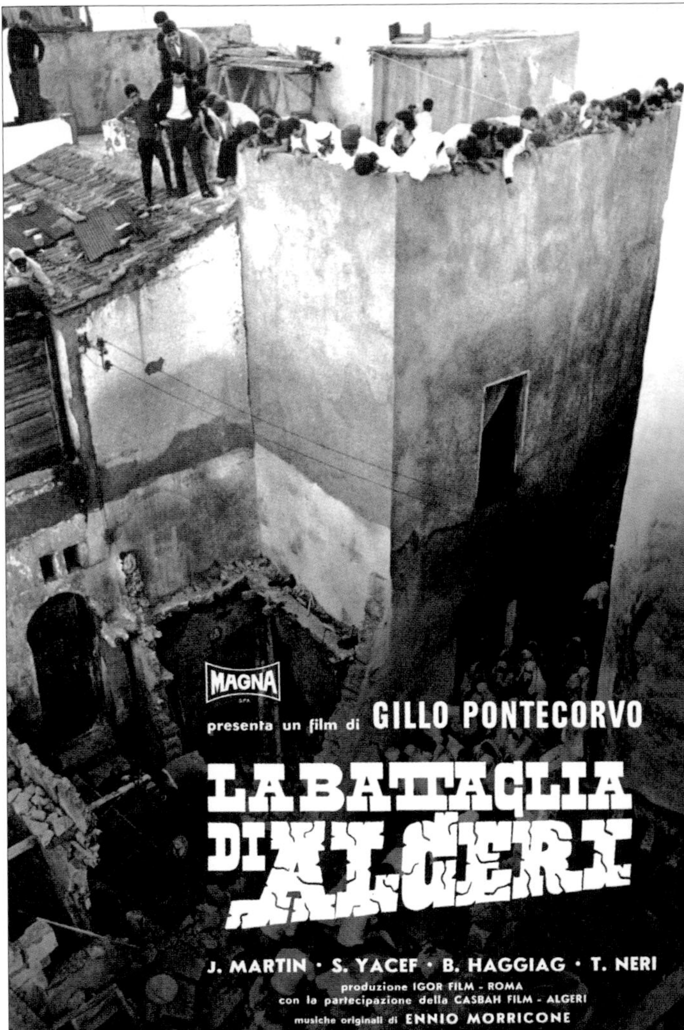
MAGNA
presenta un film di GILLO PONTECORVO
LA BATTAGLIA DI ALGERI
J. MARTIN · S. YACEF · B. HAGGIAG · T. NERI
produzione IGOR FILM - ROMA
con la partecipazione della CASBAH FILM - ALGERI
musiche originali di ENNIO MORRICONE
Prodotto da ANTONIO MUSU · Sceneggiatura di FRANCO SOLINAS

THE BATTLE OF ALGIERS 1966 (ITALY · ALGERIA)

Director Gillo Pontecorvo **Producers** Antonio Musu, Saadi Yacef
Screenplay Gillo Pontecorvo, Franco Solinas **Cinematography** Marcello Gatti
Music Ennio Morricone, Gillo Pontecorvo **Cast** Brahim Hadjadj, Jean Martin, Saadi
Yacef, Samia Kerbash, Ugo Paletti, Fusier El Kader, Mohamed Ben Kassen

A co-production between Italy and Algeria subsidized by the
Algerian government, *The Battle of Algiers* (a.k.a. *La Battaglia di
Algeri*) is notable for maintaining an objective distance from its
main theme of terrorism and refusing to take sides between the
French occupiers of Algeria and the Algerian resistance. In 2004
the Pentagon screened a restored version of the picture as a
guide for military personnel to fighting terrorism. The fact that
The Black Panthers had previously also used it as a training guide
serves as a reminder, as the film suggests, that counter-terrorism
and terrorism mirror each other.

    The Battle of Algiers is set during the struggle in 1950 by the
Algerians for independence from France (which had occupied
Algeria since 1830). Originally conceived as agitprop (political
propaganda), *The Battle of Algiers* relies on neorealist devices
(hand-held cameras, grainy film stock, and so on) to offer an
objective commentary on the struggle between colonized and
colonizer that is still relevant today. The film's producer, Saadi
Yacef, plays the central role as Djafar, the military leader of the
F.L.N. (Algerian Liberation Front) who is politicized by his
experiences in prison. His opposite is Colonel Mathieu (Martin),

◄

**Art meets agitprop
in this neorealist
documentary-
style classic where
counter-terrorism
and terrorism are
shown as two sides
of the same coin.**

previously a member of the anti-Nazi resistance party. The torture methods Mathieu uses to gain information about terrorist cells are no more legal than those utilized by Djafar and the F.L.N. At a Press Conference, Mathieu justifies the use of illegal interrogation techniques by arguing that legal methods would be too slow and would not produce the necessary results. In other words, the ends justify the means.

"INTERROGATION BECOMES A METHOD SO AS ALWAYS TO OBTAIN A RESULT."

COL. MATHIEU

The similarity between the methods of the Algerian resistance and those of the French Army is made clear through the film's images of destruction and death. At the beginning of the picture we see the French commissionaire set a bomb in the Casbah before been driven off. The bomb explodes and the camera pans in on the victims being carried away. Later, four Algerian women set bombs in the European Quarter. One by one the bombs explode—once again, the camera focuses in on the dead and dying lying amongst the destruction.

▶

With scenes like this it's perhaps not surprising that the film was banned in some countries, notably France for five years.

This mirroring that dominates the narrative trajectory of the picture is never as clear as when the Algerian women transform themselves into Europeans in order to enter the European Quarter without being searched. Here the Algerian/Colonized is rendered indistinguishable from the French/Colonizer. The message is clear, that violence only leads to more violence. **CB**

ostře
sledované
vlaky

Filmový přepis novely Bohumila Hrabala

Scénář: Bohumil Hrabal a Jiří Menzel

Režie: JIŘÍ MENZEL

Kamera: Jaromír Šofr

Hudba: Jiří Šust

V hlavní roli:

VÁCLAV

NECKÁŘ

CLOSELY OBSERVED TRAINS

1966 (CZECHOSLOVAKIA)

Director Jiří Menzel **Producers** Zdenek Oves, Carlo Ponti **Screenplay** Jiří Menzel, Bohumil Hrabal (from his novel) **Cinematography** Jaromír Sofr **Music** Jiří Sust **Cast** Václav Neckář, Josef Somr, Vlastimil Brodský, Vladimír Valenta, Alois Vachek, Ferdinand Kruta, Jitka Scoffin, Jitka Zelenohorská, Nada Urbánková

Closely Observed Trains (a.k.a. *Ostře sledované vlaky*) is the paragon of Czech New Wave cinema, especially notable for its gentle humor and its fond observance of life's little details. Director Jiří Menzel collaborated with Czech novelist Bohumil Hrabal on the script, adapted from one of Hrabal's works. Writer and director shared an exceptionally close and cordial relationship, so much so that Menzel, when accepting his Oscar for Best Foreign Language Film, attributed all the credit to the novelist. Hrabal, in turn, always claimed that he preferred the film to his original work.

The main focus of *Closely Observed Trains* is the sentimental education of the shy, sensitive young Miloš, played by Václav Neckář with a wide-eyed, guileless gaze that calls to mind Buster Keaton. Miloš takes pride in his new uniform for his job as a station guard that allows him "to stand on a platform and avoid hard work." Desperately in love with a pretty conductress on a local train, he falls into despair when his lack of romantic experience causes him to botch his first night with her. His role model is his cynical, womanizing older colleague Hubička

◄

Released as *Closely Watched Trains* in the U.S., this New Wave Czech film blends comedy and tragedy, eroticism and satire, and naturalism and absurdity into a highly idiosyncratic and beguiling mix.

(Somr), who spends his time quietly subverting authority and chasing any female who comes his way.

It is the film's setting, however, that really sets it apart: a remote railroad station during the last years of World War II. As the film proceeds, the war, at first largely disregarded, slowly comes to overshadow events, adding layers of complexity and tragedy to Miloš's story. Menzel dismantles the myths of the

"FILLED WITH WRY MOMENTS OF AWKWARD SEDUCTIONS . . . OF AN INNOCENT." MATTHEW KENNEDY

war by approaching this period (previously depicted in Czech cinema as a time of heroic struggle against the Occupation) from an oblique, ironic angle. There are no heroes in *Closely Observed Trains*: Hubička is far more concerned with his love life than with his contribution to the Resistance, and Miloš's involvement in it is mostly accidental. There are likewise no real villains: a group of German soldiers, longingly watching a train full of good-looking nurses, are not arrogant fascist killers but instead confused, homesick adolescents. Even the pro-Nazi Czech collaborator (Brodský) is more of a fool than a true enemy, accompanied by a pompous soundtrack that ridicules his Wagnerian haughtiness. Explicit reference to the Soviet domination of Czechoslovakia is not made, but it is there in the subtext and would certainly have been noticed at the time by the Czech public. **PK**

▶
Miloš (Václav Neckář), the wide-eyed station master, caught in the cultural Czech crossfire of World War II.

TRAIN THEM! EXCITE THEM! ARM THEM!

...THEN TURN THEM LOOSE ON THE NAZIS!

In 70 mm.
wide screen
and full
stereophonic
sound!

METRO-
GOLDWYN-
MAYER presents
A KENNETH HYMAN
PRODUCTION

The Dirty Dozen

Starring LEE **MARVIN** ERNEST **BORGNINE** CHARLES **BRONSON** JIM **BROWN** JOHN **CASSAVETES** RICHARD **JAECKEL**

GEORGE **KENNEDY** TRINI **LOPEZ** RALPH **MEEKER** ROBERT **RYAN** TELLY **SAVALAS** CLINT **WALKER** ROBERT **WEBBER**

screenplay by NUNNALLY JOHNSON and LUKAS HELLER From the novel by E.M. NATHANSON Produced by KENNETH HYMAN Directed by ROBERT ALDRICH IN METROCOLOR

THE DIRTY DOZEN 1967 (U.S.)

Director Robert Aldrich **Producer** Kenneth Hyman **Screenplay** Nunnally Johnson, Lukas Heller (based on the novel by E. M. Nathanson) **Cinematography** Edward Scaife **Music** Frank De Vol **Cast** Lee Marvin, Ernest Borgnine, Charles Bronson, Jim Brown, Robert Ryan, John Cassavetes, Richard Jaeckel, Trini Lopez, Telly Savalas

The "dirty dozen" comprises a group of American military prisoners given the chance to redeem themselves on a dangerous wartime mission. Ostensibly, they are dirty because they are unshaven and unkempt. But that dirtiness also clearly denotes an amorality and brutality; it indicates that these individuals will not play by the rules but instead will cheat and lie in order to get to where they need to be. This is what makes them criminals, but at the same time—the film *The Dirty Dozen* perversely suggests—it is also what makes them effective soldiers. Many of director Robert Aldrich's films possess iconoclastic qualities, and *The Dirty Dozen* is no exception. It reflects the increasing willingness to question established social authority that was evident in late 1960s culture, and the misfit characteristics of the Dozen align them with a generation that was about to start dropping out of the mainstream lifestyle and questioning conventional social values.

After a bleak sequence depicting a military execution, the movie's opening half is mainly comedic in tone as a rebellious Major (Marvin) assembles and trains his team of reprobates. Much of the humor derives from the contrast between the ill-

◄

Aldrich's anti-war, anti-authority, anti-just-about-anything movie resonated with young 1960s audiences. The special effects (mainly pyrotechnics) also went down well and won an Oscar.

behaved Dozen and the more conventional—and by late 1960s standards, "square"—troops led by a by-the-book Colonel (Ryan). Thereafter, the tone shifts disconcertingly to something much darker. The Dozen's mission involves assassinating a group of senior German officers while they relax in what in effect is an upmarket brothel located out in the countryside. Needless to say, there is nothing particularly

"... THE MOST TWISTED, ANTI-SOCIAL BUNCH OF PSYCHOPATHIC DEFORMITIES I HAVE EVER RUN INTO." CAPT. STUART KINDER

noble or heroic about such a mission, and the details of the attack, while undoubtedly exciting, do not do much to ameliorate the squalid nature of the enterprise. Indeed, Aldrich seems to take pleasure in rubbing his audience's nose in the unpleasantness of it as one of the Dozen goes mad and murders an innocent woman in the country house, while the rest trap the officers and their women in a cellar, drop hand grenades and petrol into the air vents, and finally set off an explosion that destroys the house.

► Charles Bronson and John Cassavetes who, along with Donald Sutherland, all went on from this movie to make their own special contributions to 1970s American film culture.

In this and other ways, *The Dirty Dozen* provides a remarkably cynical portrayal of war, of battle as irredeemably brutal, and of conflict as meaningless and absurd. As Aldrich himself put it: "I want people to know that war is hell." *The Dirty Dozen* can also be seen as one of those late-1960s movies that ushered in a new edgy American cinema. **PH**

One weekend Major Smith, Lieutenant Schaffer, and a beautiful blonde named Mary decided to win World War II.

They must do what no army can do…go where no army can go…
penetrate the "Castle of the Eagle", nerve-center of the Gestapo, and blow it up!

Metro-Goldwyn-Mayer presents a Jerry Gershwin · Elliott Kastner picture starring

Richard Burton · Clint Eastwood · Mary Ure

"Where Eagles Dare"

also starring Patrick Wymark · Michael Hordern story and screenplay by Alistair MacLean
directed by Brian G. Hutton · produced by Elliott Kastner · Panavision® and Metrocolor

MGM

WHERE EAGLES DARE 1968 (U.K. • U.S.)

Director Brian G. Hutton **Producer** Elliott Kastner **Screenplay** Alistair MacLean
Cinematography Arthur Ibbetson **Music** Ron Goodwin **Cast** Richard Burton,
Clint Eastwood, Mary Ure, Patrick Wymark, Michael Hordern, Donald Houston,
Peter Brakworth, William Squire, Robert Beatty, Brook Williams, Neil McCarthy

Where Eagles Dare is an action-packed suicide-mission war
movie of the highest caliber. A team of British commandos led
by Major Smith (Burton), and an American specialist Shaffer
(Eastwood), are sent into enemy territory to liberate a general
from the Nazi's impenetrable Eagle's Nest in the Bavarian Alps.
It turns out the general is just an actor whose capture was
designed to unmask German infiltrations into the British Secret
Service. Those infiltrations, as it begins to emerge in the plot,
have even affected the mission.

With this revelation, Alistair MacLean's story (he also wrote
the screenplay) abandons the cliché of the heartfelt
amateurism of drafted soldiers sticking up for each other in
favor of a cynical view of merciless professionals who stick
knives in each other's backs—or throats, as is often the case
here. *Where Eagles Dare* has occasionally been criticized for
glorifying war because of its high degree of violence, and
because it does not discriminate between the causes of the
good and the bad. With the commando team permanently
wearing German Army uniforms, such lack of differentiation is
indeed very palpable. In fact the film replaces the idea of

◀
A rollicking
adventure with
a hefty dose of
adult gratuitous
violence. The real
star of *Where Eagles
Dare* was as much
the cable car as the
cable guys Burton
and Eastwood.

fighting for a cause with that of fighting as a game. It all looks extremely cool too, as if that game is only for highly skilled professionals. Smith, in his devious wit, and Shaffer, in his ruthless executing of dozens of opponents, top the bill. Still, *Where Eagles Dare* reminds us that *all* of war is hell. In its prominent use of bright blood-red colors, its throat injuries, and in the architecture of the mountain castle, *Where Eagles*

"IN THE NEXT 15 MINUTES WE HAVE TO CREATE ENOUGH CONFUSION TO GET OUT OF HERE ALIVE." MAJOR SMITH

Dare resembles the vampire genre. It also references Italian spaghetti westerns, especially in its extended periods of silence. When Smith and Shaffer fight their way out of a compound and sneak into the castle (which is only accessible via a cable lift), fifteen suspense-filled minutes pass without much more than a snarled order. Immediately afterwards, however, when the Nazis and the commando team confront each other in the large hall of the castle, the verbal barrage of twists is more akin to a Shakespeare plot—with Burton strutting across the "stage," eloquently pitting foe against foe.

► The high tension cable car scenes were the signature settings for the movie, with spectacular jump stunts that put the audiences' hearts in their mouths.

Today, *Where Eagles Dare* is recognized as a major influence on many videos, DVDs, and videogames. Recently, interest in the film was heightened when maverick director Quentin Tarantino identified it as his favorite war movie, and added that he would like to remake it. **EM**

Out of violence, compassion.
Out of suspicion, trust.
Out of hell, hope.

LEE
MARVIN

TOSHIRO
MIFUNE

HELL
IN THE
PACIFIC

SELMUR PICTURES and HENRY G. SAPERSTEIN present

MUSIC BY   SCREENPLAY BY   STORY BY
LALO SCHIFRIN · ALEXANDER JACOBS · ERIC BERCOVICI · REUBEN BERCOVITCH

EXECUTIVE PRODUCERS   PRODUCED BY   DIRECTED BY
HENRY G. SAPERSTEIN · SELIG J. SELIGMAN · REUBEN BERCOVITCH · JOHN BOORMAN

PANAVISION · TECHNICOLOR   FROM   CINERAMA RELEASING CORPORATION

HELL IN THE PACIFIC 1968 (U.S.)

Director John Boorman **Producers** Reuben Bercovitch, Henry G. Saperstein, Selig J. Seligman **Screenplay** Alexander Jacobs, Eric Bercovici (story by Reuben Bercovitch) **Cinematography** Conrad L. Hall (with art direction by Anthony Pratt and Masao Yamazaki) **Music** Lalo Schifrin **Cast** Lee Marvin, Toshirô Mifune

A World War II film that deconstructs the conflict down to two members of opposing sides, *Hell in the Pacific* asks audiences a key question: is war inherent in human nature or the by-product of man-made influence?

On an isolated Pacific Island, a marooned Japanese naval officer (Mifune) discovers an American pilot (Marvin) in his midst. Equally surprised to see the enemy, the two men initially feud with each other over the Japanese soldier's improvised water collector. After a period where both men spend time as each other's prisoner, the incommunicative duo realize that the open question of their survival depends on each man being able to work with each other. Together they construct a raft and set sail in search of civilization. They reach a group of islands, only to find an abandoned, bombed-out military base with no one in sight.

An idiosyncratic entry in the history of war films, *Hell in the Pacific* sets itself apart with a humanist approach. Driven by the struggles of the two leads, the picture asks audiences to emotionally invest in their plight as humans rather than nationalities. According to the film, war and intolerance are not

◄

Boorman took a brave approach by reducing the Pacific War to its bare essentials with just a cast of two. His idiosyncratic approach to war movies was repeated with his autobiographical *Hope and Glory* in 1987.

innate, whereas man needs no guidance in order to try and survive. Ironically, having established this co-operative relationship, the two men see their prejudices resurface when they reach the military base and both are re-exposed to propaganda from their respective military authorities. Beyond that, the film can be read as an allegory for Hell itself as both men seem doomed to repeat the same Sisyphean tasks.

"WIN SOME, LOSE SOME. OH, FOR A SECOND I THOUGHT YOU WERE A JAP."

AMERICAN PILOT

Boorman took tremendous commercial risk creating a movie that features only two characters. Marvin is his typical coarse self, and Mifune provides the perfect counter-balance with his stern eyes and gruff voice. Both actors transform their characters mentally and physically over the course of the film to great effect.

► **American pilot Lee Marvin gets the upper hand against Captain Kuroda (Mifune), both of whom did see combat for their respective countries during World War II.**

An additional risk involves all of Mifune's dialogue being presented in Japanese with no subtitles, hoping to give Western audiences the sense of frustration that Marvin's character undergoes in his inability to communicate. Ironically, *Hell in the Pacific*'s original, respectful ending—where both men shake hands and go their separate ways—was removed by the studio in favor of an abrupt ending where both men are killed by a bomb while in a heated argument. The original ending is offered on the DVD release. **WW**

THE MUSICAL SHOT IN THE ARM!

OH! WHAT A LOVELY WAR 1969 (U.K.)

Director Richard Attenborough **Producers** Richard Attenborough, Brian Duffy, Len Deighton (uncredited) **Screenplay** Len Deighton, Charles Chilton, Joan Littlewood **Cinematography** Gerry Turpin **Music** Alfred Ralston **Cast** John Mills, Dirk Bogarde, Laurence Olivier, Ralph Richardson, Phyllis Calvert, John Gielgud, Maggie Smith

Billed as "The ever popular war game with songs, battles and a few jokes," Richard Attenborough's directorial debut is a satire on social inequalities and a plea against the futility of war, unique in its manner of comment. *Oh! What a Lovely War* was originally a radio play, transferred to the stage by Joan Littlewood in 1963. The film owes much to the latter, but it was Len Deighton and John Mills who had the idea of using Brighton's West Pier—now sadly demolished—to symbolize World War I. The pier's carnival-esque space, with its ability to have all kinds of fantasies projected onto it, makes a neat setting for social comment, and enables a rich exploration of the parallels between fairground play and the games of war.

The picture follows members of the Smith family—allegorical representations of the nation's working and middle classes— through their experiences at war, while the ruling classes stay safely on the "pier," far away from the trenches. Field Marshall Haig (Mills) gives orders atop a helter-skelter, and the horrific cost of battles are marked on cricket scoreboards—hundreds of thousands dead yet zero ground gained. Clever cutting, thanks to the innovative camerawork of Gerry Turpin, intensifies

◀

A satire revolving around songs, but not a musical, the movie had a disturbing surrealism about it that made its anti-war message much more effective than any documentary-style polemic.

the moral message and links across space and time. The shooting of a photograph becomes the shooting of Archduke Franz Ferdinand in a flash; fireworks to entertain the upper classes become shell-fire over the trenches. With a direct address, Joe Melia in various roles leads the audience from scene to scene, while battles can be watched on "What the Butler Saw" machines.

> ## "THE LAMPS ARE GOING OUT ALL OVER EUROPE. WE WILL NOT SEE THEM LIT AGAIN IN OUR LIFETIME." *SIR EDWARD GREY*

Often too ambitious, Brechtian, and stilted to work well on the big screen, there are nevertheless some powerfully moving moments, such as the scene (based on fact) in which German and British troops venture into no-man's-land on Christmas Day and a religious service when a solitary soldier challenges hypocrisy by changing the words of the hymn "What a Friend We Have in Jesus" to "When This Bloody War Is Over." Indeed, the songs, sung during the war, form the picture's emotional heart.

► The sweeping aerial shot of the crosses geometrically planted in the fields of Flanders remains a chilling epitaph to an otherwise lampoon-style movie.

Another reason for watching *Oh! What a Lovely War* is that it boasts an astonishing array of well-known faces, including most of Britain's "luvvies" of the time: Ian Holm, John Mills, Dirk Bogarde, Laurence Olivier, Ralph Richardson, John Gielgud, Kenneth More, Maggie Smith, Jack Hawkins, Michael Redgrave, Vanessa Redgrave, and Susannah York. **KM**

L'ARMEE DES OMBRES

JACQUES DORFMANN
FILMS CORONA
présente

UN FILM DE
JEAN-PIERRE MELVILLE

LINO VENTURA

PAUL MEURISSE
JEAN-PIERRE CASSEL
avec la participation de
SIMONE SIGNORET
dans le rôle de "MATHILDE"

dans
**L'ARMEE
DES OMBRES**

d'après l'oeuvre de
JOSEPH KESSEL
de l'Académie française
avec
PAUL CRAUCHET
CLAUDE MANN
et CHRISTIAN BARBIER

distribué par VALORIA FILM

ARMY OF SHADOWS 1969 (FRANCE · ITALY)

Director Jean-Pierre Melville **Producer** Jacques Dorfmann **Screenplay** Jean-Pierre Melville (based on the novel by Joseph Kessel) **Cinematography** Pierre Lhomme **Music** Eric Demarsan **Cast** Lino Ventura, Simone Signoret, Paul Crauchet, Jean-Pierre Cassel, Paul Meurisse, Claude Mann, Christian Barbier, Serge Reggiani

It's sad to think Jean-Pierre Melville died, in 1973, possibly thinking *Army of Shadows* (a.k.a. *L'Armée des Ombres*) a cinematic defeat. Poorly received in France during a radical political climate that did not appreciate any looking back—even if, in this case, upon the radicals of the past—his movie has since received critical reassessment in its home country as well as the United States, where it was finally released to wide approbation in 2006. Due to its taut pacing, focus on a series of high-tension missions, and an alternately arresting and harrowing score, the superbly suspenseful *Army of Shadows* bears more resemblance to a thriller than a war picture.

The film begins with a terrifying picture of the unthinkable: a battalion of Nazis marching on the Arc de Triomphe. After freezing on this image, the viewer is immediately dropped into the thick of the French Resistance in the person of Philippe Gerbier (Ventura), an inexplicably dapper, sober individual. Gerbier is the quintessential man of action, coming to us with no history. His character is based solely on the heroic and sometimes horrifying deeds he carries out in the name of the Resistance over the course of the movie.

◄
The poster suggests a war film subsumed by the gangster genre, and director Melville was accused of bringing noir sensibilities to the romanticized French Resistance movement.

Constantly extricating himself from seemingly impossible situations—imprisonment at Nazi headquarters, death by firing squad, a midnight skydive in utter darkness—Gerbier's apparent omnipotence and unflappability give him the air of an international spy rather than a humble tool of the Resistance. But it would be a mistake to say Gerbier saves himself. He has the help of a growing band of assistants, most operating under

"SHE SAID FIVE MINUTES, BUT SHE'LL WAIT A LIFETIME."

JEAN FRANÇOIS JARDIE

nicknames (Le Bison, Le Masque, and so on), giving the group the air of a gang. Indeed, like a gang, total fealty is expected and disloyalty harshly punished, and all are ultimately subservient to the "father" of the organization. We understand these characters through their function in each assignment, their identity subsumed into the responsibility of the larger whole. And when we do glean some personal history from a few of the cell members, we ultimately wish we had not once we learn the futility of their noble endeavors and their eventual fates: We only wish for them that they would always keep their emergency cyanide capsules handy.

▶
The gangster feel is again echoed by this drive-by shooting scene with Gerbier (Ventura), seemingly the French Resistance's action man.

Ostensibly informed by Melville's own time in the Resistance, this film is essential viewing not only for fans of war pictures or French film, but of excellent, things-that-make-your-heart-beat-faster cinema. **HB**

"Battle of Britain"

A Harry Saltzman Production

STARRING IN ALPHABETICAL ORDER:

Harry Andrews · Michael Caine · Trevor Howard · Curt Jurgens · Ian McShane · Kenneth More · Laurence Olivier
Nigel Patrick · Christopher Plummer · Michael Redgrave · Ralph Richardson · Robert Shaw · Patrick Wymark
Susannah York · PRODUCED BY Harry Saltzman AND S. Benjamin Fisz · SCREENPLAY BY James Kennaway AND Wilfred Greatorex
DIRECTED BY Guy Hamilton COLOR BY Technicolor® FILMED IN Panavision® [G] Suggested for GENERAL Audiences

United Artists

BATTLE OF BRITAIN 1969 (U.K.)

Director Guy Hamilton **Producers** S. Benjamin Fisz, Harry Saltzman
Screenplay James Kennaway, Wilfred Greatorex (from the book *The Narrow Margin*
by Derek Dempster and Derek Wood) **Cinematography** Freddie Young **Music** Ron
Goodwin **Cast** Michael Caine, Laurence Olivier, Robert Shaw, Susannah York

Battle of Britain belongs to a group of blockbuster war films
from the 1960s and 1970s that seek to tell the story of a whole
battle or campaign; others include *The Longest Day* (1962), *The
Battle of the Bulge* (1965), and *A Bridge Too Far* (1977). They are all
star-studded and spectacular, but their concern to give the
broadest possible overview of a historical event means that
they tend not to offer character-driven narratives. *Battle of
Britain* is typical in its cutting rapidly between a wide range of
British and German participants in the desperate conflict that
took place in the skies over Britain during the summer and
autumn of 1940. In many ways it is a classic underdog story,
with the British forces heavily outnumbered but securing
victory nonetheless.

   The film boasts a huge cast of familiar faces who periodically
take center stage, although none stay there for the duration.
The closest *Battle of Britain* gets to a central lead character is Air
Chief Marshall Dowding who, as memorably played by Laurence
Olivier, is a model of emotional restraint and quiet pessimism.
To a large extent it is Dowding who sets the overall tone for a
narrative that generally avoids the triumphalism that one might

◄

Star-studded
war vehicles like
Battle of Britain
were popular in
the late 1960s.
Unfortunately, the
actors always had
to play second
fiddle to the
pyrotechnics.

have expected of a battle narrative fashioned by the winning side. The German's initial overweening confidence is shown to be gradually whittled away during the course of the picture, but the British remain stoic from beginning to end. Even their moment of victory is understated; the German fighters simply fail to show up for the fight one morning, and the film concludes with British fighter pilots sitting quietly in a field.

"NEVER IN THE FIELD OF HUMAN CONFLICT WAS SO MUCH OWED BY SO MANY TO SO FEW." *WINSTON CHURCHILL*

Of course, the combat scenes are crucial in a movie such as this, and, as directed by Guy Hamilton (who was at the time best known for directing the 1964 James Bond film *Goldfinger*), *Battle of Britain* conjures up some impressive aerial duels alongside scenes of massed air attack and air-to-ground destruction. As exciting and spectacular as these scenes undoubtedly are, the impression created is less of valiant individuals jousting in the skies and more of an impersonal, machined-based combat in which likeable men on both sides are machine-gunned or burned to death. The film is never explicitly anti-war, but in these scenes the human costs of modern warfare become horribly clear. William Walton's downbeat musical score was replaced by Ron Goodwin's more strident music (although sections of Walton's score remain in the picture), but *Battle of Britain*'s surprisingly somber hues come through even so. **PH**

► Probably the real stars of the movie—the R.A.F. Spitfires and the Luftwaffe's Messerschmidts— in their overlong, choreographed dogfight sequences.

M*A*S*H 1970 (U.S.)

Director Robert Altman **Producer** Ingo Preminger **Screenplay** Ring
Lardner Jr. (from the novel by Richard Hooker) **Cinematography** Harold E. Stine
Music Johnny Mandel **Cast** Donald Sutherland, Elliott Gould, Tom Skerritt, Sally
Kellerman, Robert Duvall, Roger Bowen, Rene Auberjonois, David Arkin, Jo Ann Pflug

Despite a contentious shoot during which two of the film's
major stars, Donald Sutherland (Capt. Benjamin Franklin
"Hawkeye" Pierce) and Elliott Gould (Capt. John Francis Xavier
"Trapper" McIntyre), tried repeatedly to get Robert Altman fired,
M*A*S*H represented not only a milestone in the now-legendary
director's career, but gave rise to a long-running and critically
acclaimed television series that garnered fourteen Emmy
Awards between 1974 and 1982. Set in a mobile army surgical
hospital during the Korean War, *M*A*S*H* was ultimately an
allegory for the Vietnam War. Its scalpel-sharp satire lampooned
military imperialism and bureaucracy, while also advancing a
savage critique of the racist, sexist, homophobic, and hypocritical
ideologies rending the social fabric within the United States.

Depicted in an episodic manner sutured together by
humorous announcements over the hospital's public address
system, *M*A*S*H* tells the story of a trio of convivial surgeons—
Hawkeye, Trapper, and "Duke" (Skerritt)—who engage in witty
rejoinders and imbibe alcohol from a makeshift distillery as a
means of maintaining their sanity while laboring under a
woefully inept Lieutenant Colonel (Bowen) and two spiteful,

◄

M*A*S*H picked
up the Palme d'Or
at the Cannes Film
Festival and the
Academy Award
for Best Adapted
Screenplay.

duplicitous majors: Frank Burns (Duvall) and "Hot Lips" O'Houlihan (Kellerman). Through a series of amusing conflicts and practical jokes, the three captains manipulate their commanding officer, publicly humiliate O'Houlihan, and have Major Burns institutionalized as mentally unsuitable for duty. *M*A*S*H*, however, is far from a straightforward parody of U.S. military imperialism in Southeast Asia and the prevailing cultural

"THIS ISN'T A HOSPITAL. IT'S AN INSANE ASYLUM. AND IT'S YOUR FAULT."

MAJ. MARGARET "HOT LIPS" O'HOULIHAN

zeitgeist "at home." Altman is careful to balance scenes of verbal and slapstick humor with depictions of the human toll that armed conflicts exact. Scenes of the surgeons operating on wounded soldiers—complete with spurting arterial blood, screams of pain, and gore-soaked gauze piling up around the physician's ankles—provide sobering reminders that death in a war zone is always a heartbeat away. In addition, the depiction of the perpetual chaos that would invariably pervade a mobile Army hospital located perilously close to the front lines provided Altman with the ideal setting and scenario for experimenting with narrative and aesthetic techniques that would soon become representative of his filmmaking style. Altman's skillful management of *M*A*S*H*'s large ensemble cast anticipated similar balancing acts in *McCabe & Mrs. Miller* (1971), *Nashville* (1975), and *Gosford Park* (2001). **AK**

► Altman's decision to load *M*A*S*H* with overlapping dialogue captured a level of verisimilitude rarely evinced in Hollywood war movies. It also initiated a signature approach to the recording of sound on location.

"THE EPIC AMERICAN WAR MOVIE
THAT HOLLYWOOD HAS ALWAYS
WANTED TO MAKE BUT NEVER HAD
THE GUTS TO DO BEFORE."
—Vincent Canby, New York Times

"YOU MAY NEVER HAVE ANOTHER
EXPERIENCE LIKE IT! EVIDENTLY
SOMEONE BELIEVED THAT THE PUBLIC
HAD COME OF AGE ENOUGH TO
TAKE A MATURE FILM ABOUT A
REAL WAR WITH A HERO-VILLAIN
IN ALL HIS GLORIOUS AND
VAINGLORIOUS HUMANITY."
—Liz Smith Cosmopolitan Magazine

PATTON

20th Century-Fox presents
GEORGE C. SCOTT / KARL MALDEN
in
"PATTON"

A FRANK McCARTHY-FRANKLIN J. SCHAFFNER PRODUCTION
Screenplay by FRANCIS FORD COPPOLA & EDMUND H. NORTH
Based on "PATTON: ORDEAL AND TRIUMPH" by LADISLAS FARAGO and "A SOLDIER'S STORY" by OMAR N. BRADLEY
Music by JERRY GOLDSMITH
150
COLOR BY
DE LUXE

PATTON 1970 (U.S.)

Director Franklin J. Schaffner **Producers** Frank Caffey, Frank McCarthy
Screenplay Francis Ford Coppola, Edmund H. North (from the book *A Soldier's
Story* by Omar N. Bradley) **Cinematography** Fred Koenekam **Music** Jerry
Goldsmith **Cast** George C. Scott, Karl Malden, Stephen Young, Michael Strong

George S. Patton: not a hero, but an icon. A modern Don
Quixote running after windmills, a romantic figure of the past,
part product of his own readings, part product of his own
imagination. "Myth," states the French philosopher Roland
Barthes, "is not defined by the object of its message, but by the
way in which it utters its message." *Patton*'s script, co-written by
a young Francis Ford Coppola, emphasizes the curiosity and
contrariness of the controversial World War II general. He
believes in reincarnation and is a passionate Christian; he writes
sensitive poetry and despises fear in the field. It is the honor of
battle he lives for, obsessed with the idea of guts and glory.

Director Franklin J. Schaffner belonged to a lost generation in
American cinema just as Patton did in the American armed
forces. Both were the right men in the wrong place. Together
with fellow filmmakers like John Frankenheimer, Martin Ritt,
Norman Jewison, and Sydney Pollack, the young Schaffner
served his apprenticeship in television during the early 1950s,
bringing a new sensibility to American cinema in the following
decade. Constituting the first "New Hollywood," these directors
approached their subjects with a disenchanted, highly wary

The poster echoes
the stunning
opening scene
where Gen. Patton
(Scott), standing
in front of a giant
American flag,
orates a superbly
understated
call to arms.

attitude. It was the last generation of directors trained by life before the movie brats took over Hollywood; these were mavericks who brought a rugged individualism and nervous energy to their movies just like General Patton brought to the armed forces during World War II. Schaffner shot *Patton* like one of his early TV documentaries: detached but imaginative, with a registering camera and dynamic editing.

"THE OBJECT OF WAR IS NOT TO DIE FOR YOUR COUNTRY BUT TO MAKE THE OTHER BASTARD DIE FOR HIS." *PATTON*

▶ **George C. Scott won the Oscar for Best Actor for his portrayal of the all-American, cigar-chewing General Patton. The movie also cleaned up, winning six other Academy Awards.**

Patton was made at the height of the protests against the Vietnam War. Many critics accused the film of not articulating a decided anti-war message, that is, not condemning Patton's credo: always attack, never back down. They wanted to claim the universal in the concrete, losing sight of the concrete itself. Every depiction of combat generates visual pleasure, attracting the viewer through spectacle. Even when indicting acts of violence, generic conventions demand to show these very acts of violence. Combat films exploit what becomes visible on the screen; they inevitably celebrate violence even while tending (or pretending) to denounce it. There is no such thing as a true anti-war movie. All that *Patton* does is to teach us that combat is a dirty job, so you better act without mercy in order to get it finished quickly. Those who need movies to be able to reason against war won't find those reasons in this movie either. **IR**

PARAMOUNT PICTURES CORPORATION IN ASSOCIATION WITH FILMWAYS, INC. PRESENTS

A MIKE NICHOLS FILM
ALAN ARKIN
IN
CATCH-22
BASED ON THE NOVEL BY
JOSEPH HELLER

STARRING:
MARTIN BALSAM; RICHARD BENJAMIN; ARTHUR GARFUNKEL; JACK GILFORD; BUCK HENRY; BOB NEWHART; ANTHONY PERKINS; PAULA PRENTISS; MARTIN SHEEN;
JON VOIGHT & ORSON WELLES AS DREEDLE SCREENPLAY BY BUCK HENRY PRODUCED BY JOHN CALLEY & MARTIN RANSOHOFF DIRECTED BY MIKE NICHOLS

PRODUCTION DESIGNER - RICHARD SYLBERT TECHNICOLOR PANAVISION A PARAMOUNT PICTURE "R" UNDER 17 REQUIRES PARENT OR ADULT GUARDIAN

CATCH-22 1970 (U.S.)

Director Mike Nichols **Producers** John Calley, Martin Ransohoff **Screenplay** Buck Henry (based on the novel by Joseph Heller) **Cinematography** David Watkin **Music** Richard Strauss ("Thus Spake Zarathustra") **Cast** Alan Arkin, Art Garfunkel, Paula Prentiss, Jon Voight, Jack Gilford, Bob Balaban, Orson Welles, Martin Balsam

---

Joseph Heller's inspired ode to the deadly insanity of war is brought to the screen by Oscar-winning director Mike Nichols (*The Graduate*) and an overstuffed ensemble of Hollywood mainstreamers. Buck Henry's screenplay makes a valiant effort to distill Heller's epic World War II panorama into a digestible size, but too many characters and too many subplots combine to dull the rapier-sharp black humor of the 1961 novel.

Catch-22 describes the bureaucratic dilemma wherein Alan Arkin's Yossarian is trapped in a hell of military making. A bombardier for the giant B-25's the Allies fly out of Italy against the Axis powers, Yossarian can never fulfill an ever-increasing requirement for how many missions will qualify him to go home. When he considers claiming insanity as a reason to be grounded, he discovers a catch, Catch-22: "In order to be grounded, I've got to be crazy. And I must be crazy to keep flying. But if I ask to be grounded, that means I'm not crazy anymore, and I have to keep flying."

Highlights of the film's desperate lunacy include Milo Minderbinder (Voight) turning the airbase into a for-profit venture, contracting with the enemy to bomb the Americans'

◄

Joseph Heller's absurdist anti-war novel proved immensely difficult to capture on celluloid—though director Nichols and screenwriter Henry had a pretty good stab at it.

own airstrip: "What's good for M & M Enterprises will be good for the country." Doc Daneeka (Gilford) finds himself a non-person when the plane he's signed onto (but not actually in) crashes, leaving him officially dead, while still very much alive.

The film was one of the most anticipated of 1970, but it bombed commercially after not meeting the high standards set by Oscar-winning *Patton*, military spectacular *Tora! Tora! Tora!*,

"IN INDIVIDUALS, INSANITY IS RARE; BUT IN GROUPS, PARTIES, NATIONS, AND EPOCHS, IT IS THE RULE." *FRIEDRICH NIETZSCHE*

and especially Robert Altman's ultimate anti-establishment, anti-war film, *M*A*S*H*, all released that same year. The picture, however, has held up remarkably well over time. Any movie that can successfully engage the viewer in finding the dark and corrupt side of World War II, the great and morally sanctified American military crusade of the 20th century, can easily resonate with an audience steeped in the highly contentious legacy of more recent martial (mis)adventures.

The satirical spirit of *Catch-22* is perhaps best captured when naive Capt. Nately (Garfunkel) ripostes with an old man in a whorehouse (Dalio) about the morality of life, death, and war: "What you don't understand is it's better to die on your feet than to live on your knees." The old man then replies to him: "You have it backwards. It's better to live on your feet than to die on your knees. I know." **WSW**

► **Alan Arkin and Jack Gilford are up to some nefarious dealings and comic acting in *Catch-22*.**

TORA! TORA! TORA!

The most spectacular film ever made.

The incredible attack on Pearl Harbor as told from both the U.S. and Japanese sides.

20th Century-Fox presents **TORA! TORA! TORA!** AN ELMO WILLIAMS-RICHARD FLEISCHER PRODUCTION
For the United States Sequences: For the Japanese Sequences:
Starring MARTIN BALSAM as "Admiral Kimmel"·JOSEPH COTTEN as Starring SOH YAMAMURA as "Admiral Yamamoto"·TATSUYA MIHASHI as
"Henry L. Stimson"·E.G. MARSHALL as "Lt. Col. Bratton"·JAMES WHITMORE "Cdr. Genda"· TAKAHIRO TAMURA as "Lt. Cdr. Fuchida"· EIJIRO TONO
as "Admiral William F. Halsey"·AND as "Adm. Nagumo"· KOREYA SENDA as "Prince Konoye"· Directed by
JASON ROBARDS as "General Short"· TOSHIO MASUDA and KINJI FUKASAKU Assoc. Producer OTTO LANG
Screenplay by LARRY FORRESTER · HIDEO OGUNI · RYUZO KIKUSHIMA
Directed by RICHARD FLEISCHER Produced by ELMO WILLIAMS
Music by JERRY GOLDSMITH PANAVISION® Color by DE LUXE®

G ALL AGES ADMITTED
General Audiences

TORA! TORA! TORA! 1970 (U.S. • JAPAN)

Directors Richard Fleischer, Kinji Fukasaku, Toshio Masuda **Producers** Elmo Williams, Richard Fleischer **Screenplay** Larry Forrester, Hideo Oguni, Ryuzo Kikushima **Cinematography** Charles F. Wheeler, Sinsaku Himeda, Masamichi Satoh, Osami Furuya **Music** Jerry Goldsmith **Cast** Martin Balsam, Soh Yamamura, Jason Robards

The titular phrase comes from the first syllables of "Totsugeki" (attack) and "Raigeki" (torpedo attack) and the resulting TO-RA, TO-RA, TO-RA has the same pronunciation as "tiger" repeated thrice. You won't learn this from the film, though, since it doesn't bother to tell you. Also, you won't learn here how and why, exactly, Japan decided to side with Germany and attack "the sleeping giant" of America. Since many Japanese officers are presented in this picture as opposed to the war, the only explanation seems to lie with the "hotheads" higher up, who we never see. As for the American side, the Pearl Harbor fiasco (as depicted here) seems to have been made possible by the tiresome bureaucracy and too much self confidence among some of the giant's own hotheads.

In theory, the idea of a two-sided account of what led to Pearl Harbor is an excellent one (and precedes a similar attempt at dealing with the U.S.–Japan conflict in World War II by Clint Eastwood by more than three decades). In practice, however, the Japanese episodes do not really add much to the whole picture, but at least they are livelier than their American counterparts and their protagonists seem more human.

◄ The premise was to show the attack on Pearl Harbor from both American and Japanese perspectives. It didn't quite pan out like that, being Hollywood, but the action scenes were undeniably riveting.

Luckily at least, the film eschews the melodramatic excess of later films in this vein, such as Michael Bay's *Pearl Harbor* (2001), and instead does a good job of sticking to the facts.

Tora! Tora! Tora! is an official, military-approved production, and as such its main preoccupation lies in reconstructing who did what and who said what, or at least choosing the bits that won't hurt anyone's feelings too much. It is not interested in

"I FEAR ALL WE HAVE DONE IS TO AWAKEN A SLEEPING GIANT."

VICE-ADMIRAL ISOROKU YAMAMOTO

individuals and does not care to provide drama or suspense related to rounded characters; rather, it deals with grand gestures placed in a large scope. As an almost-documentary reconstruction it is not without value, especially in its climactic scenes of the partial destruction of the American Pacific fleet. A big budget for the time (an estimated $25 million) enabled a convincing depiction of the large-scale devastation, and in terms of pyrotechnics, models, miniatures, and visual effects it has more than stood the test of time.

► **As with all the other all-star-cast epic war movies of the 1970s, the script, spectacle, and pyrotechnics tended to overwhelm the performances of the actors.**

With an overblown budget and a troubled production (Akira Kurosawa departed in the early stages of shooting, replaced by a stalwart of Japanese *yakuza* action dramas, the great Kinji Fukasaku), at the time of its release it was considered a flop. In retrospect, *Tora! Tora! Tora!* seems pretty close to being the most accurate cinematic version of this fateful episode. **DO**

LACOMBE LUCIEN
un film de Louis Malle

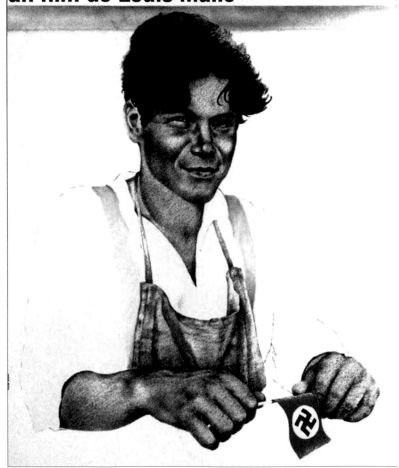

LACOMBE LUCIEN 1974 (FRANCE)

Director Louis Malle **Producers** Louis Malle, Claude Nedjar **Screenplay** Louis Malle, Patrick Modiano **Cinematography** Tonino Delli Colli **Music** Stéphane Grappelli **Cast** Pierre Blaise, Aurore Clément, Holger Löwenadler, Therese Giehse, Stéphane Bouy, Loumi Iacobesco, René Bouloc, Pierre Decazes, Jean Rougerie

Set in German-occupied France during World War II, Louis Malle's *Lacombe Lucien* fuses naturalistic performances with allegory to explore the politics of collaboration, the allure of power, and human beings' potential for forgiveness and redemption. Brilliantly portrayed by newcomer Pierre Blaise, the movie's eponymous antihero is a distressed, casually cruel young man working in a country hospital and eking out a strained existence with his adulterous mother. Too young to join the Resistance and fight alongside his father and brother, Lucien turns to the only community seemingly willing to welcome him into their fold; a duplicitous and violent collection of men and women angling to improve their economic and social status through their collaboration with the Nazi soldiers who have conquered their homeland.

While visiting a frightened and horribly exploited Jewish tailor (Löwenadler), Lucien finds himself attracted to the man's beautiful daughter, a young woman aptly named France (Clément). Eventually, learning that he has been targeted for assassination by the very Resistance fighters who rejected him earlier in the film, and whom he subsequently betrayed, Lucien

◄

One of the most deeply considered films in Malle's impressive oeuvre, and arguably one of the most important works in French cinema.

escapes with France and her stalwart grandmother, Bella (Giehse). With Switzerland as their ultimate goal, the three fugitives form a tender, virtually wordless bond, and Malle's direction leads us to believe that Lucien and France may have found the sanctuary necessary to heal one another's troubled souls. Unfortunately for the makeshift family, happiness is not to be. In an abrupt sequence of shots that seemingly anticipates

"I DON'T LIKE PEOPLE TALKING DOWN TO ME."

LUCIEN LACOMBE

the finale of his 1987 film, *Au revoir les enfants*, Malle brings this unconventional coming-of-age film to a sudden, tragic close. Casually cruel and selfish, Lucien is a difficult figure with whom to sympathize. These facets of his persona, however, constitute the thematic core of Malle's film. Rejected as too young by the French Resistance, and almost certainly confused by his country's rapidly shifting social and political terrain, spectators are challenged to discern the logic informing Lucien's actions. Is his allegiance to the Nazi collaborators driven by a genuine embrace of Vichy ideology? Or are his behaviors motivated by a desire for acceptance in a world in which he feels hopelessly insecure? Similarly, is Lucien's attraction to France motivated by her position as a disenfranchised woman he feels he can control? Or does he love her yet cannot articulate his emotions, thus rendering his fate all the more disturbing? **JM**

► Lucien's (Blaise) quandary as a collaborator acts as a metaphor for a traumatized nation rent asunder by humiliating defeat.

THE EAGLE HAS LANDED 1976 (U.K.)

Director John Sturges **Producers** David Niven Jr., Jack Wiener **Screenplay** Tom Mankiewicz (from the novel by Jack Higgins) **Cinematography** Anthony Richmond **Music** Lalo Schifrin **Cast** Michael Caine, Donald Sutherland, Robert Duvall, Donald Pleasence, Jenny Agutter, Anthony Quayle, Larry Hagman, Jean Marsh, John Standing

Based on the bestselling novel by Jack Higgins, *The Eagle Has Landed* was a relatively late addition to the ranks of fictional World War II super-productions typified by the likes of *Kelly's Heroes* (1970) and *Where Eagles Dare* (1968). It plays as something of a cross between *Went the Day Well?* (1942) and *The Day of the Jackal* (1973) with Michael Caine as a Nazi colonel whose regiment infiltrates a small English town disguised as Poles as part of a plot to kidnap Winston Churchill. But like the interlopers of *Went the Day Well?* they prove somewhat careless, in this case wearing their real uniforms under their disguises, and are soon exposed and forced to besiege the town.

It was the last film directed by John Sturges, who in a career spanning 30 years had established a solid track record in action movies and westerns, as well as helming *The Great Escape* (1963). *The Eagle Has Landed* shows his customary virtues of tense action sequences and well-photographed locations, and shows every sign of a large budget being thoroughly spent. It is, however, somewhat compromised by its unhurried pace, a plethora of different subplots, and the

◄
Some interesting casting or miscasting pervades the male roles. Jenny Agutter and Jean Marsh however add some real tension.

consequent lack of focus they cause, not to mention the central miscasting of Donald Sutherland as a wisecracking I.R.A. mercenary and Michael Caine as the Nazi leader, his accent explained away as the result of a British education. However, the movie did redeem itself somewhat by giving Donald Pleasence the chance to add Himmler to his already extensive gallery of villainous characterizations. And after the

"IF ANYTHING HAPPENS TO CHURCHILL, THEY'RE GOING TO HANG YOU FROM BIG BEN BY YOUR BALLS." COL. PITTS

leisurely first half it builds to a number of sprawling action sequences and an effectively suspenseful climax, leading to a bizarre twist ending reminiscent of some of the stranger 1950s war films, such as *The Man Who Never Was* (1956) and *I Was Monty's Double* (1958).

The Eagle Has Landed is also notable as one of very few war film entries that attempt to show relatively sympathetic Nazi characters. This can obviously be effective in creating a more complex and layered portrait of Nazi hierarchy and society, as was achieved for instance in Anatole Litvak's underrated *The Night of the Generals* (1968). Here, however, it seems rather more forced and contrived, serving no deeper purpose than to keep Caine's character—who we first see facing a court martial for obstructing an SS officer in the act of rounding up Jews—comparatively likeable. **MC**

▶ The casting of Robert Duvall as a Nazi was about as eccentric as casting Michael Caine as a Nazi leader and Donald Sutherland as a proto-I.R.A. terrorist.

CROSS OF IRON 1977 (U.K. · GERMANY)

Director Sam Peckinpah **Producers** Wolf C. Hartwig, Arlene Sellers, Alex Winitsky
Screenplay Julius J. Epstein, James Hamilton, Walter Kelley (from Willi Heinrich's
novel *The Willing Flesh*) **Cinematography** John Coquillon **Music** Ernest Gold
Cast James Coburn, Maximilian Schell, James Mason, David Warner, Klaus Löwitsch

Among the most cynical of war movies, *Cross of Iron* is also
without a doubt one of the most violent. It has rightly been
described as *The Wild Bunch* at the Russian Front. Yet it is also a
powerful criticism of the ideologies that lead to war.

The film tells the story of a platoon of German soldiers on
the Eastern European front line in 1943. They are joined by the
aristocratic Prussian officer Captain Stransky (Schell), who has
volunteered for the Russian Front in order to "earn" an Iron
Cross, the highest military honor given by the German army.
Stransky immediately finds himself at odds with Sergeant
Steiner (Coburn in imperious form), the veteran leader of the
platoon—who has already been awarded two such Iron
Crosses. The antagonism between the two men leads to
Stransky neglecting to inform Steiner's platoon of a retreat.
Soon enough, they are isolated behind enemy lines. Relying
on their wits, the platoon makes it back to the front line. But as
Steiner's troop crosses no man's land, Stransky orders them
to be gunned down. Only Steiner and a few others survive.
Instead of killing Stransky, Steiner challenges him to join him in
close battle, to show him "where the Iron Crosses grow."

◄
Peckinpah's
slow-motion,
blood-spurting,
violent Western
oeuvre translated
remarkably well
to this nihilistic tale
of antiheroes on
the Russian Front.

The clash of Establishment figure against Everyman is pure Peckinpah—a theme he constantly raises in his westerns. As Stransky embarrasses himself (he falls into a puddle, is unable to reload his gun, puts on his helmet backward), the frame freezes, and to the roar of the battle is added a cheerful German children's tune (*"Hanschen klein"*). All Steiner can do is laugh uncontrollably. His laughter continues over the credits,

"STEINER IS A MYTH. MEN LIKE HIM ARE OUR LAST HOPE AND . . . HE IS A TRULY DANGEROUS MAN." *KIESEL*

which show pictures of some of the worst atrocities of war. *Cross of Iron* is both realistic and hyperbolic. The equipment featured is historically accurate, and the entire story is based on true events. But as the ending makes clear, it is the style of *Cross of Iron* that hammers home the message. That message comes courtesy of veteran director Peckinpah. By the time he directed *Cross of Iron*, Peckinpah was said to have passed his prime, re-hashing the same styles and themes time and again.

▶
The bleak, bullet-ridden, body-strewn Russian Front could be the wild Mexican border as far as Peckinpah is concerned. It has the same themes, but a different genre and location.

Yet, somehow, his trademark approach of slow-motion bloody violence, male cynicism, misogyny (blatant here when the men encounter a Russian female platoon), and tough sarcasm from the characters seemed to work extremely well for the World War II material—the hysterical laughter, children's tune, and freeze-frames indicting the lunacy of war better than any carefully worded message. **EM**

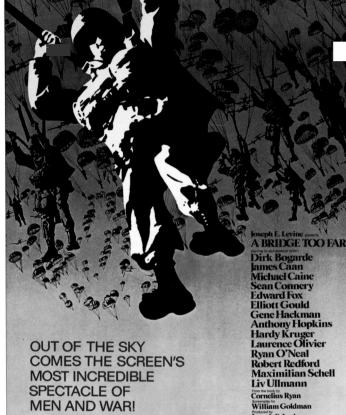

A BRIDGE TOO FAR 1977 (U.K. • U.S.)

Director Richard Attenborough **Producers** Joseph E. Levine, Richard P. Levine
Screenplay William Goldman (from Cornelius Ryan's book) **Cinematography** Geoffrey
Unsworth **Music** John Addison **Cast** Dirk Bogarde, James Caan, Michael Caine, Sean
Connery, Edward Fox, Elliott Gould, Gene Hackman, Robert Redford, Anthony Hopkins

An adaptation of Cornelius Ryan's true-life bestselling World
War II book, *A Bridge Too Far* portrays the planning and execution
of Operation Market Garden, a daring but ultimately disastrous
plan to bring the war to a swift end by capturing a series of
bridges on the way to Berlin. Boasting an impressive
international all-star cast, the film touchingly demonstrates the
brave efforts of a multinational army trying to deal with a plan
that had very quickly turned sour: airborne troops were
dropped into enemy territory without supply lines, armored
units were backed-up and harried on what became known as
"Hell's Highway," and civilians were caught in the cross-fire as
the operation slowly unraveled.

Crucial to the film's impact is John Addison's stirring score
and Attenborough's unfussy direction, which ensures that,
despite the all-star cast, the everyday heroism of the men
involved is never lost. When it comes to hard-bitten warfare, *A
Bridge Too Far* is hard to beat. The picture's constant stream of
jeeps, tanks, entire parachute battalions leaping from airplanes
and against-all-odds derring-do merely reflects a fraction of
the true cost of Operation Market Garden.

◄

**A screenplay from
William Goldman
gave the all-star
cast a chance to
deliver some telling
lines among the
authentic set pieces.**

Attenborough's film was groundbreaking in the scale of its deployment of both men and machine and in daringly portraying an Allied military failure. Nearly 25 years later the HBO mini-series *Band of Brothers* (2001) would recreate parachute drops into enemy territory using up-to-the-minute CGI effects. In *A Bridge Too Far* the only way to recreate Operation Market Garden was to actually drop thousands

"I'M AWFULLY SORRY, BUT I'M AFRAID WE'RE GOING TO HAVE TO OCCUPY YOUR HOUSE." *LT. COLONEL FROST*

upon thousands of parachutists into the Netherlands once again on a truly epic scale. This time, though, they were being filmed: shot but not shot at.

The movie is at its best when showing the consequences of a plan that went catastrophically wrong, the crisscrossing narrative slowly leading to what we know will be the most "un-Hollywood" of endings as tired and poorly supplied troops either surrender, are captured, or are killed. Operation Market Garden was pure hubris from the start, and *A Bridge Too Far* shows the extent to which it was part of the race between the British and American allies toward Berlin. But it is perhaps Attenborough's portrayal of Lt. Col. Frost's (Hopkins) fearless assault on, and ultimately unsuccessfully protracted defense of, Arnhem Bridge that is the most damning assessment of Operation Market Garden: gritty and heroic but ultimately doomed to failure. **RH**

► The film highlights a desperate attempt by the British military to outdo their American counterparts by coming up with a plan to reach the German capital before them.

THE DEER HUNTER

EMI Films present

ROBERT DE NIRO IN A **MICHAEL CIMINO** Film **THE DEER HUNTER**

co-starring

JOHN CAZALE · JOHN SAVAGE · MERYL STREEP · CHRISTOPHER WALKEN

Music composed by STANLEY MYERS · Director of Photography VILMOS ZSIGMOND, a.s.c.

Associate Producers MARION ROSENBERG · JOANN CARELLI · Production Consultant JOANN CARELLI

Story by MICHAEL CIMINO, DERIC WASHBURN and LOUIS GARFINKLE, QUINN K. REDEKER

Screenplay by DERIC WASHBURN   Produced by BARRY SPIKINGS · MICHAEL DEELEY · MICHAEL CIMINO and JOHN PEVERALL

Directed by **MICHAEL CIMINO**

THE DEER HUNTER 1978 (U.S.)

Director Michael Cimino **Producers** Michael Cimino, Michael Deeley, John Peverall, Barry Spikings **Screenplay** Michael Cimino, Deric Washburn, Louis Garfinkle, Quinn K. Redeker **Cinematography** Vilmos Zsigmond **Music** Stanley Myers **Cast** Robert De Niro, John Cazale, John Savage, Christopher Walken, Meryl Streep, George Dzundza

The Deer Hunter won the Oscar for Best Picture in 1978, with the horrors of the Vietnam War still in recent memory. Cimino looks at the war through the lens of a group of friends, three steel workers from western Pennsylvania: Michael (De Niro), Steven (Savage), and Nick (Walken). Opening just days before they are to report to combat duty, *The Deer Hunter* is divided into three hour-long acts: before, during, and after the war.

Unlike other Vietnam movies, we see part of just one small battle scene. The remainder of the second act is spent in an aquatic chamber of horrors. Rather than entice with the spectacle of battle, Cimino devotes the first hour of the movie to documenting the lives of the town folk. This first act culminates in a twenty minute long wedding scene that provides a sentimental glimpse into a fragile world about to be destroyed by the war taking place on the other side of the globe. As a frightening preview of what is to come, a shell-shocked soldier accidentally interrupts the wedding reception. He wants only to drink in silence and to forget the jungle. Cimino presents Russian roulette as a metaphor for war, which despite being fairly obvious, remains effective. Getting out of

◄

Cimino's blockbuster used its violent content to show the gruesome nature of war, although a large part of the film took place "back home" in Pennsylvania.

the war alive is largely a mater of luck. Walking into a jungle battle is, indeed, much like spinning the chamber of a revolver. Few can live for long this close to death without suffering some form of psychological devastation. The hardiest of the triad, Michael, manages to make it through relatively unscathed (although in real life De Niro claims it was his most exhaustive role), but the others are not so lucky. Paradoxically, Nick, the

> ## "A DEER HAS TO BE TAKEN WITH ONE SHOT. I TRY TO TELL PEOPLE THAT BUT THEY DON'T LISTEN." MICHAEL

luckiest of the three, becomes involved in a twisted underground gambling circuit, where he serially competes in games of Russian roulette for money.

The Deer Hunter is often misunderstood as a *post hoc* protest film, critical of the recent Vietnam War. But the movie presents no such argument. Cimino directs an anti-war movie, not necessarily an anti–Vietnam War protest movie. There is no criticism of U.S. involvement or of this war in particular. Cimino portrays the Vietcong as child-killing sadists who are fighting to keep their prison camps filled with contestants for an endless game of Russian roulette.

Regardless of Cimino's demonized portrayal of the Vietcong, he insightfully depicts the way the enemy feels to soldiers thrown into a dangerous jungle. *The Deer Hunter* allows us to see the impact of war on individuals, families, and entire towns. **AS**

► Robert De Niro gave one of his grittiest ever performances as Michael, but it was hard to outshine Walken's mesmerizing portrayal of Nick.

APOCALYPSE NOW 1979 (U.S.)

Director Francis Ford Coppola **Producer** Francis Ford Coppola **Screenplay** John Milius, Michael Herr (based on the novel *Heart of Darkness* by Joseph Conrad) **Cinematography** Vittorio Storaro **Music** Carmine Coppola, Francis Ford Coppola **Cast** Martin Sheen, Marlon Brando, Robert Duvall, Frederick Forrest, Harrison Ford

"This film is not about Vietnam, this film *is* Vietnam," said Coppola in 1979 on its release. *Apocalypse Now* was shot over four years in the Philippines under disastrous conditions with the set burning down and the main actor having a heart attack. Based on a screenplay by John Milius itself based on Conrad's classic novel *Heart of Darkness*, the script was constantly re-written by Michael Herr during the shoot. The version Coppola finally presented to a stunned audience in Cannes was always considered an "interim" version, but hit the theaters nonetheless.

In disturbingly beautiful images the film tells the story of army-executioner Willard's (Sheen) journey to find and exterminate former U.S. Colonel Kurtz (Brando) who has seemingly gone mad somewhere beyond the Cambodian border. Together with a small platoon, Willard sails up the river and continuously faces his own abyss. When he finally meets Kurtz he realizes that this very sophisticated man has established a neo-barbarian kingdom in the jungle, crowning himself God-King. The first half of *Apocalypse Now* focuses on the madness of the Vietnam War: U.S. soldiers on drugs, loaded

The brooding presence of Marlon Brando pervades the film, even though he doesn't appear in most of it. The overweight actor kept arguing about his role, and the film's costs spiraled from $12 million to $30 million.

with modern weaponry, unable to even see the enemy. In the film's most famous sequence the helicopter-squadron of Col. Kilgore (Duvall) napalm bombs a small, peaceful village just to go surfing on the beach. The second half of the picture is more philosophical: Willard realizes more and more that he has left modern civilization behind and now faces barbarism. In modern culture Kurtz is the incarnation of evil turning back

> ## "YOU HAVE A RIGHT TO KILL ME . . . BUT YOU HAVE NO RIGHT TO JUDGE ME."
>
> *KURTZ*

toward a mythical age and establishing a kingdom of human sacrifice and bloody rituals. Kurtz really is the "heart of darkness." He reads James Frazer's *The Golden Bough*, a book that focuses on the ritual killing of the king.

The title, *Apocalypse Now*, which first appears as graffiti on a temple wall, also refers to the world of Kurtz, who has transcended the profane age and invoked the mythical one. Kurtz has reached his ultimate goal when Willard calls the air force to bomb his compound and replaces him. Willard finally unleashed the Apocalypse. The fact that the film actually begins with the burning jungle scored by The Doors' "The End" is critical: the cycle is closed. *Apocalypse Now* is not an anti-war film—it is a radical mythological allegory on the eternal presence of war. To this day *Apocalypse Now* remains the most visionary and philosophical entity in the war film genre. **MS**

► Kurtz's (Brando) renegades await Willard's (Sheen) visit. The film's title is written on the wall—awaiting the biggest-ever explosion then staged for the screen.

Only
chance
could have
thrown them together.

Now,
nothing can pull them apart.

SAMUEL FULLER'S

THE
BIG
RED
ONE

LORIMAR PRESENTS LEE MARVIN   MARK HAMILL
IN SAMUEL FULLER'S "THE BIG RED ONE"
CO-STARRING ROBERT CARRADINE   BOBBY DI CICCO   KELLY WARD   SIEGFRIED RAUCH   STEPHANE AUDRAN
MUSIC BY DANA KAPROFF   PRODUCED BY GENE CORMAN   WRITTEN AND DIRECTED BY SAMUEL FULLER   DOLBY STEREO   A LORIMAR RELEASE THRU ☦ United Artists
A Transamerica Company

PG PARENTAL GUIDANCE SUGGESTED   ©1980 LORIMAR DISTRIBUTION INTERNATIONAL   READ THE BANTAM PAPERBACK

THE BIG RED ONE 1980 (U.S.)

Director Samuel Fuller **Producer** Gene Corman **Screenplay** Samuel Fuller
Cinematography Adam Greenberg **Music** Dana Kaproff **Cast** Lee Marvin,
Mark Hamill, Robert Carradine, Bobby DiCicco, Kelly Ward, Stéphanie Audran,
Siegfried Rauch, Serge Marquand, Charles Macaulay, Alain Doutey, Maurice Marsac

The Big Red One is based on writer/director Samuel Fuller's own
experiences in the First Infantry Division during World War II. In
this film, Fuller exemplifies what American cinema could be:
made for a fraction of what a typical Hollywood production
costs, there is no sense of waste on screen, just solid and
powerful filmmaking.

The First Infantry Division of the American Army, known
affectionately as "the Big Red One" due to their insignia, were
often the first squads to engage the enemy in combat. The film
follows one particular squad of four privates and their sergeant
through North Africa, Sicily, the D-Day invasion, across France
and Belgium (including Bastogne), and finally into
Czechoslovakia and the liberation of a concentration camp.
Through their eyes, we experience the major European theaters
of combat in World War II.

As the picture is largely based on Fuller's own combat
experiences (Pvt. Zab [Carradine] is Fuller's stand-in), we get a
private's-eye-view of the battle, and the movie is particularly
noteworthy for the minute details of warfare from this
perspective, like using condoms to cover the barrels of their

◀
**Fuller built up
an impressive list
of taut and tough
war movies kicking
off with *The Steel
Helmet* (1950),
and *Fixed Bayonets*
(1951), but this
stylized movie
is his masterpiece.**

rifles when making amphibious landings to prevent sea water getting into their guns. The seemingly surreal image of soldiers wading ashore carrying aloft, not the American flag, but rolls of toilet paper, makes perfect sense without having to see the problems involved with personal hygiene while in the field. Yet such scenes underline the real and tangible concerns common soldiery would have (beyond simply not getting shot).

"YOU'RE GOING TO LIVE, EVEN IF I HAVE TO BLOW YOUR BRAINS OUT."

THE SERGEANT

The film's individual episodes are, in themselves, lovely little snapshots of life on the front line. The squad help a young Sicilian boy bury his dead mother in exchange for information about the location of a camouflaged German tank; the soldiers help a French woman give birth inside a tank, with her feet in ammunition belts as stirrups; and perhaps most poignantly of all, there is a moving concentration camp rescue. As Fuller himself boasted: "Any war picture I made, [and he made a few B movies in the genre] you're in the war!"

In 2004 the film underwent a "reconstruction" and was re-released with close to an hour of footage previously removed in 1980 added. This version is a great deal closer to what Fuller originally intended to be seen. Visually and philosophically, it's Fuller's equivalent of Kurosawa's *Kagemusha* (1980), although Fuller's film is more complex, absurd, and haunting. **MK**

▶
Perhaps the single most beautiful moment in American combat cinema, as the Sergeant (Marvin) carries a young boy he has just rescued from a concentration camp.

From a place you may never have heard of...
a story you'll never forget.

A Peter Weir Film

GALLIPOLI

A

ROBERT STIGWOOD–RUPERT MURDOCH FOR ASSOCIATED "GALLIPOLI" MEL GIBSON Executive FRANCIS O'BRIEN Screenplay DAVID WILLIAMSON
R & R FILMS PTY LTD. PRESENT A PETER WEIR FILM MARK LEE Producer by

Based on a Story by PETER WEIR Produced by ROBERT STIGWOOD and PATRICIA LOVELL Directed by PETER WEIR

A PARAMOUNT PICTURE DISTRIBUTED BY CINEMA INTERNATIONAL CORPORATION

GALLIPOLI 1981 (AUSTRALIA)

Director Peter Weir **Producers** Robert Stigwood, Patricia Lovell **Screenplay** Peter Weir, David Williamson (from Ernest Raymond's novel) **Cinematography** Russell Boyd **Music** Brian May **Cast** Mark Lee, Mel Gibson, Bill Kerr, Harold Hopkins, Charles Lathalu Yunipingli, Heath Harris, Ron Graham, Bill Hunter, David Argue, Reg Evans

The advertising tag line for the international release of Peter Weir's *Gallipoli* has a curious double meaning: It either refers to the film's eponymous battlefield in Turkey, where Australian troops suffered devastating casualties in a diversionary action for the benefit of British troops elsewhere; or to Australia itself, a remote post-colonial backwater to which Peter Weir, with an auteurist vision typical of his early career, draws a striking psychological profile.

Gallipoli tells the story of Archie Hamilton (Lee) and Frank Dunne (Gibson), who cross the Australian outback together to fight in the Great War. We follow the friendship from their first encounter and enlistment in Australia, to the battlefield at Gallipoli. As Frank, recruited as a messenger, fails to deliver in time the command that would save his friend and comrades, a freeze-frame of Archie ends the movie.

Unlike war films which illustrate how war calls and allows for the systematic perversion and deformation of human character, *Gallipoli* has a less spectacular yet ultimately more sobering point to make: that war's savagery is merely an extension of peaceful civil society.

◄
The tagline ("From a place you may never have heard of . . . a story you'll never forget") was Weir's way to wryly suggest that the time for Australian auteurs had arrived.

The film opens with two programmatic scenes, one showing young, innocent Archie pushing himself to the limit as a runner to please his uncle, a stern yet benevolent father figure; the other following Archie as he outruns one of his father's farmhands on horseback in an exuberant display of youthful play. Neither scene is ominous; both are shot in beautiful Australian landscapes, bathed in the same light of the magic

"THE THING I CAN'T STAND ABOUT YOU MATE IS YOU'RE ALWAYS SO BLOODY CHEERFUL." *FRANK DUNNE*

hour that gives the entire film a serene elegiac beauty.

Like most of his fellow Australians, Archie has no answer for anyone who expresses indifference to the war or even hostility to the British cause. Beyond Archie's narrow perspective, the picture never provides a reasonable rationale for war, painting the Australians as children oblivious to peril. Only a career officer's wife knows exactly what is in store for her husband as they say their farewells; the enlisted men tussle like puppies or frolic in the surf like schoolboys.

► **Mel Gibson was given the Australian Film Institute Award for Best Actor for his role as Frank Dunne.**

Without a political rationale for war, *Gallipoli* concentrates upon the play of ideologies; among them, most tragically, a burgeoning nationalism and striving for recognition that barely mask a fundamental uncertainty about Australian national identity. It also remains a tribute to the ANZACS who perished for the Allied cause in World War I. **SH**

Das Boot

Eine Reise ans Ende des Verstandes

BAVARIA ATELIER zeigt DAS BOOT ein Film von WOLFGANG PETERSEN nach dem Roman von LOTHAR-GÜNTHER BUCHHEIM

mit JÜRGEN PROCHNOW, HERBERT GRÖNEMEYER, KLAUS WENNEMANN, HUBERTUS BENGSCH, MARTIN SEMMELROGGE, BERND LAUBER, ERWIN LEDER, MARTIN MAY, HEINZ HÖNIG, UWE OCHSENKNECHT, CLAUDE OLIVER RUDOLPH, JAN FEDDER, RALPH RICHTER, JOACHIM BERNHARD, OLIVER STRITZEL, KONRAD BECKER, LUTZ SCHNELL, MARTIN HEMME, als Gäste GÜNTER LAMPRECHT, OTTO SANDER

Produzent GÜNTER ROHRBACH   Co-Produzent MICHAEL BITTINS   Schnitt HANNES NIKEL   Musik KLAUS DOLDINGER   Buch und Regie WOLFGANG PETERSEN   Herstellungsleitung JÖST VACANO   Bildgestaltung ROLF ZEHETBAUER, GÖTZ WEIDNER   Szenenbild MONIKA BAUERT   Spezial-Effekte KARL BAUMGARTNER   Kamera-Modelltrick ERNST WILD   Eine Produktion der BAVARIA ATELIER GESELLSCHAFT   in Co-Produktion mit RADIANT FILM   ein Film im Verleih der

DAS BOOT 1981 (WEST GERMANY)

Director Wolfgang Petersen **Producer** Günter Rohrbach **Screenplay** Wolfgang Petersen (based on the novel by Lothar G. Buchheim) **Cinematography** Jost Vacano **Music** Klaus Doldinger **Cast** Jürgen Prochnow, Herbert Grönemeyer, Klaus Wennemann, Hubertus Bengsch, Martin Semmelrogge, Bernd Tauber

Das Boot is the ultimate submarine film, a sea-warfare movie beyond comparison. Its trajectory from gung-ho glory to dumb defeat exemplifies the story of so many crews and their beloved "buckets."

The picture tells of German submarine U-96 and its hunt for British and American ships in the Atlantic Ocean. Over the course of a few months, the boat and its crew encounter several Allied convoys and sink several freighters. They almost collide with another U-boat, get battered by a three-week-long storm that drifts them off-course, and are severely damaged by destroyers and aircraft whose relentless chase forces them into the deepest corners of the ocean—well beyond what the vessel is supposed to endure. In between, the crew copes with the hardship and on-board dread. When U-96 finally returns home, home is gone. Upon anchoring, the ship is bombed and destroyed. Upon seeing his ship sink, the captain's fate is sealed too.

At the time, *Das Boot* was Europe's answer to Hollywood's ownership over "big war stories." *Das Boot*'s budget and logistics were designed to match Hollywood blockbusters—with the historical accuracies intact.

◄
The movie picked up half a dozen Academy Award nominations but failed to win any. Nevertheless it gave Hollywood blockbusters of the war genre a good run for their money.

The story of simple German sailors told through a German film became a source of pride, and a symbol in debates over the cinematic historiography of war. Petersen and crew enlisted real U-boat captains as consultants to get the tiniest details right. The tools helped evoke the claustrophobic feeling of being on a submarine and revolutionized "at sea" cinema—the film's traveling shots inside the narrow U-boat, the gyroscopic surface

"TAKE PICTURES OF RETURNING CREWS, NOT OF DEPARTING CREWS. BECAUSE IT MEANS SOMETHING." *LEHMAN*

rolling effects and the intimidating use of sonar sounds are still unparalleled. It is uncommon for war movies to shake off their topicality. But in the case of *Das Boot*, its almost mythical qualities lift it well above the status of naval epic. *Das Boot* takes the viewer on a journey from blue-sky opportunity to inferno and, as the film's tagline promised, "to the edge of the mind."

► **Not for claustrophobics: Prochnow goes to action stations. Petersen's use of edgy, hand-held camera in confined spaces gives *Das Boot* a sense of documentary realism.**

After a successful release that saw *Das Boot* outclass the Hollywood competition, its popularity was sustained across a television mini-series, a hugely successful video shelf-life and a rave techno version of the theme song that became of one of the emblems of the 1990s. A re-release in 1997 and various DVD versions (of up to 293 minutes) only intensified its reputation. It also made the boat's mascot image of the laughing sawfish an icon of international renown and cemented the film into the canon of cinema history. **EM**

THE KILLING FIELDS

Every so often, there is a film that is destined to be
talked about and remembered for years to come.

THE KILLING FIELDS 1984 (U.K.)

Director Roland Joffé **Producer** David Puttnam **Screenplay** Bruce Robinson
Cinematography Chris Menges **Music** Mike Oldfield **Cast** Haing S. Ngor,
Sam Waterston, John Malkovich, Julian Sands, Craig T. Nelson, Spalding Gray,
Bill Paterson, Athol Fugard, Graham Kennedy, Katherine Krapum Chey

Based on a true story, *The Killing Fields* centers on post-Vietnam fallout in Cambodia in the mid-1970s, and the enduring friendship between two men as one of them struggles to survive the country's ethnic cleansing.

The film begins in Cambodia as *New York Times* journalist Syd Schanberg (Waterston) covers the war alongside his assistant and interpreter Dith Pran (Ngor). With the United States pulling out in 1975, the totalitarian Khmer Rouge under the control of Pol Pot seizes control of the country. Knowing the certain peril his friend Pran faces as a U.S. sympathizer, Schanberg conspires with fellow journalist Jon Swain (Sands) and photographer Al Rockoff (Malkovich) to get Pran out of the country with a fake passport. When the plan fails, Pran is forced to leave the Embassy and disappear into a forced labor camp. Back in the U.S., Schanberg helps Pran's family settle and begins a four-year journey to locate his friend.

Based on Schanberg's article *The Death and Life of Dith Pran*, *The Killing Fields* is the first major film to deal with the Cambodian genocide under Pol Pot. Delineating the cost of human life of the nearly two million killed would be epic, so

◀

Roland Joffé's slow-paced, roving camerawork managed to convey the horrors of Pol Pot's genocide without the need for shock tactics. The movie won an Oscar for Best Cinematography.

Pran's remarkable true account is the perfect vessel to give the story a human focus. Marking theater and TV veteran Roland Joffé's debut as a feature director, the film begins with a slow-building hysteria punctuated by moments of sudden terror like a suicide bombing at an outdoor café. The film's second half is more emotionally draining as Pran's harrowing escape dominates the action. Juxtaposed with Pran's physical struggle

"IF THE WAR KEEPS GOING LIKE THIS, THE FUTURE COULD BE VERY BAD."

DITH PRAN

are scenes of Schanberg back home, mentally struggling with his conscience with both the guilt of keeping Pran in the country and the agony of failing to save him.

The picture's two lead performances are impeccable. Waterston, a dedicated humanitarian, brings a brooding intensity to the haunted writer and is entirely believable. Newcomer Ngor lived a remarkably similar life to unassuming hero Dith Pran, having lost family and escaped the Khmer Rouge in Cambodia during the 1970s.

▶

Haing Ngor deservedly won an Oscar for Best Supporting Actor for his portrayal of Dith Pran, despite having no previous acting experience.

Ngor brings a genuineness to the role that won him the Academy Award for Best Supporting Actor. Tragically, he was killed during a random robbery in San Francisco in 1996. A film about the beauty and simplicity of friendship during wartime, *The Killing Fields* is as powerful as it is daring in its depiction of its subject matter. **WW**

RAN 1985 (JAPAN · FRANCE)

Director Akira Kurosawa **Producers** Masato Hara, Serge Silberman
Screenplay Akira Kurosawa, Hideo Oguni, Masato Ide **Cinematography** Asakazu
Nakai, Takaeo Saito, Masaharu Ueda **Music** Toru Takemitsu **Cast** Tatsuya Nakadai,
Akira Terao, Jinpachi Nezu, Daisuke Ryu, Mieko Harada, "Peter," Masayuki Yui

While *Ran* was not Kurosawa's final film, it stands as a definitive
statement of the director's artistry, along with *Kagemusha*
(1980). It is a magnificent epic of Medieval Japan made all the
more remarkable in that the director was almost entirely blind
by the time he made it, painting the film's remarkable images in
his head and describing them to his cinematography team
who realized those images brilliantly

Based largely on Shakespeare's *King Lear*, *Ran* opens with
the aging warlord Hidetora (Nakadai) dividing his hard-won
estate among his three sons. While Taro (Terao) and Jiro (Nezu)
sycophantically honor their father, the youngest son, Saburo
(Ryu), rejects the great lord's legacy as foolishness and is
banished for his insolence. Hidetora's plan is simple enough:
He retains his title but renounces his power to his eldest son,
Taro, and the other two sons support the new lord. Saburo
points out to his esteemed father that titles without power
are meaningless, and that such a scheme would only work in
a world where honor and loyalty are respected. Very quickly,
Saburo's predictions are proven correct and the blood-soaked
legacy sown by Hidetora is reaped by the next generation:

◄
**Kurosawa's use
of deep-focus
photography
enabled him to
keep his large-scale
armies amassing
their ranks on
a far hillside
in perfect focus.**

Taro and Jiro form an alliance, manipulated by Taro's wife, Lady Kaede (Harada), to oust Hidetora once and for all. Betrayed by his two eldest sons, unable to turn to Saburo for help (as he'd been banished), and further unable to save face by committing *hari-kiri*, Hidetora can only slip into madness and exile accompanied by his fool Kyoami (Peter) and one loyal vassal (Yui).

"MEN PREFER SORROW OVER JOY . . . SUFFERING OVER PEACE!"

TANGO HIRAYAMA

At the center of *Ran* is one of the most spectacular battle sequences ever filmed: as Jiro and Taro attack Hidetora's third castle and take control of the kingdom, Kurosawa drops the diegetic sound from the soundtrack and with Toru Takemitsu's soft and ethereal score creates one of the most haunting moments in cinema history.

Hundreds of extras running around the set decked out in the color scheme of their respective lords—gold for Taro's army, red for Jiro's, white and black for those still loyal to Hidetora—creates flowing eddies of pigment on the screen. Thousands of arrows fly through the air at the castle, soldiers impaled with multiple shafts bleed profusely and the entire sequence wrapped in the notable absence of diegetic battle sounds is simply one of the most remarkable examples of mise-en-scène ever committed to the screen. **MK**

▶
Hidetora (Nakadai) as the King Lear figure. The movie was almost swamped by its depth of color and fabulous costumes (it won an Oscar for Best Costume).

COME AND SEE 1985 (U.S.S.R.)

Director Elem Klimov **Screenplay** Ales Adamovich, Elem Klimov
Cinematography Aleksei Rodionov **Music** Oleg Yanchenko **Cast** Jüri
Lumiste, Aleksei Kravchenko, Olga Mironova, Liubomiras Lauciavicius, Vladas
Bagdonas, Viktor Laurents, Kazimir Rabetsky, Yevgeni Tilicheyev, Aleksandr Berda

World cinema has a long tradition of producing films that filter
the experience of war through the eyes of a child. Among
others, Clément's *Forbidden Games* (1952), Tarkovsky's *Ivan's
Childhood* (1962), Schlöndorff's *The Tin Drum* (1979), and closer
to home Spielberg's *Empire of the Sun* (1987) come immediately
to mind. Few, however, possess the searing emotional power
of Elem Klimov's *Come and See* (a.k.a. *Idi i smotri*). Florya Gaishun
(Kravchenko), an adolescent with one of the most expressive
faces in film history, stumbles from atrocity to atrocity in his
besieged homeland of Byelorussia.

Released forty years after the Russian victory over Germany
in World War II, Klimov's film blends a brutal realism with a
nightmarish surrealism that shifts the narrative's visual and
aural assault from a harshly "objective" depiction of Nazi
massacres to a subjective perspective that feels as though it
allows spectators to "experience" the painful disintegration of
Florya's psyche. This strategy dominates Klimov's brutal work. It
is through Florya's eyes that we *come* to the horrific tableaux of
ethnic cleansing, and it is primarily through his point of view
that we *see* these appalling events transpire.

◄

**The horrors of
war are distilled
through the eyes
of a boy, and,
with one village
massacre scene
shot in a real time
half-hour, it turns
the audience
into horrified
but compulsive
voyeurs.**

Indeed, witnessing the extent of the brutality that human beings are capable of inflicting upon one another is one of *Come and See*'s most explicit themes, and the repeated focus on Florya's ravaged visage emerges as one of the film's most conspicuous and unsettling tropes. At times, his eyes contribute to an almost skull-like countenance to a face that steadily ages as the film moves toward its memorable climax—an astounding

"AN EXPRESSIONIST NIGHTMARE, FULL OF ABSTRACT HORRORS AND HEIGHTENED SURREALISM." SCOTT TOBIAS

sequence that is not only surreal and heartbreaking, but an affirmation of humanity that feels neither forced nor overtly sentimental.

Come and See is one of those rare achievements in world cinema, an expressionist masterpiece at once harrowingly intimate and remarkably expansive. From its relatively playful opening sequence, in which Florya and a young friend find a rifle buried in a sandy makeshift grave, through Florya's short-lived dalliance with the beautiful young Glasha (Mironova) in a picturesque forest that seemingly promises sanctuary, Klimov projects a world on the verge of sudden and seemingly irrevocable collapse. A mythic narrative with the structure of an epic, and the tenor of a nightmare from which one cannot awaken, *Come and See* remains one of the most powerful indictments of the senseless horror of war ever filmed. **JM**

► In a picture punctuated by dramatic close-ups, Florya's (Kravchenko) wide, staring eyes evince the toll exacted by the plethora of traumatic events continuously unfolding before him.

**Dateline: 1980
El Salvador**

**Correspondent:
Richard Boyle
Photojournalist-
Guatemala, Iran,
Vietnam, Chile,
Belfast, Lebanon,
Cambodia...**

SALVADOR

Based on a true story.

JAMES WOODS · JIM BELUSHI · MICHAEL MURPHY And JOHN SAVAGE
ELPEDIA CARRILLO   CINDY GIBB
HEMDALE FILM CORPORATION Presents An OLIVER STONE Film SALVADOR
Executive Producers JOHN DALY & DEREK GIBSON Screenplay by OLIVER STONE AND RICHARD BOYLE
Music by GEORGES DELERUE Produced by GERALD GREEN AND OLIVER STONE Directed by OLIVER STONE

SALVADOR 1986 (U.S.)

Director Oliver Stone **Producers** Oliver Stone, Gerald Green **Screenplay** Oliver Stone, Richard Boyle **Cinematography** Robert Richardson **Music** Georges Delerue **Cast** James Woods, James Belushi, John Savage, Michael Murphy, Elpidia Carrillo, Tony Plana, Colby Chester, Cynthia Gibb, Will MacMillan, Juan Fernández

Salvador is one hell of a powerful movie. Right from the opening titles it presents us with an audiovisual assault that suggests the kind of film we're about to see: snippets of black-and-white footage of chaos and violence in the streets of El Salvador are backed by bombastic music and by credits written in a blood-red font in the foreground.

Richard Boyle (James Woods, in a captivating and career-defining performance) is a photojournalist without a job, money, or place to live (based on the real Richard Boyle's experiences in the field). With a car, some booze, and weed he is on his way back to Salvador, searching for a story and eventually finding more than he bargained for. The film thus begins as a road movie, almost like a loose adaptation of *Fear and Loathing in Las Vegas*, only in El Salvador, with some amusing banter between Boyle and his road companion Doc Rock (Belushi). But that's only the beginning of a journey into "the heart of darkness," a small silence before the barrage of in-your-face war atrocities filmed in a gritty and raw manner. *Salvador* is a bold political statement, but it never gets too preachy. Boyle is depicted as an idealist, but his idealism is not

◄

Co-written by the real Richard Boyle, on whom the story is based, the movie is a visual and aural assault on American ignorance in global politics—at the time the C.I.A. was dabbling with Latin American dictators and death squads.

overly prominent at first because he's not naive and acts as an opportunist who lies all the time. But with the proximity of death becoming tangible, Boyle gets more personally involved and focuses on two goals—the survival of the truth through the legacy of photojournalist John Cassady (Savage), and the physical survival of innocents, namely Boyle's girlfriend María (Carrillo) and her family. Something that began as Boyle's way

> ## *"FIRST I'LL TAKE YOUR ARMS, THEN I'LL TAKE YOUR LEGS! THEN YOUR BALLS, SOUNDS LIKE A FUN GAME?"* FERNÁNDEZ

of escaping all the troubles of his personal life quickly turns into his road to redemption. For him, this isn't "just another article." Woods brilliantly portrays a man who becomes almost suicidal in his willingness to do the right thing in a world gone mad, and he makes every step and stumble of Boyle's desperate journey truly believable.

Stone's first transition from screenwriter to director brings an overall sense of urgency and intensity to a number of scenes, and marks his card as a topflight director in the making. He made a movie here that was quite relevant at the time, with the civil war in El Salvador still going on. But the film's relevance and impact are preserved even today because of the way this gut-wrenching history lesson is told: through the eyes of a common man, a flawed hero on his way from Hell on Earth to his very own purgatory. **MCv**

▶
James Woods in a career-defining role as Richard Boyle—a photojournalist scrounging for a living caught up in a nasty civil war.

PLAT**OO**N

HEMDALE FILM CORPORATION
An ARNOLD KOPELSON Production   An OLIVER STONE Film
"PLATOON"   TOM BERENGER   WILLEM DAFOE   CHARLIE SHEEN
Music By GEORGES DELERUE   Co-Producer A. KITMAN HO
Executive Producers JOHN DALY and DEREK GIBSON
Produced by ARNOLD KOPELSON   Written and Directed by OLIVER STONE
An **ORION** PICTURES *Release* © 1986 Hemdale Film Corporation. All rights reserved.
DOLBY STEREO

PLATOON 1986 (U.K. · U.S.)

Director Oliver Stone **Producer** Arnold Kopelson **Screenplay** Oliver Stone
Cinematography Robert Richardson **Music** Georges Delerue **Cast** Tom Berenger,
Willem Dafoe, Charlie Sheen, Forest Whitaker, Francesco Quinn, John C. McGinley,
Richard Edson, Kevin Dillon, Reggie Johnson, Keith David, Johnny Depp

Director and former Vietnam veteran Oliver Stone's semi-autobiographical coming-of-age tale depicts the psychological effects of facing front-line combat during a chaotic and brutal war. With an immensely strong ensemble cast, including stars Charlie Sheen, Tom Berenger, and Willem Dafoe, and with outstanding support from Forest Whitaker, John C. McGinley, and Kevin Dillon, as well as a young Johnny Depp, *Platoon* secured Stone his first Academy Award in the category of Best Director, and rightly so.

Loosely regarded as the first part of a trilogy with his later *Born on the Fourth of July* (1989) and *Heaven & Earth* (1993), each segment depicting a different aspect of the Vietnam War, *Platoon* is told through the eyes and letters of Private Chris Taylor (Sheen), an initially naive young man who volunteers for duty after dropping out of college, and who becomes perilously ensnared in the rivalry between his two commanding officers, Sergeant Barnes (Berenger) and Sergeant Elias (Dafoe). These two men embody markedly different conceptions of masculinity: the former affable, kind, and protective of his men; the latter self-interested, ruthless, and destructive. The

◄
Stone plays this movie at his normal volume—maximum—to hurtle the audience into the maelstrom of a war that had already been dissected daily on television screens of the time.

ensuing tension between these two leaders proves to be almost as much a danger to the platoon as the war itself. While the action never leaves the front line, Stone employs the unrelentingly tense and suspenseful footage of the horror of battlefield gunfire, and lingering shots of the manifest terror on the soldiers' faces, to emphasize his moral outlook on war, and to make a case for its evils. As members of the platoon are

> ## "ARE YOU SMOKING THIS SH*T TO ESCAPE FROM REALITY? ME, I DON'T NEED THIS SH*T. I AM REALITY." *BARNES*

evidently traumatized by fear, the psychological effects of war manifest themselves in harmful treatment of civilians and innocent bystanders. Stone regularly draws attention to American naivety with regard to the indigenous population— labeled derogatorily and dismissively by the soldiers as "gooks"—and to the army's propensity to discount their ill-treatment of the locals with such terms. As many of Stone's films have shown, this endeavor reflects wider issues in the tense relations between sections of American society and foreign cultures, and highlights American insularity, while attempting to reveal to us that these young soldiers are as much a victim of this tension as anyone else.

Stone also somehow acquired a reputation as peacenik director, yet this movie revels in violence and brutality by which the director is totally fascinated. **SR**

► Charlie Sheen at the front line of a war where soldiers are simply brutes or made brutes. The movie picked up four Oscars (non-acting ones).

FULL METAL JACKET 1987 (U.K. · U.S.)

Director Stanley Kubrick **Producer** Stanley Kubrick **Screenplay** Stanley
Kubrick, Michael Herr, Gustav Hasford (from Hasford's novel *The Short Timers*)
Cinematography Douglas Milsome **Music** Vivien Kubrick **Cast** Matthew Modine,
Vincent D'Onofrio, R. Lee Ermey, Arliss Howard, Adam Baldwin, Kevin Major Howard

Director Kubrick's anti-militarism, begun in *Paths of Glory* (1957)
and let loose in *Dr. Strangelove* (1963), continued with this
adaptation of the memoirs of Gustav Hasford, a combat
correspondent in Vietnam. Filmed in and around London's old
docklands (in part because an increasingly hermit-like Kubrick
allegedly didn't want to drive very far from his Hertfordshire
home), the film provides a detached but damning indictment
of the Vietnam war from basic training to combat.

The story is told through the eyes of Private Joker (Modine), a
savvy and cynical recruit. We follow him through boot camp as
his ambition to be a writer gets him assigned as a war
correspondent for the army's official magazine, *Stars and Stripes*.
Growing increasingly tired of covering up the truth with army-
speak, he is reassigned to the front line, where he re-groups with
some of his old buddies from his Parris Island training camp.

Most memorably, R. Lee Ermey provides the star turn as the
intense drill instructor Gunnery Sergeant Hartman. Ermey was
originally hired as a technical consultant, and impressed Kubrick
so much that he was cast in the film after the director heard
him direct a non-stop two-minute stream of invectives at the

◀
A film of two
parts, one is a
conventional boot
camp saga with
an over-the-top
drill sergeant; the
other is a nerve-
wracking depiction
of war, made edgy
by hand-held
camerawork.

cast (never repeating himself once). In many ways the character of Joker is a cipher though which we are made to observe the dehumanizing process that turns otherwise "nice young men" into trained killers, as Gunnery Sergeant Hartman relentlessly humiliates and degrades them so as to reshape them as "fighting machines." In one memorable scene, the overweight and oafish Private Gomer Pyle, played with a slowly maddening

"THE DEAD KNOW ONLY ONE THING: IT IS BETTER TO BE ALIVE."

PRIVATE JOKER

glee by Vincent D'Onofrio, is beaten up by his fellow recruits for continually letting the squad down by regularly failing on the combat assault course and bringing punishment upon them all. His eventual crazed-eye suicide plays as the worst kind of army recruitment film in reverse, showing just what happens when the rigors of war make human decency go AWOL.

► Private Joker (Modine) and other recruits struggle in boot camp and the burned-out buildings of Vietnam. Kubrick managed to evoke Vietnam in the depths of Deptford and the old London docklands.

Given the abrupt transition between the Parris Island boot camp segment and live combat in Vietnam, *Full Metal Jacket* is really two distinct films within one. The shift in tone from the claustrophobic terror inflicted upon the soldiers by the terrifyingly acerbic presence of Hartman, and the wide open spaces of Hue City where danger lurks unseen everywhere, is notable. The latter scenes, with their jarring metallic soundscape, offer a chilling assessment of an army without a plan fighting an enemy they neither understand nor ever really see. **RH**

A celebration of family.
A vision of love.
A memoir of war.
All through the eyes of a child.

HOPE
AND
GLORY

A FILM BY JOHN BOORMAN

COLUMBIA PICTURES PRESENTS IN ASSOCIATION WITH NELSON ENTERTAINMENT AND GOLDCREST
"HOPE AND GLORY" STARRING SARAH MILES · DAVID HAYMAN · DERRICK O'CONNOR · SUSAN WOOLDRIDGE · SAMMI DAVIS ·
AND IAN BANNEN WITH SEBASTIAN RICE EDWARDS AS BILL · ORIGINAL MUSIC COMPOSED AND CONDUCTED BY PETER MARTIN · COSTUME DESIGNER SHIRLEY RUSSELL ·
PRODUCTION DESIGNER ANTHONY PRATT · DIRECTOR OF PHOTOGRAPHY PHILIPPE ROUSSELOT · EXECUTIVE PRODUCERS JAKE EBERTS AND EDGAR F. GROSS
CO-PRODUCER MICHAEL DRYHURST · WRITTEN, PRODUCED AND DIRECTED BY JOHN BOORMAN

HOPE AND GLORY 1987 (U.K.)

Director John Boorman **Producer** John Boorman **Screenplay** John Boorman
Cinematography Philippe Rousselot **Music** Peter Martin **Cast** Sebastian Rice-
Edwards, Sarah Miles, Sammi Davis, Geraldine Muir, Ian Bannen, Jean-Marc Barr,
David Hayman, Derrick O'Connor, Susan Wooldridge, Annie Leon, Amelda Brown

Based loosely on writer and director John Boorman's own childhood in World War II London, *Hope and Glory* was a hit with critics, garnering five Oscar nominations among its many other accolades. In his sole film appearance, Sebastian Rice-Edwards plays Bill Rowan, the only son in a London family whose father is sent away to fight in World War II. The film shows the war through young Bill's eyes, as he witnesses (but doesn't necessarily understand) everything from bombings to love making. Left for the majority of the picture in a home with only women around him, Bill experiences at once boyhood's rites of passage, as well as the concerns and deprivation of war.

While not eschewing the fright and panic of wartime, Boorman's lyrical film is also an affectionate account of Bill's quirky but loving family whose unity, while endangered by the very fact of war, remains a constant for him during this turbulent time. For nine-year-old Bill, the war is a fascinating, at times even pleasurable, experience. Although his father is drafted, Bill doesn't seriously question his safe return; when his own home is burned in a bombing, Bill's mother moves her son and daughters out to her parents' country home. There, although

◄
Gracing the poster, this was the only acting credit for unknown Sebastian Rice-Edwards.

the war rages, Bill passes an almost idyllic summer, learning to play cricket with his cantankerous grandfather and observing the distinctively female daily concerns of his mother, aunts, and pregnant sister. For Bill, the war is an event that rarely poses a direct physical threat to his family. During one of the bombings of London, the mother of one of his schoolmates is killed, yet even this tragedy is as unreal to Bill and his young friends as the

> ## "I'M GOING TO MISS THE WAR AND IT'S ALL YOUR FAULT."
>
> *BILL ROWAN*

war footage they see in the cinema each weekend. When his teenage sister is put in the family way by an enlisted man, rather than abandoning her or getting killed, the soldier comes back for her. Even when bombs finally encroach on the family's isolated country retreat, they don't threaten Bill's safety. Rather, the bombs destroy his school, providing Bill with a delightful and unexpected reprieve from the boredom and insults of the schoolroom. Lastly, unlike many war films, *Hope and Glory* ends not with tragedy, but with a wedding.

Boorman's film is a thought-provoking motion picture. *Hope and Glory* undoubtedly is an important and needed addition to the war film genre. Its tender reminiscences amidst an uncertain time provide the audience with the distinct and necessary perspective of a child who cannot, and should not, fully understand the potentially life-altering nature of war. **AK**

▶
Shot in faded hues,
Hope and Glory
evokes the Blitz
and the British
bulldog spirit, and
is seen through the
eyes of a young Bill
(Rice-Edwards),
here with sister
Sue (Muir).

EMPIRE OF THE SUN 1987 (U.S.)

Director Steven Spielberg **Screenplay** Tom Stoppard (from the novel by J.G. Ballard) **Producers** Kathleen Kennedy, Frank Marshall, Steven Spielberg **Cinematography** Allen Daviau **Music** John Williams **Cast** Christian Bale, John Malkovich, Miranda Richardson, Nigel Havers, Joe Pantoliano, Masatō Ib

Steven Spielberg's *Empire of the Sun* tells the story of Jim (Christian Bale in his debut), a young British boy, who separated from his parents when the Japanese attack Shanghai during World War II, comes-of-age in a Japanese prison camp.

Mentored by Basie (Malkovich), Jim finds the strength to survive through a combination of petty scavenging and an overactive imagination. Tom Stoppard's screenplay collapses much of J. G. Ballard's original quasi-autobiographical story into a collection of powerful scenes that nevertheless manage to capture much of Jim's trauma and confusion. The scenes depicting U.S. planes parachuting food for the famished survivors and Jim's witnessing, albeit at a great distance, one of the atomic bombs dropped on Japan, are particularly powerful.

The combination of Spielberg's masterful direction and John Williams' elegant score contribute to the movie's potency; the collaboration between director, cinematographer (Allen Daviau), and composer allow the standard Spielbergian theme of the family unit's "centrality" to the human condition to achieve a subtle poignancy. Consequently, *Empire of the Sun's* climactic moments elude the over-determined sentimentality

◄

The movie was based on the quasi-autobiographical novel by the celebrated British novelist J. G. Ballard.

that render sequences in similar films less effective. *Empire of the Sun*'s focus on a child's experience of war and its tragic consequences vacillates tonally between the despairing deluge of atrocities in Klimov's *Come and See* (1985) and the romanticized nostalgia of Boorman's *Hope and Glory* (1987). Bale's remarkably assured performance contributes significantly to *Empire of the Sun*'s effectiveness. From his pre-war arrogance, to his emaciated

"LEARNED A NEW WORD TODAY. ATOM BOMB. IT WAS LIKE THE GOD TAKING A PHOTOGRAPH." JIM "JAMIE" GRAHAM

body's dead-eyed and utter shuffle through a blasted, apocalyptic landscape, audience sympathies remain firmly aligned with Jim's internal and external struggles.

In one tour-de-force sequence, American planes bomb the airfield adjacent to the prison camp. The camera follows Jim as he races through the camp and across the prison's rooftops. Exploding bombs fill the air with smoke and dust. Shining metal aircraft zoom past, their wings dipping perilously close to the ground. After a series of tracking shots, the camera pushes in to capture Jim's stunned posture and astonished visage in medium full shot. Bale's wide, staring eyes convey a mixture of horror and wonder, a gaze that communicates far more about his discordant emotional state than any scene of verbal exposition could ever hope to convey. It is the look of a strong yet clearly traumatized child aged far beyond his years. **AK**

▶
Christian Bale, in a powerful debut role, conveys a disorientated shock and awe as he witnesses American planes attacking an airfield next to his Japanese prison camp.

GOOD MORNING, VIETNAM

1987 (U.S.)

Director Barry Levinson **Producers** Mark Johnson, Larry Brezner
Screenplay Mitch Markowitz **Cinematography** Peter Sova **Music** Alex North
Cast Robin Williams, Forest Whitaker, Bruno Kirby, J. T. Walsh, Tung Thanh Tran,
Robert Wuhl, Noble Willingham, Chintara Sukapatana, Richard Edson, Juney Smith

Robin Williams is the beginning, middle, and end of Barry Levinson's *Good Morning, Vietnam*, and Levinson had the good sense to let his thoroughbred run unfettered. The main attraction of this film—and the source of box-office appeal that earned it $124 million domestic (when $100 million was mighty impressive)—is the series of comic detonations that Williams set off in his guise as Adrian Cronauer, a military DJ. His enthusiastically irreverent on-air patter is the delight of the grunts in the field and the bane of his humor-challenged immediate superiors, played by Bruno Kirby and J. T. Walsh.

Levinson encouraged Williams to improvise his anti-establishment riffs, and the energy and inventiveness are truly inspired. The Academy was duly appreciative and nominated Williams for a Best Actor in a Leading Role Oscar (won that year by Michael Douglas for *Wall Street*). Had it stuck to being a "Caddyshack Goes to 'Nam" style movie, it would be a Comedy Channel regular. For better or worse, however, it felt the need to explore the complexities of a controversial war and clash of civilizations, and this yielded some unsatisfactory results.

◄
The film's basic U.S.-centric sympathies generate huge laughs and some tears, but fail to ask the rights or wrongs of U.S. foreign policy.

Williams' Cronauer interacts with the locals on three fronts: he tries romancing a lovely young woman (Sukapatana); hangs out with her brother (Tran); and teaches English in a ramshackle school. He goes into full witty-and-charming mode for his intended: "You know, you're very beautiful. You're also very quiet. And I'm not used to girls being that quiet unless they're medicated." This might work in American, but the aggressive

> ## "IT'S THE TRUTH. I JUST WANT TO REPORT THE TRUTH. IT'LL BE A NICE CHANGE OF PACE." *CRONAUER*

style incites mainly discomfort, even fear, in the innocent young Vietnamese woman—whose limited English doesn't allow her to understand how clever he may be.

This illustrates where the script has some malfunctions. Williams' humor and attitude work well for his American audience (witness the big-time box office takes), but they ring false in the context of his relations with the Vietnamese in the film. His romantic technique could easily be considered stalking. He teaches street slang to his students, which makes the film audience howl with laughter, but will probably not serve his students well in business or more polite social occasions. When his Vietnamese buddy turns out to be Vietcong, Williams feels hurt and betrayed—understandable if this were just a poker buddy, but it's not: this is war, and the Vietnamese take the stakes for their culture enormously seriously. **WSW**

► A tour-de-force performance from Williams carries the film beyond its pat exploration of America's global empire building.

GRAVE OF THE FIREFLIES 1988 (JAPAN)

Director Isao Takahata **Producer** Tohru Hara **Screenplay** Isao Takahata (from the novel by Akiyuki Nosaka) **Cinematography** Nobuo Koyama **Music** Michio Mamiya **Cast** Tsutomu Tatsumi, Ayano Shiraishi, Yoshiko Shinohara, Akemi Yamaguchi, Rhoda Chrosite, Shannon Conley, Crispin Freeman, Dan Green

Grave of the Fireflies, based upon the semi-autobiographical book by Nosaka, is arguably the most famous *anime* film to emerge from Studio Ghibli that is not directed by Hayao Miyazaki. One of the few animated war films to deal directly with the consequences of warfare on children, it was awarded The Rights of Children Award at the Chicago International Film Festival in 1988. And as has often been noted, *Grave of the Fireflies* is the only movie from Studio Ghibli that Disney does not have the distribution rights to.

The movie focuses on two siblings and their struggle to survive the final days of World War II in Kobe, Japan. The protagonists are a brother, Seita (Tatsumi), and his younger sister Setsuko (Shiraishi), whose home is destroyed in bombing raids. Their mother is seriously injured and dies before she can be transferred to a hospital. The children are reluctantly taken in by a distant aunt who resents their impact on scarce resources—at one point she forces Seita to sell his dead mother's clothes for rice—as a result of which Seita and Setsuko soon find themselves homeless again. Forced to live in a bomb shelter, the film follows Seita's desperate attempts

◀

Grave of the Fireflies (a.k.a. *Hotaru no haka*) was based on a true story—the writer lost his sister during the war as a result of malnutrition (for which he blamed himself).

to provide the basic necessities of life for himself and his sister. And yet in the midst of this struggle for existence, moments of sheer beauty animate their everyday lives. The fireflies that light up the sky at night provide momentary illumination in the darkness for Seita and Setsuko in the cave where they live. In the morning the fireflies have died, their light and lives extinguished in a moment. Like fireworks, the fireflies provide

"SEPTEMBER 21, 1945 . . . THAT WAS THE NIGHT I DIED."

SEITA

a canopy of brilliance in the dark night sky, visually mirroring the American planes that continuously firebomb Kobe. At the same time, the short life-span of the fireflies is a metaphor for the ephemeral nature of human existence.

The circular narrative begins with the death of Seita and ends with the death of Setsuko. The final shot is of Seita sitting, while Setsuko sleeps in his arms, watching as contemporary Kobe rises from the ashes. The score by Michio Mamiya follows the events but is never intrusive or manipulative, allowing—as does the frequent use of pillow shots—the viewer to experience the picture in its intensity through moments of silence known as *ma* in Japanese aesthetics. *Grave of the Fireflies* is both a powerful anti-war film and a naturalistic study of the relationship between a brother and his sister. Once watched, it cannot be forgotten. **CB**

▶
One memorable scene (of many) where fireflies light up the sky at night, mirroring the American bombers dropping their deadly cargo on Kobe.

MATTHEW BRODERICK   DENZEL WASHINGTON   CARY ELWES AND MORGAN FREEMAN

Glory

TRI-STAR PICTURES PRESENTS A FREDDIE FIELDS PRODUCTION AN EDWARD ZWICK FILM "GLORY"

CO-PRODUCER PIETER JAN BRUGGE MUSIC BY JAMES HORNER EDITED BY STEVEN ROSENBLUM PRODUCTION DESIGNER NORMAN GARWOOD DIRECTOR OF PHOTOGRAPHY FREDDIE FRANCIS

SCREENPLAY KEVIN JARRE PRODUCED BY FREDDIE FIELDS DIRECTED BY EDWARD ZWICK

A TRI-STAR RELEASE

GLORY 1989 (U.S.)

Director Edward Zwick **Producer** Freddie Fields **Screenplay** Kevin Jarre
Cinematography Freddie Francis **Music** James Horner **Cast** Matthew Broderick,
Andre Braugher, Jihmi Kennedy, Cary Elwes, Morgan Freeman, Denzel Washington,
John Finn, Donovan Leitch, J. D. Cullum, Alan North, Bob Gunton, Cliff De Young

In a number of films, including *The Last Samurai* (2003) and
Defiance (2008), director Edward Zwick has focused on the
experience of a persecuted minority who refuse to be victims
and instead chose to fight against their persecution. *Glory* was
Zwick's first, and arguably most successful, examination of this
key theme. Set during the American Civil War, the film tells the
story of the 54th Massachusetts Volunteer Infantry—one of
the very first fighting units made up of African-Americans—as
they struggle to be accepted as free men and to prove
themselves as soldiers.

The film is adapted from Peter Burchard's *One Gallant Rush*
(1965) and Lincoln Kirstein's *Lay This Laurel* (1973), as well as
from the letters of Robert Gould Shaw, the 54th's commanding
officer. Matthew Broderick's performance as Shaw strikes a deft
balance between stiff, bourgeois reticence and an instinctive
and humane egalitarianism, and his voiceover narration of
Shaw's poignant letters home inform us of his pride in his men
but also his feeling that he will never be able to understand
fully how difficult their lives are. This qualified view allows *Glory*
to grasp the complex class and racial politics of the time.

◄
Displaying the
Afro-American
viewpoint of
America's bloodiest
war, *Glory* was
beautifully shot
and won the
Oscar for Best
Cinematography.

Alongside telling the story of Shaw's command, the film describes the experiences of four African-American characters. In a key scene the angry black nationalist, Trip (an Oscar-winning performance by Denzel Washington), is mistakenly flogged for desertion. As the flogging proceeds we see that his back is already covered in scars from previous punishments as a slave. It is a tragic, dramatic, and richly imagined scene that manages

"IT'S NOT TRUE IS IT? I MEAN ABOUT NOT BEING ALLOWED TO FIGHT."

CPL. THOMAS SEARLES

to convey some sense of how, from an African-American perspective, the Civil War was a war that had to be waged on two fronts: first, against the institutionalized, knee-jerk racism of the Union army, and then against the lethal armies and militias of the slave-owning Confederacy.

Another of *Glory*'s strengths is its meticulous attention to historical detail, which combines with Freddie Francis's Oscar-winning cinematography to create a rich tapestry of the Union army's training camps, supply lines, and preparations for battle. The film closes with a scene showing the 54th leading a frontal assault on Fort Wagner: the battle has a grim, infernal quality that, in contrast to the brothers-in-arms clichés of many Civil War movies, manages to register the pointlessness and waste of America's bloodiest war while also celebrating the values being fought and died for by this particular group of men. **GW**

▶
Denzel Washington won Best Actor in a Supporting Role for his portrayal of Private Trip.

ARTUR BRAUNER - MARGARET MENEGOZ
CCC-FILMKUNST GMBH - LES FILMS DU LOSANGE
SOFIMA
avec la participation du Ministère de la Culture et de la Communication
le Centre National de la Cinématographie - ARD et Bayerischer Rundfunk
présentent
EUROPA
EUROPA
L'Histoire extraordinaire et pourtant véridique
du Jeune Salomon PEREL
UN FILM DE
AGNIESZKA HOLLAND

EUROPA, EUROPA 1991 (GERMANY)

Director Agnieszka Holland **Producers** Artur Brauner, Margaret Ménégoz
Screenplay Agnieszka Holland (based on the book by Solomon Perel)
Cinematography Jacek Petrycki **Music** Zbigniew Preisner **Cast** Marco
Hofschneider, René Hofschneider, Julie Delpy, André Wilms, Piotr Kozlowsky

Any study of cinema about the Holocaust soon reveals that the strangest and most bizarre stories are actually the true ones. *Europa, Europa* is a picaresque tale through the eyes of a young Jewish boy, a kind of Jewish *Candide*, who survives the war under the noses of those who would have destroyed him.

Salomon "Solly" Perel (Marco Hofschneider), on the day of his bar mitzvah is exiled from his middle-class German Jewish home in a Nazi pogrom. The Perel family flee to Łódź, but come the German invasion of Poland, Salomon must flee further east. He is separated from his brother, Isaac (Marco's real-life brother René), and rescued by the Soviet army. Solly is sent to a Soviet school and there is indoctrinated into the Stalinist rhetoric of the day. As the Germans move deeper into Soviet-controlled Europe, Solly is separated from his comrades and eventually picked up by a Nazi patrol. Hiding his Jewish identity, and demonstrating his proficiency in German, Polish, and Russian, Solly acts as interpreter for the German military. As the squad he is with comes under heavy Soviet fire, killing all the German soldiers, Solly is left alone and tries to get back to the Soviet front line and the relative safety of Stalinism.

◀
The original German title of the film, *Hitlerjunge Salomon* (lit. Hitler Youth Salomon), better reflects the film's content and ironic style than the anonymous *Europa, Europa*.

Inadvertently, he leads the German army to victory, capturing the Soviet platoon he was trying to escape to. Hailed as a hero of the Reich, Solly is adopted by a Nazi general and his wife and sent to an elite Nazi Youth school back in Germany, where he succeeds in passing himself off as Aryan. "Salomon" is a stereotypical Jewish name—the irony of someone thus named being in the Hitler youth (*Hitlerjunge*) is obvious. For all the Nazi

"MEIN FÜHRER!"

NAZI AGENT INNA MOYSEYEVNA (DELPHINE FOREST) WHILE HAVING SEX WITH SOLLY (HOFSCHNEIDER)

ideological pronouncements regarding their Aryan superiority, particularly in comparison with the racial inferiority of Jews, that Solly as the cuckoo in their midst is able to surpass and succeed subverts the ideology. We see Solly swimming in the school's pool, with a large swastika painted on its bottom, in full military gear, winning a race. We see Solly brought to the front of a eugenics class as the teacher demonstrates that while he may not be pure-blooded Nordic, such fine features of his skull indicate he is clearly Aryan.

► **Combining the questionable themes of sex and genocide, this somewhat tasteless movie follows the fortunes of Solly (Hofschneider).**

The one thing Solly cannot hide is his circumcision; but this doesn't stop him from seducing a high-ranking Nazi agent on the train taking him to Germany. Solly demonstrates not just his own physical prowess, but throughout the film demonstrates his sexual prowess too, literally "screwing the Nazis at their own game." **MK**

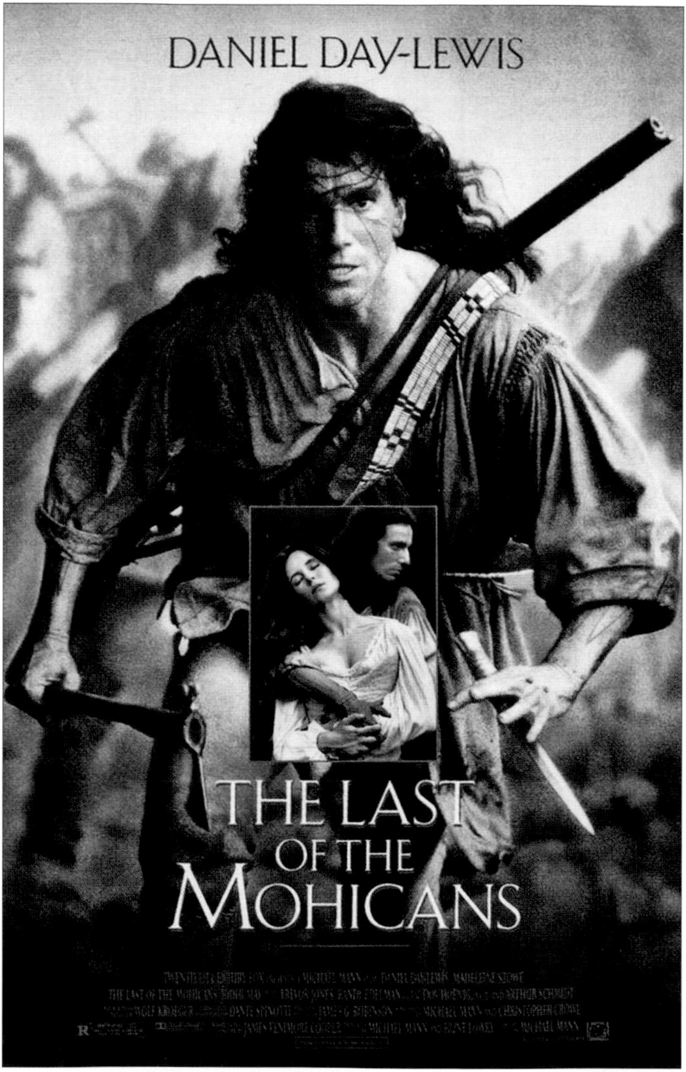
DANIEL DAY-LEWIS
THE LAST
OF THE
MOHICANS

THE LAST OF THE MOHICANS
1992 (U.S.)

Director Michael Mann **Producers** Michael Mann, Hunt Lowry **Screenplay** Michael Mann, Christopher Crowe **Cinematography** Dante Spinotti **Music** Trevor Jones, Randy Edelman **Cast** Daniel Day-Lewis, Madeleine Stowe, Russell Means, Pete Postlethwaite, Steven Waddington, Eric Schweig, Jodhi May, Wes Studi, Terry Kinney

Michael Mann, pioneer of the contemporary urban crime drama, travels back to 18th-century America in this action packed telling of James Fenimore Cooper's adventure tale. Nathaniel "Hawkeye" Poe, a white colonial orphan raised by Mohicans, meets and falls in love with Cora Munro, daughter of an English officer, amid a four-way war between the French, English, American colonials, and Native Americans.

The two lead roles (played by Day-Lewis and Stowe) have great screen chemistry, conveying the powerful attraction of two people from alien worlds, through silently exchanged looks or striking shots of their hugging forms silhouetted against rugged natural locations. As Hawkeye, adopted son of the titular last Mohican, Daniel Day-Lewis does his usual outstanding job of communicating the complex mix of his character's origins. The actor's real-life English accent works to his advantage, turning Hawkeye's diction into something indeterminate—part colloquialism, part proper English. Madeleine Stowe's Cora is luminous and willful, committing herself to Hawkeye without fear of consequence.

◀

The music should have won an Oscar but for contractual reasons was withdrawn from nomination. Guy Dagul's lush arrangements underpinned Trevor Jones's catchy themes.

Visually, the film is one of Mann's best. Frequent collaborator Dante Spinotti's cinematography is painterly and, in the 18th-century sense of the term, sublime. The positioning of figures, richly colored details, and the naturalistic portrayal of Native Americans recall such early American artists as Benjamin West or John Singleton Copley, while its wide-angle view of a magnificent wilderness has a grandeur where humanity is but

> ## "DEATH AND HONOR ARE THOUGHT TO BE THE SAME . . . I HAVE LEARNED THAT SOMETIMES THEY ARE NOT." COL. MUNRO

a traveling speck on a massive, misty canvas. The many battle scenes are beautifully shot. The Alamo-like siege on Fort Henry is an eerie night battle, with fire-lit smoke and shadows billowing across a vast expanse of rutted land. The surrender of the fort, and subsequent attack by the vengeful Huron Magua (Studi) and his fellow warriors is a masterpiece of color and violence, starting with cross-cuts between bright red British hues dwarfed by wild greenery, and the brown and black tones of near-naked warriors amassing in the trees, before building into a savage crashing of tomahawks and musket-fire. As music rises quietly underneath the chaos, Hawkeye the hero swoops Cora up in a slow-motion rescue. The film is full of noble sacrifices: a smug British officer for Cora; Uncas (Schweig), the second-to-the-last of the Mohicans, for Cora's sister Alice (May). Better to die than let someone you love die. **GC**

► **Daniel Day-Lewis as Hawkeye in one of his many running scenes across the untamed American landscape of 1757.**

EIN FILM VON

JOSEPH VILSMAIER

STALINGRAD

DOMINIQUE HORWITZ THOMAS KRETSCHMANN JOCHEN NICKEL SEBASTIAN RUDOLPH

HANNO HUTH GÜNTER ROHRBACH und B.A. PRODUKTION ... ROYAL-BAVARIA-B.A.-PERATHON-PRODUKTION ... JOSEPH VILSMAIER ... STALINGRAD ...
MINIQUE HORWITZ THOMAS KRETSCHMANN JOCHEN NICKEL SEBASTIAN RUDOLPH SYLVESTER GROTH MARTIN BENRATH und DANA VAVROVA ... JOHANNES HEIDE
JÜRGEN BÜSCHER JOSEPH VILSMAIER ... UTE HOFINGER ... RUTH PHILIPP HEINER NIEHUES ... HANNES NIKEL ... MILAN BOR und NORBERT J. SCHNEIDER
WOLFGANG HUNDHAMMER JINDRICH GOETZ ... KARL BAUMGARTNER ... JOSEPH VILSMAIER B.V.K. ... JOSEPH VILSMAIER
ORIGINAL-SOUNDTRACK AUF CD UND MC HEYNE ... BUCH ZUM FILM BEIM HEYNE VERLAG

STALINGRAD 1993 (GERMANY)

Director Joseph Vilsmaier **Producers** Hanno Huth, Günter Rohrbach
Screenplay Jürgen Büscher, Johannes Heide, Joseph Vilsmaier, Christoph Fromm
Cinematography Rolf Greim, Klaus Moderegger, Peter von Haller **Music** Enjott
Schneider **Cast** Thomas Kretchmann, Dominique Horwitz, Jochen Nickel, Dana Vávrová

There a very few films about the battle of Stalingrad, one of the defining clashes of World War II. That is not surprising. In a slaughter that cost nearly two million lives, where "hugging" front lines made delineations between sides impossible, and where both armies used each other's weapons and uniforms, even shooting their own, there is little room for individual heroism, honor, or glamour. Jean-Jacques Annaud took a pretty good stab with Jude Law and Ed Harris trying to out-sniper each other in *Enemy at the Gates* (2001), but the celluloid battle lines had been drawn by *Stalingrad*.

The movie tells the story of a platoon of German soldiers, led by the inexperienced Lieutenant Hans Von Witzland (Kretchmann), but carried by veterans Fritz (Horwitz) and Rollo (Nickel). The platoon quickly learns the main tricks to survival: keep your head low and distrust officers. After they make their way back, through basements and sewers (and with heavy losses), from a dangerous assignment, they are forced into "punishment missions." These include a suicidal anti-tank operation and execution squad duty. As the trapped German army disintegrates and command lines break down, Hans, Fritz,

◀

The movie was hard for audiences to identify with as the line between good and bad in people was so blurred that all the players ended up as indistinguishable collateral.

and Rollo realize they will not be rescued. They go into hiding to keep out of the hands of the Russians. Rollo disappears. Hans and Fritz try to escape across the plains with the help of former captive Irina (Vávrová). She is shot by her own troops. Abandoned, Hans and Fritz's bodies are covered with snow, to be enclosed in their fate. Director Joseph Vilsmaier and producer Günter Rohrbach (of *Das Boot* [1981]), have given

"THE MEN TRUSTED YOU, FOUGHT WITH YOU. ARE WE NOTHING BUT A FLAG ON YOUR DAMN MAP?" *LT. VON WITZLAND*

Stalingrad a tremendously bleak outlook. Perpetual suffering is punctuated by brutal images of debris, ruins, twisted metal, carcasses, blood, and severed limbs. Everything is damaged. Not a single plan succeeds. Even dying seems horrendous, as guns jam and injuries are left unattended. At several points, the platoon encounters wounded soldiers begging to be killed, and they are denied even that request. Throughout, a barrage of roars, cries, shrieks, and pounding artillery creates an aural onslaught that shows there is never a moment's relief from this hellish nightmare.

►
Palpable fear shows in the face of German Lieutenant Hans Von Witzland (Kretchmann).

Stalingrad had a reasonably wide release, but was only moderately successful. Outside Europe, the film was criticized for implying *Stalingrad*'s soldiers are *only* "innocent victims," never perpetrators of evil—harsh criticism for a movie that actually concentrated on action set pieces. **EM**

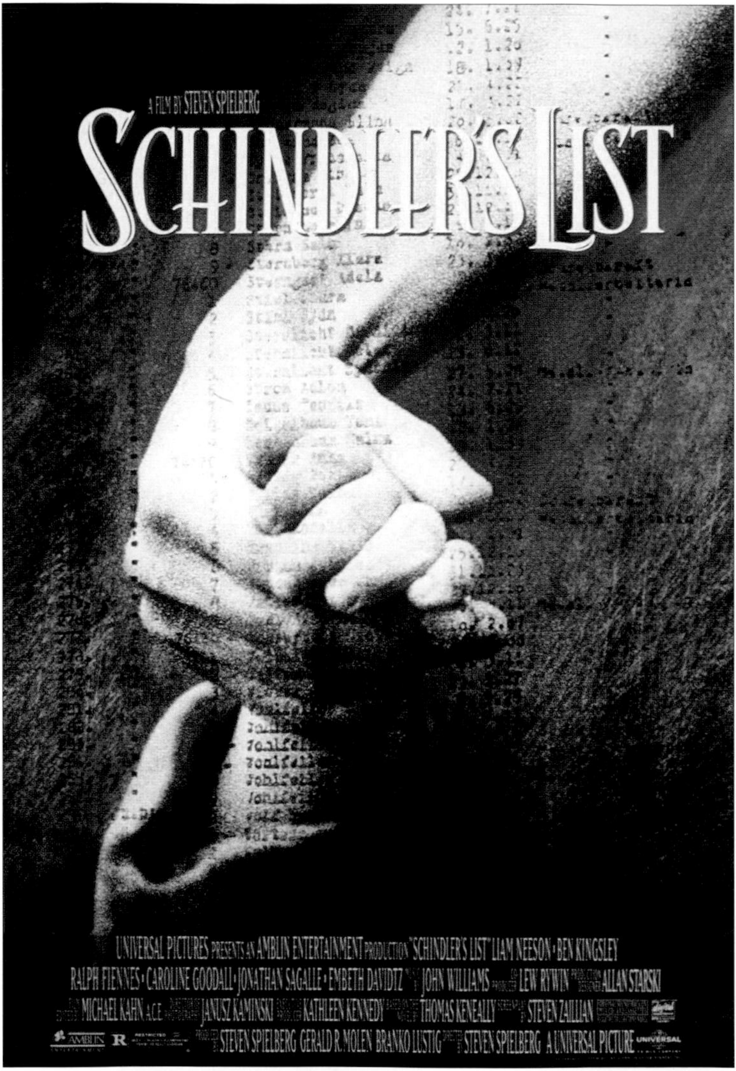
A FILM BY STEVEN SPIELBERG
SCHINDLER'S LIST
UNIVERSAL PICTURES PRESENTS AN AMBLIN ENTERTAINMENT PRODUCTION "SCHINDLER'S LIST" LIAM NEESON • BEN KINGSLEY
RALPH FIENNES • CAROLINE GOODALL • JONATHAN SAGALLE • EMBETH DAVIDTZ JOHN WILLIAMS LEW RYWIN ALLAN STARSKI
MICHAEL KAHN A.C.E. JANUSZ KAMINSKI KATHLEEN KENNEDY THOMAS KENEALLY STEVEN ZAILLIAN
AMBLIN R
STEVEN SPIELBERG GERALD R. MOLEN BRANKO LUSTIG STEVEN SPIELBERG A UNIVERSAL PICTURE
UNIVERSAL

SCHINDLER'S LIST 1993 (U.S.)

Director Steven Spielberg **Producers** Branko Lustig, Gerald R. Molen, Steven Spielberg **Screenplay** Steven Zaillian (based on the book by Thomas Keneally) **Cinematography** Janusz Kaminski **Editor** Michael Kahn **Music** John Williams **Cast** Liam Neeson, Ben Kingsley, Ralph Fiennes, Embeth Davidtz, Malgoscha Gebel

Based on the historical novel *Schindler's Ark* by Thomas Keneally, *Schindler's List* tells the story of a Nazi wartime profiteer, Oskar Schindler (Neeson) While starting out as a self-interested businessman, his perspective changed, and by using his enamel work factory in Poland and bribing the right Reich officials, he managed to save more than 1,100 Jewish workers from the gas chambers of Auschwitz

Schindler's List very quickly became the film in vogue to loathe within academic circles it was criticized for its trivialization of the Holocaust, turning the Shoah into "Shoah-business" (a truly offensive pun), not because of anything inherent in the film, but simply because Spielberg's name was attached to it. Spielberg was accused of turning the death of ten million people and six million Jews into a theme-park adventure ride. Millions of cinemagoers and the Academy of Motion Picture Arts and Sciences, which organizes the Oscars, disagreed with this prejudiced view of *Schindler's List*. Their consensus? That Spielberg appeared to prove he could make such a serious film. The bottom line? The man does know how to make a winning picture. While a filmmaker such as

◄

After a period of cloyingly sentimental films that pandered to America's immature cinemagoers, Spielberg tackled the Holocaust and, contrary to most predictions, did a creditable job.

Spielberg is able to raise hundreds of millions of dollars for his production budgets, and while he often relies on almost a hundred years of Hollywood tricks to tell the story, and while the film does end in overwrought sentimentality, it is still an incredibly effective picture. However cynical or detached you may feel about Spielberg's oeuvre, the final images of the film—of the actual Schindler survivors, along with the actors

"IF THIS FACTORY EVER PRODUCES A SHELL THAT CAN ACTUALLY BE FIRED, I'LL BE VERY UNHAPPY." *SCHINDLER*

who played them, placing a stone on the actual grave of Oskar Schindler (a Jewish memorial ritual)—may be highly manipulative, but they are incredibly moving nevertheless. This is the film to win over Spielberg sceptics.

Having mined a vast movie vein pandering to immature America, Spielberg was doubted by many critics who questioned whether the director was a sufficiently mature filmmaker to tackle the Holocaust. This was especially pertinent because in interviews of the period, Spielberg would always seem to point out his film school credentials, and how influenced he was by the French New Wave; yet it was debatable just how invisible such influences seemed to be in his own cinema. So the odds were stacked against Spielberg pulling off such a movie. But, with *Schindler's List*, he regained all his old credibility. **MK**

► Filmed in grainy black-and-white to lend it a sense of documentary neorealism, Spielberg's film won Oscars in most of the technical categories, and for Best Picture and Best Director.

Tierra y Libertad

Una película de
Ken Loach

LAND AND FREEDOM 1995 (U.K. • SPAIN)

Director Ken Loach **Producer** Rebecca O'Brien **Screenplay** Jim Allen
Cinematography Barry Ackroyd **Music** George Fenton **Cast** Ian Hart,
Rosana Pastor, Icíar Bollaín, Tom Gilroy, Marc Martínez, Frédéric Pierrot, Andrés
Aladren, Sergi Calleja, Eoin McCarthy, Suzanne Maddock, Angela Clarke

Land and Freedom (a.k.a. *Tierra y libertad*) begins with Kim
(Maddock) discovering her recently deceased grandfather's
effects, including, much to her surprise, clippings from Socialist
newspapers and Communist pamphlets dating back to the
1930s. There are several old photographs in this box too, of
people she has never heard of or knew about. Most significantly
are a series of letters her granddad wrote to her grandmother
Kitty (Clarke) in the 1930s when he was a volunteer in the
Republican militia during the Spanish Civil War. Kim's discovery
of her grandfather's anti-Fascist activism is the structuring
narrative device that draws in the audience to Loach's film; as
Kim discovers her grandfather's past, so do we.

David Carr (Hart) is a committed Mancunian Communist.
While at a rally on behalf of the anti-Franco forces in Manchester,
Carr feels it is wrong to simply support the Republican
movement and is compelled to sneak into Spain and literally
fight for what he believes in. Once in Spain, Carr joins an
international squad of idealistic young Socialists from around
the world—American, British, German, French, Italian, and
Irish—and together they engage the Nationalists.

◄
**The movie
ultimately is more
about selling anti-
Franco Socialism
to the Anglo-
Americans, than
developing the
protagonists'
story and plotline.**

It doesn't take long, however, before ideological in-fighting breaks out amongst the various Leftist factions—pro-Stalinist Communists versus Spanish Socialists—and ultimately the movie suggests that Franco's victory was due in no small part to the lack of coherence among the Republican factions.

Land and Freedom is an unapologetically left-wing propaganda film; Carr's journey into disillusionment is too

"WE ELECT THE OFFICERS . . . IT'S SOCIALISM IN ACTION—NOT LIKE THE ARMY BACK HOME." *CARR*

clichéd and underdeveloped to be the center of the story. Instead, the picture explains one step at a time the Spanish Civil War to the audience. *Land and Freedom* uses a double identification structure: as Kim discovers her grandfather's involvement in 1930s Spain, when the film flashes back we are positioned alongside Carr himself as he discovers the importance of the Spanish Republican movement. It is through both his and his granddaughter's eyes that our two-hour history lesson is presented.

By first using Kim and then Carr as narrative devices the effect is somewhat preachy and didactic; we are shown, through the eyes of Carr, the Fascist atrocities in the civilian population (like using them as human shields), the political in-fighting between the Leftist factions and the camaraderie among the militia themselves. **MK**

► Marc Martínez as Juan Vidal, one of the leaders of P.O.U.M. (the Workers' Party of Marxist Unification).

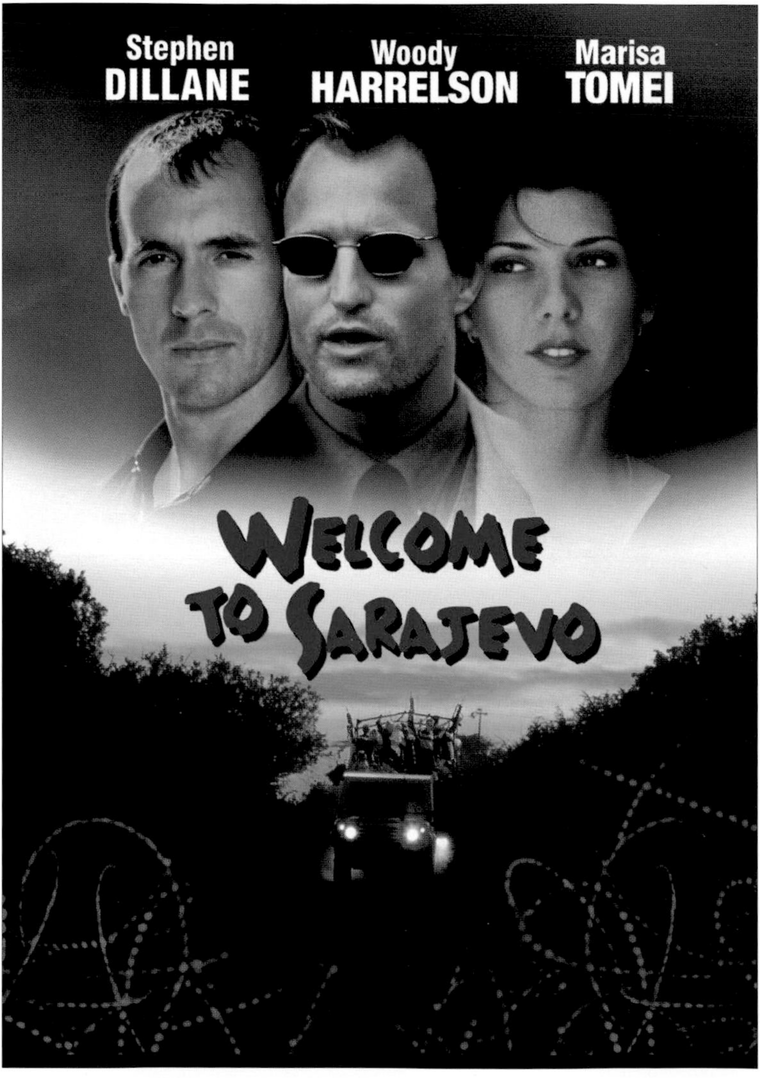
Stephen
DILLANE
Woody
HARRELSON
Marisa
TOMEI
WELCOME
TO SARAJEVO

WELCOME TO SARAJEVO 1997 (U.K. · U.S.)

Director Michael Winterbottom **Producers** Graham Broadbent, Damian Jones
Screenplay Frank Cottrell Boyce (from the book *Natasha's Story* by Michael Nicholson)
Cinematography Daf Hobson **Music** Adrian Johnston **Cast** Stephen Dillane,
Woody Harrelson, Marisa Tomei, Goran Višnjić, Emira Nušević, James Nesbitt

Based on the non-fiction book *Natasha's Story* by English
reporter Michael Nicholson, *Welcome to Sarajevo* is a powerful
film illustrating the singular impact made by one person during
the Bosnian War.

The story focuses on Michael Henderson (Dillane), a British
war correspondent riding around the capital city of Sarajevo
with his driver/interpreter Risto (Višnjić) and fearless American
journalist Flynn (Harrelson). Disillusioned by the West's
indifference to the escalating war in Bosnia-Herzegovina, and
haunted by two incidents involving war-weary children,
Henderson turns his attention to an orphanage housing roughly
two-hundred youths that is situated on the front lines. Looking
to counter the United Nation's general unresponsiveness,
Henderson creates a series of reports about the children before
working with aid representative Nina (Tomei) to move the kids
to safety. Among the children is Emira (Nušević), a young girl
abandoned by her mother that Henderson has promised a
better future in England. Using a mix of real war footage and
scripted drama, director Michael Winterbottom skillfully
recreates the urban warfare of the conflict. The authenticity is

◀

**Winterbottom's
direction gives
a human face to
one of the 20th
century's most
misunderstood
conflicts.**

helped by the fact that the filmmakers began shooting in war-torn locations literally months after the 1995 cease-fire. Winterbottom pulls no punches in the depiction of war and the ethnic cleansing that occurred, juxtaposing images of world leaders speaking about the conflict with gruesome results of the war. The decision to use unknown locals alongside professional actors gives the picture additional credibility and

"NO ONE SHOULD HAVE TO COME BACK TO THIS."

RISTO BAVIC

reality. Like its cinematic predecessors *Catch-22* (1970) and *M*A*S*H* (1970), (but without the humor) the film centers on a group of people growing accustomed to being trapped in the insanity and tedium of wartime. The reporters convene in the hotel bar nightly and pack the streets during conflicts; they are oblivious to the rocket attacks and unmoved when a UN ambassador gives a cursory visit or they are told that a Royal Family divorce has bumped a war story on a newscast.

► Henderson (Dillane) has promised Emira (Nušević) sanctuary back in the U.K., and here they run the gauntlet of sniper fire and bombs in downtown Sarajevo.

Ultimately, it is Henderson's struggle with the idea of maintaining his professional objectivity and his moral conscience that defines the film as he opts to try and make a difference in the war he is seeing. The movie's second half—where Henderson and Emira make the treacherous expedition and he must return to Sarajevo to meet Emira's mother—is the most lingering, as viewers are emotionally invested in the journey. **WW**

JONATHAN PRYCE   JAMES WILBY   JONNY LEE MILLER

R E G E N E R A T I O N ⑮

A FILM BY GILLIES MACKINNON

BASED ON THE FIRST PART OF THE TRILOGY BY THE BOOKER PRIZE-WINNING AUTHOR, PAT
BARKER, THE MOVING STORY OF A REAL-LIFE ENCOUNTER BETWEEN W.H.R. RIVERS, AN
ARMY PSYCHIATRIST AND THE WAR POETS SIEGFRIED SASSOON AND WILFRED OWEN.

REGENERATION 1997 (U.K. • CANADA)

Director Gillies MacKinnon **Producers** Allan Scott, Peter R. Simpson, Mark Shivas, Saskia Sutton, Eddie Dick, Kathy Avrich-Johnson **Screenplay** Allan Scott **Cinematography** Glen MacPherson **Music** Mychael Danna **Cast** Jonathan Pryce, James Wilby, Stuart Bunce, Jonny Lee Miller, Tanya Allen, David Hayman, Paul Young

Set in Scotland in 1917 at the end of World War I, *Regeneration* is a thoughtful war drama that focuses on the moral consequences of war and its psychological toll. Based on the prize-winning author Pat Barker's 1991 novel, the film tells the story of three soldiers and the psychiatrist who treats them at Craiglockhart Hospital, which specializes in restoring shell shocked soldiers to good mental health and returning them to the battlefield, if at all possible.

With great sensitivity, Jonathan Pryce plays Dr. William Rivers, a pioneering psychiatrist feeling his way through the profession's infancy and treating his patients with whatever common sense he can apply. He is clearly feeling the impact of his close involvement with his patients' terrors as he practices his talking cures and is dismayed by his colleagues' more invasive shock treatment methods. He questions the validity of taking already fragile minds and making them insane enough to want to go back to the front. The eminent poet and war hero Siegfried Sassoon (Wilby) is sent to the hospital because he has had a change of heart about the war and has written a pamphlet that denounces its shift from a war of

◄
A post-traumatic-stress movie before such a condition was recognized, *Regeneration* explores the mental breakdown of brave men caught up in flashbacks they cannot deal with.

liberation to one of aggression. He is given the choice of being court-martialed or being sent to the madhouse. While there he meets another budding poet, Wilfred Owen (Bunce), whose work Sassoon encourages and steers toward realistic coverage of the war. Another patient at the hospital is Billy Prior (Miller), a soldier who has gone mute from the horrors he's seen on the battlefield. The depiction of the turmoil of these true historical

"MANAGES TO CONVEY WAR THROUGH THE EYES OF ITS VICTIMS."

FIONA CLAGUE

figures is challenging for the audience to witness. Ultimately, *Regeneration* is a film of ideas and ideologies and, interestingly, was given an American release during a period of renewed Hollywood interest in the war film genre; consider *Saving Private Ryan* and *The Thin Red Line*, for example, both of which came out in 1998. The screenplay by Allan Scott (who also produced) is intelligent and provocative. However, the film's dramatic pull does not always involve the viewer at the deepest emotional levels. The narrative skips evenly among the four compelling leads, but never lights on any single dramatic conflict or character as its central focus. It may be a futile search for heroes in a movie that questions the very validity of heroes. Yet *Regeneration* is a war film that engages us at a mostly conceptual level rather than a visceral one. This anomaly is also what makes it a particularly distinctive work. **MB**

▶

Wilfred Owen (Bunce) comforts Billy Prior (Miller), in this harrowing tale of the psychological impact of war in the trenches.

LIFE IS BEAUTIFUL 1997 (ITALY)

Director Roberto Benigni **Producers** Gianluigi Braschi, Elda Ferri
Screenplay Roberto Benigni, Vincenzo Cerami **Cinematography** Tonino
Delli Colli **Music** Nicola Piovani **Cast** Roberto Benigni, Nicoletta Braschi,
Giorgio Cantarini, Giustino Durano, Sergio Bustric, Marisa Paredes, Horst Bucholz

Perhaps more controversial than Steven Spielberg's *Schindler's List* (1993), Roberto Benigni's *Life Is Beautiful* (a.k.a. *La Vita è Bella*) was much lauded by many film critics and at awards ceremonies, academically disdained for its sentimentality, and raised debates surrounding whether or not comedy was an appropriate mode in which to discuss the Holocaust.

The film is largely in two parts: the first concerns Guido Orefice (Benigni), an Italian Jew subverting Mussolini's Racial Laws and his wooing of Dora (Braschi—and the real-life Mrs. Benigni), a seemingly unobtainable Gentile woman engaged to an up-and-coming Fascist bureaucrat.

The second part takes place several years later: Dora and Guido are now married and have a five-year-old son, Giosué (Cantarini). Despite living under the worst of conditions for Italian Jews, Guido tries to keep the realities of Fascist anti-Semitism away from his boy. Guido's ingenuity is put to the ultimate test when he and Giosué are deported to an unnamed concentration camp. Guido tries to shield his son from the realities of the Holocaust by pretending that the concentration camp experience itself is nothing but a big game.

◄
Should comedy be used as a cinematic vehicle to explore the dark nightmare of the Holocaust? The U.S. film academy certainly thought so, awarding it Best Foreign Language Film and making Benigni Best Actor.

Holocaust comedies are a highly problematic and controversial mode to discuss the historical extermination of Europe's Jews. While few have much of a problem with the undercutting of Fascist authority in the first part of this picture, portraying the Shoah as a "game," even within the narrative confines of trying to protect Giosué, seemed to trivialize and falsify the seriousness of the topic. Historically, children

"IF YOU SPEAK MY NAME, I VANISH. WHAT AM I? SILENCE."

GUIDO OREFICE

Giosué's age would have been immediately put to death in most camps, so the impossibility of *Life Is Beautiful*'s very premise is highly problematic.

More problematic, however, although few academic critics choose to discuss this, is the film's overwhelming sentimentality. Even more than Spielberg's abilities to manipulate his audience's emotions, Benigni wrenches out every single tear from his audience he can. But the film does raise the significant question of the role of sentimentality and melodrama in Holocaust cinema. Is this the right emotion to evoke for the topic? Filmmakers like Claude Lanzmann, whose *Shoah* (1985) is often considered the definitive Holocaust film, would posit that the murder of six million Jews needs to be understood intellectually and definitively, not emotionally. It is a debate that certainly needs to be aired and further examined. **MK**

► Orefice (Benigni) pokes fun at his Nazi camp guard to keep up the pretense for his son that the concentration camp is just an elaborate game.

A STEVEN SPIELBERG FILM

tom hanks

saving private ryan

edward burns   matt damon   tom sizemore

the mission is a man.

SAVING PRIVATE RYAN 1998 (U.S.)

Director Steven Spielberg **Producers** Ian Bryce, Mark Gordon, Gary Levinsohn, Steven Spielberg **Screenplay** Robert Rodat **Cinematography** Janusz Kaminski **Music** John Williams **Cast** Tom Hanks, Matt Damon, Tom Sizemore, Edward Burns, Barry Pepper, Adam Goldberg, Vin Diesel, Giovanni Ribisi, Jeremy Davies, Ted Danson

In 1999, *Saving Private Ryan* won the Oscar for Steven Spielberg as Best Director, but lost to *Shakespeare in Love* as Best Picture; statistically speaking, Director/Picture splits are fairly rare. Notwithstanding the obvious absurdity of the Oscar celebrations, within the remit of the Academy Awards this split does make logical sense: despite the remarkable direction in *Saving Private Ryan*, which certainly deserved that award, the screenplay by Robert Rodat is not particularly noteworthy.

Saving Private Ryan is loosely based on a true story: all three of Pvt. James Francis Ryan's (Damon) brothers have been killed in action during World War II. Capt. John Miller (Hanks) and his squad, having just survived the Normandy invasion, are sent by the War Office to find Private Ryan and send him home in recognition of the supreme sacrifice his family has already made, under what is known as the "Sole Survivor Policy."

The film is memorable above all for the remarkable direction and cinematography of the D-Day landing sequences. Remembering the 50th anniversary of these momentous events, the men-on-a-mission's opening sortie at Omaha Beach had been suggested while reworking the pedestrian script.

◄
The film's visual and aural impact on other war movies—such as *Enemy at the Gates*, *Three Kings*, *The Patriot*, and the Spielberg-Hanks TV production *Band of Brothers*—has been colossal.

Running almost thirty minutes at the beginning of the picture, these sequences are brutal, relentless, and incredibly graphic. Just as important, they have been recognized as being strongly historically accurate by veterans of the invasion, and a close approximation of the actual experience. Throughout the film, the battle sequences (of which there are several) are cinematically breathtaking. The action to hold the bridge at

"HE BETTER BE WORTH IT. HE BETTER CURE A DISEASE, OR INVENT A LONGER-LASTING LIGHT BULB." *CAPT. MILLER*

Ramelle is just as visceral—dull thuds and pops rather than howling explosions, and hand to hand combat to the death. It is truly gut-wrenching and graphic for the audience.

However, the script itself is fairly tedious, rehearsing many of the same combat film clichés Hollywood has been trotting out for decades, including, but not limited to: the lone Nazi sniper encounter; the mixed bag squad reflecting the diversity of American servicemen; the no-nonsense and dedicated Captain whom the squad will follow into the worst kinds of combat; the Southern redneck sharpshooter; and so on. We don't learn anything particularly new about the war (as we do, say, from the related Spielberg/Hanks-produced HBO television series, *Band of Brothers*), but what we *see* is new (at least for a Hollywood war movie)—the visceral contributions combat veterans make in war. **MK**

► Capt. Miller (Hanks) is a sane voice on a seemingly insane mission. The movie doesn't glorify war but simply asks "what is heroism?"

SEAN PENN

ADRIEN BRODY

JIM CAVIEZEL

BEN CHAPLIN

GEORGE CLOONEY

JOHN CUSACK

WOODY HARRELSON

ELIAS KOTEAS

NICK NOLTE

JOHN C. REILLY

JOHN TRAVOLTA

THE
THIN RED LINE

EVERY MAN FIGHTS HIS OWN WAR

FOX 2000 PICTURES PRESENTS FROM PHOENIX PICTURES IN ASSOCIATION WITH GEORGE STEVENS, JR. A GEISLER · ROBERDEAU PRODUCTION
"THE THIN RED LINE" MUSIC BY HANS ZIMMER EDITED BY BILLY WEBER, LESLIE JONES PRODUCTION DESIGNER JACK FISK DIRECTOR OF PHOTOGRAPHY JOHN TOLL, A.S.C. EXECUTIVE PRODUCER GEORGE STEVENS, JR.
PRODUCED BY ROBERT MICHAEL GEISLER · JOHN ROBERDEAU, GRANT HILL BASED ON THE NOVEL BY JAMES JONES SCREENPLAY AND DIRECTED BY TERRENCE MALICK

PHOENIX   20
                                                                            FOX

TERRENCE MALICK

THE THIN RED LINE 1998 (U.S.)

Director Terrence Malick **Producers** Robert Michael Geisler, Grant Hill, John Roberdeau **Screenplay** Terrence Malick (based on the novel by James Jones) **Cinematography** John Toll **Music** Hans Zimmer **Cast** Sean Penn, Adrien Brody, Jim Caviezel, Ben Chaplin, Nick Nolte, John Cusack, John Travolta, George Clooney

Director Terrence Malick is one of cinema's most celebrated and elusive figures. He first came to the attention of cinema-goers and critics alike with *Badlands* (1973), his poetic re-telling of the Starkweather-Fugate killing spree in 1950s America. He followed this with *Days of Heaven* (1978) which, after a troubled production, arrived to mixed reviews and left Malick exhausted and disillusioned enough to retreat from Hollywood. His return to filmmaking after an almost 20-year self-imposed exile in France came in 1998 with *The Thin Red Line*, a loose adaptation of a novel by James Jones.

Much anticipation and rumor surrounded Malick's take on the story of a group of U.S. soldiers sent to capture Guadalcanal, an island under the control of Japanese troops during World War II. In the early days of its production, due to their reverence of Malick, many high-profile actors flocked to work on the picture. In fact, the ensemble cast was to become so vast that some found their contributions reduced from a major role to nothing more than a walk-on cameo. Gary Oldman, Mickey Rourke, and Billy Bob Thornton even had the misfortune to find their work totally cut from the final movie.

◀

Malick's hyper-reality in the Pacific jungle evokes something of a Coppala-esque quality, and the film appropriately earned several Oscar nominations.

Although the film cannot be said to have a clear lead character, it is Jim Caviezel's Private Witt with whom the audience is first-acquainted and it is he who provides the majority of the poetic voiceover throughout. His conflicts with nihilistic commanding officer Sergeant Welsh (Penn) paint Witt as something of an innocent, clearly anti-war but dedicated to his fellow soldiers. At various points Witt is seen

"ONLY ONE THING A MAN CAN DO, FIND SOMETHING THAT'S HIS, MAKE AN ISLAND FOR HIMSELF." SERGEANT WELSH

wandering contemplatively, at one with nature while war rages around him, desperate to find beauty in the ugly reality of his surroundings.

Such scenes tend to jar with the matter-of-fact portrayal of the battle for Guadalcanal and Witt's cavalier yet selfless bravery during combat hints at a conflict within both character and movie. Indeed, at the heart of the film is the contrast between creation and destruction. The calm beauty of nature is compromised viciously by the violence that is enacted upon it.

However, by *The Thin Red Line*'s closing scene comes evidence of nature beginning the slow, but sure, renewal that will wipe away the scars left by man. Malick offers no such solace in the fates of those caught up in the brutal uncertainty of war. **MW**

► Pfc. Doll (Dash Mihok) is shown here in a typical "man versus nature" scene.

GEORGE
CLOONEY   MARK   WAHLBERG   ICE CUBE

THREE
KINGS

A DAVID O. RUSSELL FILM

WARNER BROS. PRESENTS
IN ASSOCIATION WITH VILLAGE ROADSHOW PICTURES/VILLAGE-A.M. PARTNERSHIP
A COAST RIDGE FILMS/ATLAS ENTERTAINMENT PRODUCTION A DAVID O. RUSSELL FILM GEORGE CLOONEY MARK WAHLBERG ICE CUBE "THREE KINGS" SPIKE JONZE
NORA DUNN JAMIE KENNEDY MYKELTI WILLIAMSON CLIFF CURTIS SAID TAGHMAOUI MUSIC BY CARTER BURWELL CO-PRODUCERS KIM ROTH DOUGLAS SEGAL EDITED BY ROBERT K. LAMBERT, A.C.E.
PRODUCTION DESIGNER CATHERINE HARDWICKE DIRECTOR OF PHOTOGRAPHY NEWTON THOMAS SIGEL, A.S.C. EXECUTIVE PRODUCERS KELLEY SMITH-WAIT GREGORY GOODMAN AND BRUCE BERMAN STORY BY JOHN RIDLEY SCREENPLAY BY DAVID O. RUSSELL
R RESTRICTED RATED R FOR GRAPHIC WAR VIOLENCE, LANGUAGE AND SOME SEXUALITY. PRODUCED BY CHARLES ROVEN PAUL JUNGER WITT EDWARD L. McDONNELL DIRECTED BY DAVID O. RUSSELL
VILLAGE ROADSHOW PICTURES   Soundtrack Album on COLUMBIA and MP3.com
www.three-kings.com   www.warnervideo.com
©1999 Warner Bros.   © 2000 Warner Home Video.   All rights reserved.

THREE KINGS 1999 (U.S. • AUSTRALIA)

Director David O. Russell **Producers** Bruce Berman, Paul Junger Witt, Chuck Roven
Screenplay David O. Russell, John Ridley (story) **Cinematography** Newton Thomas
Sigel **Music** Carter Burwell **Cast** George Clooney, Mark Wahlberg, Ice Cube, Spike
Jonze, Cliff Curtis, Nora Dunn, Jamie Kennedy, Saïd Taghmaoui, Mykelti Williamson

Three Kings is a redemption story set against the backdrop of
the first Iraq war. Archie Gates (Clooney) leads a band of soldiers
on a trip to steal a stash of gold the Iraqis lifted from Kuwait.
The heist goes bad, but the troop is able to find redemption in
an unsanctioned humanitarian mission.

Three Kings is best known, or at least best remembered, for its
viscera cam shot that follows a bullet deep into the body of its
target. Early in the film, Archie tells us that it's not the immediate
pain from the bullet that you need to worry about, but sepsis
(blood poisoning)—the condition one will likely develop after
bile and bacteria-rich fluids fill the cavity carved out from the
slug as it makes its way through the torso. Using a variety of
special effects, Director David O. Russell lets us see the
beginnings of this process.

Russell takes great pains to direct our attention to the
physical impact of violence. The principal firefight in the village
square doesn't involve a hail of bullets, but a tit for tat, ping-
pong battle. A shot is fired. It hits its target, tearing through his
flesh. Repulsive bile fills the shrapnel-tunneled passage. In this
way, Russell presents the violence in a manner akin to Homer in

◄
Three Kings is
more than just
a war movie.
It's a war movie-
cum-spaghetti
western-cum-heist
thriller-cum-SFX
movie-cum-
media satire.

the *Iliad*: "Meriones ran him down from behind / And hit him in the right buttock. The spear point / Slid beneath the bone clear through the bladder. / He fell to his knees, and groaned as death took him." (*Iliad*, 5.78 trans. Lombardo). Both focus on the vulnerability of our bodies to the weapons of war. But unlike the *Iliad*, Russell presents all of the guts and none of the glory. In another scene reminiscent of *The Matrix*'s slick slow-motion,

> *"YOU KNOW YOU'RE ON THE PATH TO TRUTH WHEN YOU SMELL SH*T, ISN'T THAT WHAT THEY SAY?" GATES*

bullets float between the Desert Storm posse and a ragtag bunch of Iraqi soldiers. This war is violent, cool, satiric, and very darkly humoresque.

Three Kings is often referred to as critical of the Iraqi war, but any such claim must be qualified. Russell criticizes the execution of the war more than the war itself. He suggests that the motivation for the invasion was to secure the flow of oil, whereas it should have been humanitarian—to free the populace from their mass-murdering dictator.

Three Kings suggests that the United States left the job incomplete. Saddam did indeed remain in power. Unfortunately, just such a justification was offered for the second Iraq war, but here again Russell would have us ask what the real reasons were behind the invasion. Regardless, *Three Kings* directs our attention to the very real human costs of warfare. **AS**

► Mark Wahlberg, George Clooney, and Ice Cube are a wayward "band of brothers" (more like brigands) brought together for a humanitarian cause.

RIDE WITH THE DEVIL 1999 (U.S.)

Director Ang Lee **Producers** Robert F. Colesberry, Ted Hope, James Schamus
Screenplay James Schamus (from the novel *Woe to Live On* by Daniel Woodrell)
Cinematography Frederick Elmes **Music** Mychael Danna **Cast** Tobey Maguire,
Skeet Ulrich, Jeffrey Wright, James Caviezel, Jonathan Rhys-Meyers, Glenn Q. Pierce

Ride with the Devil's lack of commercial success upon its release
seems inversely proportional to its power to thrill and instruct.
Based on Daniel Woodrell's novel, *Woe to Live On* (1987), Ang
Lee's Civil War epic focuses on a group of pro-Southern irregular
forces, or Bushwackers as they were known, who wage guerrilla
warfare against the Union Army and pro Northern Jayhawkers
along the Kansas Missouri border in the early 1860s. The group
includes social misfits, Southern gentlemen, psychopaths, and
even a freed slave still loyal to his master. As neighbor betrays
neighbor, the fighting they engage in is grim, compromised
and bloody—resonating with the intractable ethnic warfare
that had destroyed Yugoslavia in the years immediately
preceding the film's release.

   Beautifully crafted, the film is meditative in tone: from the
haunting, bleached-out cinematography by regular Lee
collaborator Frederick Elmes, through the pacing of the
narrative, to the faithful reconstruction of the cadences and
locutions of regional dialect and 19th-century custom. That
said, there is also no shying away from the grotesqueries and
gruesomeness of war, especially in the scenes that show

◄

Ride with the Devil
spans diverse
stories as ethnic,
class, and gender
differences are
fractured and
reformed in the
crucible of the
Civil War.

Quantrill's Raid on Lawrence, Kansas, and the massacre of 200 of its inhabitants. Also remarkable is Tobey Maguire's understated performance as the 19-year-old Jake Roedel, which manages to subtly convey the strain of reconciling his first generation German-American ethnicity (siding him with the Unionists) with his allegiance to his Southern friends. Jeffrey Wright's freed slave, Holt, is a similarly important figure, loyal to

"DON'T THINK YOU ARE A GOOD MAN. THE THOUGHT WILL SPOIL YOU."

BLACK JOHN

his master even as the whole condition of slavery is turned on its head. The film concludes with Holt facing a tough decision—stay in a society in which he will always be thought of as a slave, or ride out into the territory a free man.

The film inhabits the between and betwixt lesser-known portions of the war, avoiding well-known set piece battles of Gettysburg and Antietam of which much has already been said and shown. This is the terrain of earlier Hollywood films such as Ray Enright's *Kansas Raiders* (1950), Clint Eastwood's *The Outlaw Josie Wales* (1976), and Walter Hill's *The Long Riders* (1980). The perspectives of both insider and outcast give the viewer a strong structural sense of both the conflict between North and South and also, most distinctively, how the historical event is lived out by marginal characters, each with their own allegiances, hybrid identities, fears, and desires. **GW**

► **Skeet Ulrich as Jack Bull Chiles joins the Bushwhackers, irregulars loyal to the South, along with his friend Jake Roedel (Maguire).**

DIVIDED WE FALL 2000 (CZECH REPUBLIC)

Director Jan Hrebejk **Producers** Pavel Borovan, Ondrej Trojan **Screenplay** Jan Hrebejk, Petr Jarchovský **Cinematography** Jan Malír **Music** Ales Brezina **Cast** Bolek Polívka, Anna Sisková, Csongor Kassai, Jaroslav Dusek, Martin Huba, Jirí Pecha, Simona Stasová, Vladimir Marek, Richard Tesarík, Karel Hermánek

Divided We Fall (a.k.a. *Musíme si pomáhat*), a movie created by Czech director Jan Hrebejk, tells the true story of a childless couple in a small Czech town during World War II who find themselves making some dangerous choices when they decide to hide a Jewish man in their pantry for two years.

Bolek Polívka plays Josef Cizek, a man who has been living on disability and spends most of his time napping. His lovely wife Marie (Sisková) dutifully looks after him, all the while praying to the Madonna to bless them with a child. The couple's quiet life is regularly interrupted by unannounced visits from Josef's ex colleague and supposed friend, Horst Prohaska (Dusek), who is excited by the Third Reich to the extent that he sports a Hitler-style moustache. Horst is laughable, obnoxious, and dangerous.

In the beginning of the film, Josef, Horst, and others help their Jewish boss and his family pack up and travel to their new state-appointed camp; the Czechs do not yet realize what this means and assume they will be back soon. After the youngest son, David (Kassai), escapes from the hellhole where his family has been killed, he returns to Josef and Marie for help. After

◄
A tragi-comedy about ordinary people trying to do the right thing—in this instance harboring a Jew—when the banality of evil is everywhere.

much panicking, the couple stashes David in the pantry—along with a giant pig carcass—until the danger clears. After Horst makes unwanted advances on Marie and she rejects him, he gets his revenge by attempting to move a Nazi clerk into their home. On the spot, Marie declares herself pregnant and insists that they will be needing the extra room for a nursery. Alas, on this very same day Josef pays a visit to the

"A TENDER AND HEARTBREAKINGLY LOVELY STORY OF RISK AND SACRIFICE IN THE SHADOW OF THE TERROR." *SEAN AXMAKER*

doctor and finds out he is sterile. You need to get pregnant, Josef tells her, and fast. The only solution, of course, is David.

The characters are all imperfect and capable of realization and growth. There is so much chaos all the time that the one solid in the middle of everything is David, the quiet, tortured young man who is shy, unassuming, and supposed to be dead. It is difficult to believe the terror his existence evokes in the lives of decent people like Josef and Marie.

With a strong script, brilliant acting, and an intense plot, the picture is a masterpiece of mixed emotions. Though it deals in serious fashion with war and death, there is enough comic relief not to feel drained after leaving the theater. Nominated for an Academy Award for Best Foreign Language film, *Divided We Fall* is an outstanding addition to the World War II movie subgenre. **KW**

►

Josef Cízek (Polívka) is caught napping in more ways than one when a Nazi lodger is imposed on his household.

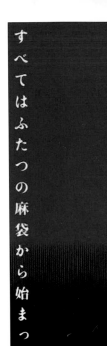

すべてはふたつの麻袋から始まった。

鬼が来た！

DEVILS ON THE DOORSTEP

二〇〇〇年カンヌ国際映画祭グランプリ

主演：姜文
香川照之

監督・脚本・出演●アン・ウォン（姜文）
撮影監督●ク・チャンウェイ（顧長衛）
音楽●ツイ・ジェン（崔健）
主演●アン・ウォン（姜文）、香川照之
●アン・スンホー（姜宏波）、ユエン・ティン（袁丁）他
製作総指揮●夏雨田地

配給●OAGA アジアグループ
発売元●PUG POINT JAPAN
宣伝協力●ソニー・ピー・シー・ビー（株）
配給●キネマ旬報

FORTISSIMO フィルムズ

原題●鬼子来了

DEVILS ON THE DOORSTEP 2000 (CHINA)

Director Jiang Wen **Producer** Jiang Wen **Screenplay** Jiang Wen, Haiying Li, Xing Liu, Ping Shu, Jianquan Shi, Fengwei You (from the novella *Shengcun* by Fengwei You) **Cinematography** Changwei Gu **Music** Jian Cui, Haiying Li, Xing Liu **Cast** Jiang Wen, Jiang Hongbo, Kagawa Teruyuki, Yuan Ding

Like so many of the great black comedies set against the grim backdrop of war—Billy Wilder's *Stalag 17* (1953), Robert Altman's *M*A*S*H* (1970), Emir Kusturica's *Underground* (1995)—Jiang Wen's scathing satire *Devils on the Doorstep* (a.k.a. *Guizi lai le*) is rooted in an inhuman scenario: Japan's brutal occupation of China during the 1930s and 1940s.

The year is 1945, and for the past eight years, Japanese troops have been marching up and down the switchbacks of the tiny northern Chinese village of Rack-Armour Terrace, routinely humiliating villagers like Ma Dasan (Jiang) and forcing them to subsist on near-starvation rations. Late one winter night, Dasan is summoned to his door by a loud knock. An unseen figure claiming to be an anti-Japanese fighter dumps two sacks on his doorstep and, waving a gun under Dasan's nose, orders him to interrogate the Japanese prisoners tied up inside. The voice with the gun tells him he'll be back on New Year's Eve, five days hence, then disappears into the night. The directive puts Dasan, his mistress, and their neighbors in a terrible predicament.

Dasan knows that keeping the prisoners alive is in itself an act of collaboration, but if they return the prisoners to the Imperial

◄
Guizi lai le won the Grand Jury Prize at the Cannes Film Festival, but it was banned in its native country— hence only this Japanese poster being available.

Army, they'll be branded traitors and risk reprisal by the resistance movement. If they don't turn them in and are later caught, they'll surely be executed. After much bickering, Dasan agrees to sit tight for the next five days and interrogate the two prisoners—Chinese-born collaborator Dong Hanchen (Yuan), who begs for mercy, and Japanese soldier Hanaya Kosaburo (Kagawa), who begs for death—but New Year's Eve comes and

"A GRIMLY IRONIC TREATMENT OF THE MADNESS OF WAR AND THE INNOCENTS SWEPT UP BY HISTORY." *SCOTT TOBIAS*

goes with no sign of Dasan's mysterious visitor. Six months later, the prisoners are still with them, now hidden in a section of the Great Wall, and Ma Dasan is deeply mired in an untenable situation exacerbated by miscommunications and cultural dissonance from which there can be no peaceful escape.

The extreme violence and deprivation suffered by the Chinese during the occupation is hardly the stuff of fast-paced, rollicking farce, but Jiang manages to tap directly into the fundamental absurdity of ordinary people attempting to do the right thing in a world without morality, where basic survival is no longer a given. Jiang draws a great deal of humor from the situation, but the film inevitably explodes in terrible violence. This boisterous comedy serves up a cruel reminder of the fate of hundreds of thousands of Chinese, one which can only qualify as a terrible tragedy. **KF**

► Japanese occupying forces march along the dusty switchbacks of northern China. Although it is the Chinese who suffer, the movie was deemed unsuitable for home consumption.

FROM THE DIRECTOR AND PRODUCER OF THE ACADEMY AWARD® WINNING 'KOLYA'

"An epic! Brilliantly directed and sublimely acted, with a respect for complex characters and a refreshing lack of sentimentality, 'Dark Blue World' blends action, romance and tragedy in a work that has both intensity and entertainment value."
-Rex Reed, THE NEW YORK OBSERVER

DARK BLUE WORLD

IN WORLD WAR II THERE WERE SO MANY FORGOTTEN HEROES

SONY PICTURES CLASSICS

www.columbiafilms.com.au

DARK BLUE WORLD 2001 (CZECH REPUBLIC)

Director Jan Svěrák **Producers** Eric Abraham, Jaroslav Kucera, Iva Prochazkova, Jan Svěrák **Screenplay** Zdeněk Svěrák **Cinematography** Vladimír Smutný **Music** Ondrej Soukup **Cast** Ondřej Vetchý, Kryštof Hádek, Tara Fitzgerald, Charles Dance, Oldřich Kaiser, David Novotný, Linda Rybová, Jaromír Dulava, Lukáš Kantor

In case proof is needed that you don't need a $150-million-dollar-plus budget, Michael Bay, Ben Affleck, or Jerry Bruckheimer to create a memorable war film (*Pearl Harbor*, anyone?), there is always *Dark Blue World* (a.k.a. *Tmavomodrý svět*). Hollywood could certainly take some notes from this Czech production with its strong script (by the director's father, who also teamed with his son on the Oscar-winning *Kolya* in 1996), compelling performances, and authentic World War II backdrops.

Franta Sláma (Vetchý) is captain of a squad of trained Czech fighter pilots who are forced to turn over their base to the Nazis when their country is invaded. Instead of simply giving up and hoping for the best, they travel to England and join the Air Force there in order to battle the enemy. Franta leaves his girlfriend behind while bringing along the youngest pilot in the bunch, a good-looking lad named Karel Vojtisek (Hádek). Franta, Karel, and the others have to prove themselves by learning English and training for several months before they are ever allowed up in the air. Much of the subsequent drama revolves around their interacting with British Wing Commander Bentley (the excellent Dance), their initial missions, getting shot

◀

The fact that the Czech resistance fighters were treated no better by the victorious Communist regime than the former SS enemy is grimly ironic.

down, losing comrades, and also the love of a woman. After surviving a crash, Karel is rescued by a married lady named Susan Whitmore (Fitzgerald), who is waiting for her missing husband to return home while taking care of evacuated children from London. The couple share an intimate evening and Karel quickly finds himself falling in love with her. As fate would have it, however, he introduces Susan to Franta and she

> ## "IT WAS HARD, MR. SLÁMA, TO BE A GERMAN AND NOT BE PROUD."
>
> *DOCTOR BLASCHKE*

falls for him instead. Karel and Franta's friendship is soon put to the test and they are forced to decide whether the love of a woman is worth sacrificing everything else for.

While all this is taking place, a second story is also played out on a much larger scale. After the war ends and the surviving pilots manage to return home alive, the brutal Communist regime then imprisons them in hard labor camps for supposedly betraying their country. They have been "contaminated" by spending the war years in the West and cannot be trusted to be good comrades. The only way out is death, and the men find themselves sharing quarters with members of the SS who are also being punished. The cruel irony of their situation and the courage of the pilots rings true, and gives *Dark Blue World* a potency not found nearly often enough in contemporary Hollywood war movies. **KW**

► For its aerial dogfights, the movie was spliced with action scenes taken from the epic war film *Battle of Britain* (1969).

NO MAN'S LAND
2001 (BOSNIA-HERZEGOVINA • SLOVENIA)

Director Danis Tanović **Producers** Marc Baschet, Frédérique Dumas-Zajdela, Čédomir Kolar **Screenplay** Danis Tanović **Cinematography** Walther van den Ende **Music** Danis Tanović **Cast** Branko Đjuric, Rene Bitorajac, Filip Šovagović, Georges Siatidis, Katrin Cartlidge, Simon Callow, Serge-Henri Valcke, Sacha Kremer

A biting and darkly comic satire of the Bosnian War, *No Man's Land* (a.k.a. *Ničija zemlja*) speaks to the futility of war on both the dangerous front lines and in the safety of war rooms.

The story concerns three soldiers (two Bosnians and one Serb) trapped in an abandoned foxhole in "no man's land," the unclaimed terrain between two front lines. Following an ambush, wounded Bosnian soldier Ciki (Đjuric) takes refuge in the trench before a two-man Serbian scouting crew arrives. Ciki kills one Serb and wounds Nino (Bitorajac), but not before the duo place a mine underneath Cera (Šovagović), one of Ciki's fellow soldiers believed to be dead. But Cera is very much alive and this cruel trap has immobilized all three men. Both sides alert the United Nations Protection Force (UNPROFOR), and before long the situation becomes an international incident thanks to overzealous U.N. envoy Sgt. Marchand (Siatidis) and reporter Jane Livingstone (Cartlidge).

Alternating between comedy and drama, Tanović satirizes the relief efforts of the United Nations and international reporters' coverage of the situation. The U.N.'s bureaucratic

◄

A bleak satire on blinkered warring factions who refuse to resolve enmity, and the uselessness of the U.N. in resolving anything, the film picked up an Academy Award for Best Foreign Language Film.

system is shown as something that ultimately gets in the way of the peace process. Marchand is frustrated by the inaction and having to depend on higher-ups to get approval to do anything. The Jane Livingstone character offers a glimpse of reporters more concerned with a story than human life, as news editors miles away hope for a dramatic interview with the man on the mine. The film also has lighter moments, including

"WHAT THE HELL MADE YOU RUIN THIS BEAUTIFUL COUNTRY?"

CIKI

a running joke that the only language all the international participants understand is English. Utilizing a realistic approach, director Tanović rejects the sentimental notion that warring factions will embrace peace when faced with their enemy one-on-one. On the contrary, both Ciki and Nino decline the idea of helping each other and constantly bicker about who started the war. Ciki rejects Nino's offer of friendship outright, stating that the next time they see each other it will be through the sights of their guns. In the end, the film serves as an allegory for the war itself: Ciki and Nino represent their respective sides that dislike each other's existence and refuse to work together, ultimately sealing their fates; the U.N. proves to be entirely ineffectual in providing a solution; and poor Cera—the individual caught between the two sides—is left all alone for the film's haunting final image. **WW**

▶
**Branko Đjurié,
Rene Bitorajac, and
Filip Šovagović as
the main
protagonists
representing the
ethnic enmity that
erupted after the
collapse of
Yugoslavia.**

ENIGMA 2001 (U.K. • U.S.)

Director Michael Apted **Producers** Lorne Michaels, Mick Jagger **Screenplay** Tom Stoppard (from the novel by Robert Harris) **Cinematography** Seamus MacGarvey **Music** John Barry **Cast** Dougray Scott, Kate Winslet, Saffron Burrows, Jeremy Northam, Nikolai Coster Waldau, Tom Hollander, Donald Sumpter, Richard Leaf

Except for one cheaply staged naval battle, a car chase at 25 miles an hour, and a manhunt by train culminating in a fist-fight on a boat, there is no action in *Enigma*. Instead, we get to watch smart people think.

A motley group of British intellectuals at Bletchley Park in 1943 are trying to crack the German military code; meanwhile an MI5 officer is searching for a mole inside the British decoding operation. At the same time a disheveled young mathematician is trying to solve the puzzle of his beautiful and sexually adventurous lover's mysterious disappearance, finding himself, in the film's closing scene, married to another, slightly less beautiful, though all the more sensible woman. Can this multi-generic combination of the British murder mystery, the espionage thriller, and the melodramatic love story distract from the array of frowning faces, rubbed temples, and contrived "Eureka!" moments advancing the plot?

It is to the credit of the combined star power behind the film—from its high-profile producers, its fine screenwriter, and seasoned director, to a cast assembled from the best of British actors—that the film nonetheless succeeds in turning Robert

◄
This movie made coding sexy. This aspect of the British wartime effort now became part of World War II history rather than the prehistory of modern computers.

Harris's creaky bestselling novel (1996) into an entertaining experience. There is a hint of novelist Alan Furst in the doomed wartime romance between Thomas Jericho (Scott) and the "enigmatic" Claire (Burrows); a hint of Thomas Pynchon's *Gravity's Rainbow* in the eccentricities of the scientific effort behind the military machinery of World War II; and, even though the film predates it by a year, *Enigma* is reminiscent of

"I LIKE NUMBERS, BECAUSE WITH NUMBERS, TRUTH AND BEAUTY ARE THE SAME THING." *THOMAS JERICHO*

Anthony Horowitz's smart television series *Foyle's War*. Besides the discovery of the Katyn Forest massacre as a major plot point, the film's thematic hook, and contribution to the genre of the war film, is its popularization of the science and technology of coding. Though *Enigma*'s intention is the recuperation of historical facts, the film keeps a cautious distance from history. Harris might have based Tom Jericho on Alan Turing, but Turing himself never appears—a casualty of mainstream appeal, replaced by a fictional character, who can steer, untroubled by Turing's homosexuality, straight for the film's happily heterosexual end. The picture's avoidance of controversy, its celebration of British ingenuity, and its mild nostalgia for the adventure of war may stand as a compensatory reflex to a public discussion that, by the 1990s, had begun to touch upon the moral ambiguity of some British wartime policy. **SH**

▶
Thomas Jericho (Scott) and Hester Wallace (Winslet) going for brain over brawn.

LEAVE NO MAN BEHIND

A JERRY BRUCKHEIMER PRODUCTION · A RIDLEY SCOTT FILM

BLACK HAWK DOWN

REVOLUTION STUDIOS AND JERRY BRUCKHEIMER FILMS PRESENT A RIDLEY SCOTT FILM A JERRY BRUCKHEIMER PRODUCTION IN ASSOCIATION WITH SCOTT FREE PRODUCTIONS STARRING JOSH HARTNETT
"BLACK HAWK DOWN" ERIC BANA EWAN McGREGOR TOM SIZEMORE WILLIAM FICHTNER AND SAM SHEPARD CASTING BY BONNIE TIMMERMANN MUSIC BY HANS ZIMMER EDITOR PIETRO SCALIA, A.C.E.
PRODUCTION DESIGNER ARTHUR MAX DIRECTOR OF PHOTOGRAPHY SLAWOMIR IDZIAK EXECUTIVE PRODUCERS SIMON WEST MIKE STENSON CHAD OMAN AND BRANKO LUSTIG BASED ON THE BOOK BY MARK BOWDEN SCREENPLAY BY KEN NOLAN AND STEVE ZAILLIAN
PRODUCED BY JERRY BRUCKHEIMER AND RIDLEY SCOTT DIRECTED BY RIDLEY SCOTT

REVOLUTION STUDIOS

sony.com/blackhawkdown

BLACK HAWK DOWN 2001 (U.S.)

Director Ridley Scott **Producers** Jerry Bruckheimer, Ridley Scott
Screenplay Ken Nolan (based on Mark Bowden's book) **Cinematography** Slawomir
Idziak **Music** Hans Zimmer **Cast** Eric Bana, Ewen Bremner, William Fichtner, Josh
Hartnett, Ewan McGregor, Tom Sizemore, Sam Shepard, Gabriel Casseus, Kim Coates

As its first caption informs viewers, *Black Hawk Down* is "based
on an actual event." Filmed with a sense of authenticity, the
U.S. military provided assistance to director Ridley Scott, even
supplying Black Hawk helicopters for filming. (However, such
collaboration can often mean a propagandist/recruitment film
much like Ridley's brother Tony's war effort *Top Gun* [1986].)
Scott's work was also inspired by a journalistic account of the
Somalian incursion, highlighting U.S. military intervention in
parallel with the United Nations' mission.

Co-produced by Jerry Bruckheimer, infamous for his gung
ho action flicks, *Black Hawk Down* celebrates the U.S. military's
heroism, but not much else. Matt Eversmann (Hartnett) is
appalled that America's presence can do nothing to protect
Somalian civilians, massacred by militia linked to warlord
Mohamed Farrah Aidid. Rules of engagement prevent the U.S.
from firing unless they are fired upon. Pursuing a military
strategy aimed at destabilizing Aidid's power base, U.S.
personnel go into Mogadishu to "extract" key militia leaders.

Operating under the command of General Garrison
(Shepard), U.S. forces are denied armored air support by

◀
The movie
blatantly
advertises a
populist message,
while fighting
shy of tougher
political questions,
stressing military
realism over any
assessment of the
Somalian conflict.

Washington, and vulnerable helicopters are duly shot down by militia armed with rocket-propelled grenades. The first crash —"Black Hawk down"—is shown via the film's reddish-brown, saturated hues strikingly morphing into the blue, surveillance-camera tones of Garrison's control center. Contrasting the deadly situation on the ground with the General's mediated vision, the movie's feeling of tense realism is reinforced.

"NOBODY ASKS TO BE A HERO, IT JUST SOMETIMES TURNS OUT THAT WAY."

MATT EVERSMANN

Moments of stylization tend to book-end military action sequences, such as the helicopters flying into their mission, accompanied by suspenseful music, or soldiers emerging eerily from the fog of warfare.

▶
Josh Hartnett as Eversmann gives a great "grunt" performance, but you have to ask what on earth were British actors Ewan McGregor and Orlando Bloom doing in this piece of U.S. military revisionism?

Delta forces including "Hoot" Gibson (Bana) and U.S. Rangers such as Eversmann are caught up in efforts to help stranded U.S. personnel. Essentially a rescue flick, American forces are pitted against marauding hordes of Somalian fighters; the scenario resembles a classical Western—Indians circling the wagon train . Eversmann's initial humanitarianism gives way to the desire to help his fellow soldiers. Rather than an "everyman" fighting for the universal good, Eversmann, like "Hoot," can ultimately do no more than defend the men next to him. A reluctant hero, he muses that "sometimes it turns out that way." **MH**

A ROMAN POLANSKI FILM

THE
PIANIST

MUSIC WAS HIS PASSION. SURVIVAL WAS HIS MASTERPIECE.

A D R I E N   B R O D Y   T H O M A S   K R E T S C H M A N N

A FOCUS FEATURES RELEASE ALAIN SARDE AND ROBERT BENMUSSA PRESENT A ROMAN POLANSKI FILM "THE PIANIST" FRANK FINLAY MAUREEN LIPMAN EMILIA FOX ED STOPPARD JULIA RAYNER
JESSICA KATE MEYER CAST. BY CELESTIA FOX MUSIC WOJCIECH KILAR COSTUME RAINER R.SCHAPER PRODUCER GENE GUDWSKI EDITOR ANNA SHEPPARD PHOTOGRAPHY ALLAN STARSKI DESIGN BY PAWEL EDELMAN
PRODUCERS LEW RYWIN HENNING MOLFENTER TIMOTHY BURRILL PRODUCED BY ROMAN POLANSKI ROBERT BENMUSSA ALAIN SARDE BASED ON A BOOK BY WLADYSLAW SZPILMAN SCREENPLAY BY RONALD HARWOOD DIRECTED BY ROMAN POLANSKI

R   READ THE PICADOR BOOK
PICADOR   SOUNDTRACK AVAILABLE
STUDIO CANAL   ON SONY CLASSICAL   BASED ON A TRUE STORY   www.thepianistmovie.com

F O C U S
F E A T U R E S

THE PIANIST 2002 (FRANCE · POLAND · GERMANY · U.K.)

Director Roman Polanski **Producers** Robert Benmussa, Roman Polanski, Alain Sarde **Screenplay** Ronald Harwood (from the autobiography by Władysław Szpilman) **Cinematography** Pawel Edelman **Music** Wojciech Kilar **Cast** Adrien Brody, Thomas Kretschmann, Frank Finlay, Maureen Lipman

Despite having survived the Nazis and the Kraków Ghetto as a young child, Roman Polanski seems to have shied away from making World War II movies. Perhaps his childhood during that period was simply just too painful to explore in cinema, or at least until the right story came his way. The story made here is based on the autobiography of Władysław Szpilman (portrayed by Adrien Brody), a Polish-Jewish pianist of some acclaim before the start of the war.

We are introduced to Szpilman at the height of his career in 1939 Warsaw playing Chopin on Polish radio. His family live well in a middle-class apartment and life seems to be relatively good, at least until the Nazis march in. We follow Szpilman throughout the war, from his relocation to the Warsaw Ghetto; his escape from a transport to Treblinka, which ultimately will claim the lives of his family in the Holocaust; living in hiding in the Gentile section of the city; and finally his abandonment in the bombed-out city as the Soviets approach.

The sequences in the Warsaw Ghetto are the film's strongest. We can only speculate as to the extent to which elements of Polanski's own World War II memories are involved. There are

◄

Roman Polanski deservedly won Best Director for his Holocaust movie.

certainly some devastatingly detailed sequences. Two elderly people fight over a rusty tin of soup that spills on the filthy street and the elderly man gets down on the ground to literally lick the pavement stones to get as much food as he can; emaciated corpses are left in the gutters; and people gone mad aimlessly wander the streets looking for murdered loved ones they still imagine to be alive. These are the images of an all-too-

"THEY ALL WANT TO BE BETTER NAZIS THAN HITLER."

WŁADYSŁAW SZPILMAN

real Hell on Earth. It is this intimacy and the real sense of immediacy and credibility of the personal eyewitness account that make the story so disarming.

It may not have the broad sweep of some other films that deal with this subject matter, but it is emotively charged and that makes it just as compelling. The pace is allowed to slow right down in later scenes, in particular where Szpilman survives alone in the ruins of the ghetto, but this adds to its sense of realism. Brody manages to carry the film throughout the desolation and isolation of the empty streets of the now-liquidated ghetto. Through him we experience the Warsaw Ghetto uprising in 1943, but rather than as a participant, as an impotent and helpless spectator in hiding from the other side of the ghetto walls, and finally to his animal-like existence in the ruins of his once-great city. **MK**

▶

The entire picture rests on Brody's shoulders and he does a remarkable job with the role. His winning of the Best Actor Oscar was a shoo-in in 2003.

RUSSELL CROWE

MASTER AND COMMANDER
THE FAR SIDE OF THE WORLD

11.14

MASTER AND COMMANDER 2003 (U.S.)

Director Peter Weir **Producers** Samuel Goldwyn Jr., Duncan Henderson, Peter Weir **Screenplay** Peter Weir, John Collee **Cinematography** Russell Boyd **Music** Iva Davies, Christopher Gordon, Richard Tognetti **Cast** Russell Crowe, Paul Bettany, James D'Arcy, Edward Woodall, Chris Larkin, Max Pirkis

Propelled by artistic direction and Oscar caliber performances, *Master and Commander: The Far Side of the World* is a cinematic marvel. This historical, seafaring epic commands the stage with as much bravado and breadth as *Spartacus* (1960) or *Gladiator* (2000); yet between the swells and surges course gentle undercurrents of human intimacy. And despite being very much a period costume piece, *Master and Commander* has a certain universal appeal that renders it timeless.

Set in 1805 during the Napoleonic Wars, *Master and Commander* is the story of swashbuckling sea legend Captain Jack Aubrey (Crowe) and the crew of the H.M.S. *Surprise*, whose orders are to search the Pacific Ocean for the French frigate *Acheron*. Though vastly undermanned, outgunned, and undersized, the H.M.S. *Surprise* and its men must either take the French crew prisoner and pilot the *Acheron* back to England as a prize for the King, or else destroy it at sea.

After his ship is outmaneuvered and crippled by the *Acheron*, Captain Jack disregards everyone's advice, including the cogent protests of his closest friend, surgeon-cum-naturalist Dr. Stephen Maturin (Bettany), and refuses to head

◀

Director Peter Weir joined forces with John Collee to distill this screenplay from two of Patrick O'Brian's twenty popular historical novels about life in the 19th-century British navy.

home for repairs. Captain Jack's mission has evolved into a personal vendetta, and pride will be the force billowing his ship's sails in the direction of that phantom French frigate now assuming the role of his Moby Dick.

What's most striking about *Master and Commander* is not only its comprehensive attention to detail, but the sharp contrasts between some of the minutiae. For instance, scenes

"THOUGH WE BE ON THE FAR SIDE OF THE WORLD, THIS SHIP IS OUR HOME. THIS SHIP IS ENGLAND." *AUBREY*

echoing with cannon blasts, sword clanks, and howling storms are tempered by musical interludes, featuring Captain Jack on violin and Dr. Maturin on cello. Any appeal of seafaring—picturesque seascapes, honor amongst officers, and camaraderie-induced chants—is offset by gory depictions of war casualties below deck (amputations, self-surgeries, and crude skull patches involving hammers and nails). And the juxtaposition of the officers roasting and toasting overhead while the lowly marines dine on slop and grog below serves to emphasize both their inherent naval hierarchy and the resentment it invokes. These combinations are effective at establishing equal shares of glory and gloom, a cinematic harmony often absent in Hollywood productions. Underpinning this, the movie deservedly won Academy Awards for Best Cinematography and Best Sound Editing. **CR**

► Period detail and authenticity are the name of the game as Captain Aubrey (Crowe) here struts his stuff on deck.

우린 반드시 살아서 돌아가야 해
태극기 휘날리며
|2004 한국영화의 위대한 도전|
강제규 감독 작품
장동건 원빈 이은주
김수로 최민식

BROTHERHOOD 2004 (SOUTH KOREA)

Director Kang Je-gyu **Producer** Lee Seong-hun **Screenplay** Kang Je-gyu
Cinematography Hong Kyung-pyo **Music** Lee Dong-jun **Cast** Jang Dong-kun,
Won Bin, Lee Eun-ju, Kong Hyoeng-jin, Lee Yeong-ran, Ahn Kil-kang, Joe Cappellitti,
Choi Min-sik, D. C. Douglas, Jang Min-ho, Jeong Dae-hoon, Jeon Jae-hyeong

A stirring portrayal of the Korean War, *Brotherhood* (a.k.a.
Taegukgi hwinalrimyeo) chronicles the devotion of two brothers
during wartime and shows the collateral damage that war can
inflict on families.

After receiving a call from Korean War historians regarding a
recently unearthed skeleton, Jin-seok Lee (Won) reflects back to
when the Korean War began and he and older brother Jin-tae
(Jang) were drafted into service by the South Korean military.
Wanting to protect his younger, educated brother, Jin-tae
discovers that he can send Jin-seok home if he wins a medal for
bravery, which leads to Jin-tae volunteering for every risky
mission. As the war goes on, Jin-seok uncovers Jin-tae's ulterior
motive for his perilous behavior, but also notices the bloodlust
that seems to be overtaking his brother with every mission.

Having ushered in the South Korea New Wave with the
thriller *Shiri* (1999), director Kang Je-gyu here delivers a war film
that is both epic in scale and intensely intimate with its drama.
With the two brother characters, Kang examines the
psychological pressure men face in war, and how the individual
reacts to war's dehumanizing effects; Jin-tae becomes more

◄
**Despite
incongruent
elements of love
and war, this is
a compelling
and emotional
dramatization of
the Forgotten War.**

unstable with each conflict, whereas Jin-seok becomes stronger. Family relations are the strongest force in the picture, as this dictates all of Jin-tae's actions, from protecting his brother to losing faith and joining the enemy when he mistakenly believes South Korean Nationalists have killed his entire family. This brotherhood extends symbolically to the men in the fighting squad, featuring several vivid supporting

"YOU AND I SHOULD BE TOGETHER. WE LIVE AND DIE TOGETHER."

LEE JIN-SEOK

players, and even to the enemy, such as when Jin-seok saves a former friend fighting for the enemy from execution. At the same time, *Brotherhood* elicits drama in human cruelty.

A rare example in war movies, the film refrains from generic heroic labels as both sides are shown committing atrocities and characters question the idea of mindless patriotism. The many battle scenes are simultaneously exciting, deadening, and disheartening. Kang follows the squad through several major conflicts with each successive encounter growing fiercer, allowing audiences to empathize with the experiences of the soldiers. While the portrait of realistic combat is impressive, the film benefits mainly from the strong family bond displayed on screen, culminating with a beautifully emotional scene where Jin-seok stands over his brother's skeleton with the contentment of finally knowing his protector's fate. **WW**

▶
Director Kang Je-gyu ekes out some highly realistic battle scenes as the brothers look out for each other.

BRUNO GANZ
ALEXANDRA MARIA LARA
CORINNA HARFOUCH
JULIANE KÖHLER
ULRICH NOETHEN
THOMAS KRETSCHMANN
„WENN DER KRIEG VERLOREN GEHT, IST ES VOLLKOMMEN EGAL, WENN DAS VOLK MIT UNTERGEHT. ICH KÖNNTE DARÜBER NOCH KEINE TRÄNE WEINEN, DENN ES HÄTTE NICHTS ANDERES VERDIENT."
CONSTANTIN FILM UND BERND EICHINGER ZEIGEN
DER UNTERGANG
EIN OLIVER HIRSCHBIEGEL FILM EINE BERND EICHINGER PRODUKTION
ARD Degeto
ORF
WWW.UNTERGANG.FILM.DE
List
Constantin Film

DOWNFALL 2004 (GERMANY)

Director Oliver Hirschbiegel **Producer** Bernd Eichinger **Screenplay** Bernd Eichinger **Cinematography** Rainer Klausmann **Music** Stephan Zacharias **Cast** Bruno Ganz, Alexandra Maria Lara, Christian Berkel, Ulrich Matthes, Heino Ferch, Juliane Köhler, Traudl Junge, Matthias Habich, Thomas Kretschmann, Rolf Kanies

The first German film to directly deal with Adolf Hitler in nearly half a century, *Downfall* (a.k.a. *Der Untergang*) is a powerful re-creation of the final ten days of the Fuhrer and the devastation he brought to the German people and those around him.

Culled from several books by historical witnesses, *Downfall* opens with Traudl Junge (Lara) securing the position of being Hitler's (Ganz) personal secretary. Three years later, in 1945, Junge, Hitler, and his closest advisors are secluded inside a bunker as the Soviet army advances into Berlin. While Hitler makes inept decisions, above ground the battle rages as a professor (Berkel) tries to save patients and tattered members of the Hitler Youth blindly provide the final front line.

More than just a reconstruction of the private world of a madman, *Downfall* is a powerful personal drama about a group of men and women struggling not only to survive, but to understand how they followed a leader to such a point of despair. The film is bookended with actual interview footage of the real Junge, who articulates just how unaware she was of the depths of Hitler's misdeeds and madness. The film never depicts Hitler as either a tragic or sympathetic character.

◄

This harrowing movie is based on the book *Inside Hitler's Bunker: The Last Days of the Third Reich* by Joachim Fest, and *Until the Final Hour: Hitler's Last Secretary* by Traudl Junge and Melissa Mueller.

Instead, he is a selfish man who blankly stares at a follower when she cries for his leadership. He blames others for his failings and, by rejecting surrender, refuses to acknowledge his country's suffering.

As an intense war film, Hirschbiegel creates a grim, bloody rendering of inner city combat that rivals the realistic scenes in *Saving Private Ryan* (1998). Hirschbiegel painstakingly re-creates

"I MUST FORCE AN OUTCOME IN BERLIN OR FACE MY DOWNFALL."

ADOLF HITLER (BRUNO GANZ)

Hitler's final quarters with its slate-gray walls, corridors, and confined conference rooms that offer a claustrophobic quality. Swiss actor Ganz—who methodically studied Hitler's mannerisms and accent—offers a portrayal of pure commitment and intensity. While the outbursts draw the most attention, it is in the film's reserved moments—when Hitler muses over a miniature scale replica of his vision of Berlin or discusses the survival of the fittest over dinner—that showcase how deep into the psyche of Hitler the filmmakers went.

► Hitler (Ganz) emerges from his bunker for the last time on his birthday to award medals to members of the Hitler Youth and tells them how he wishes his generals had their bravery.

Two scenes perfectly encapsulate the insanity during these final days. In one, Eva Braun (Köhler) forces everyone to dance in a ballroom during an air raid. Later, Magda Goebbels gently murders her six children first with sleeping pills, so they won't know what is happening and then with the horrid short, sharp snap of poisonous phials implanted in their mouths. **WW**

When the world
closed its eyes,
he opened his arms.

DON CHEADLE
SOPHIE OKONEDO
NICK NOLTE

A FILM BY TERRY GEORGE

HOTEL
RWANDA
A TRUE STORY

WINNER
AGF People's Choice Award
Toronto International
Film Festival

HOTEL RWANDA 2004 (U.K. • U.S.)

Director Terry George **Producers** Terry George, A. Kitman Ho **Screenplay**
Keir Pearson, Terry George **Cinematography** Robert Fraisse **Music** Afro Celt
Sound System, Rupert Gregson-Williams, Andrea Guerra **Cast** Don Cheadle,
Desmond Dube, Hakeem Kae-Kazim, Sophie Okonedo, Neil McCarthy, Nick Nolte

Hotel Rwanda dramatizes the story of Paul Rusesabagina, who
sheltered 1,268 people at the Hotel des Mille Collines in Kigali
during the Rwandan conflict of 1994. The narrative focuses on
Paul (Cheadle), as he struggles to protect his family and then as
he extends his notion of family to include anyone who comes
to him seeking help, regardless of ethnicity, class, or even
previous association. All the while powerful nations such as the
United States, France, and Belgium and organizations like the
U.N. play with words, ignoring the genocide.

Paul's understanding of the people he protects as simply
people, an extension of family and neighbors, and his refusal to
allow those people to be identified as Hutu, Tutsi, or even by
room number—a rejection of the labels and classifications
being used to commit and ignore genocide—effectively
exposes the hypocrisy and fallacies of the arguments made by
both the Interahamwe committing the genocide and the
international community that forsook Rwanda. The film
highlights the difficult decisions Paul heroically makes and the
role personal relationships play in his desperate efforts to save
the lives of more than a thousand people, whether he is

◄
**A steely yet
vulnerable
performance
from Don Cheadle
earned him a
Best Actor Oscar
nomination.**

negotiating with the Interahamwe or Hutu army, or appealing to the president of Sabena for assistance. *Hotel Rwanda* makes a deliberate decision to place the details of the genocide in the background in an attempt to personalize the human cost of war as well as our best hope against war. Drawing from documentary sources, the film does show the massacres happening outside the hotel and strategically places particular

> ## "I AM GLAD THAT YOU HAVE SHOT THIS FOOTAGE AND THAT THE WORLD WILL SEE IT." PAUL RUSESABAGINA

details—such as dogs belonging to Westerners being evacuated while Rwandans are left to die or bloody electric drills being wielded as weapons of tortuous murder distilling the emotional and psychological impact of the graphic details—in order to focus on the people *to whom* this was happening in contrast to *what* was happening.

Thus, while certain characters are composites of several people and particular details of the genocide may have been rearranged for dramatic purposes, *Hotel Rwanda* succeeds in presenting a genuine examination of the Rwandan genocide that allows viewers to understand the magnitude of the tragedy, and identify with Rwandans as individuals rather than faceless victims. This makes Paul's story *our* story. Through Paul, we are reminded of our responsibility as human beings, and we are given hope about the future of humanity. **KB**

► Paul (Cheadle) and Tatiana Rusesabagina (Okonedo) support each other in the midst of the Tutsi-Hutu conflict.

MERRY CHRISTMAS 2005 (FRANCE)

Director Christian Carion **Producer** Christophe Rossignon **Screenplay** Christian Carion **Cinematography** Walther van den Ende **Music** Philippe Rombi **Cast** Diane Kruger, Natalie Dessay, Benno Fürmann, Alex Ferns, Guillaume Canet, Gary Lewis, Daniel Brühl, Steven Robertson, Bernard Le Coq, Robin Laing

Harmony and peace on the front lines of World War I. That is the unlikely scenario played out by a small contingent of French, British, and German soldiers on Christmas Eve, 1914. *Merry Christmas* (more widely known by its French title, *Joyeux Noël*), is a European co-production based on a true story. The daily slaughters were halted when officers and soldiers put down their weapons to share Christmas carols, food, and wine, and to exchange photographs in a show of extraordinary goodwill. The Germans were led by Horstmayer (Brühl), the French by Lieutenant Audebert (Canet), and the Scottish contingent by Gordon (Ferns).

Among the German force was the famous tenor Nikolaus Sprink (Fürmann), who is allowed a visit from his Danish girlfriend Anna Sorenson (Kruger), also an opera singer. They too find themselves in the trenches on Christmas Eve. When they hear the sound of Scottish bagpipes, they begin to sing with neither fear nor protection. The feeling of sentimentality and peace they convey through their voices, however, leads the respective commanding officers to call a temporary truce. This heartfelt and compelling story sees each side's officers join

◄
Perhaps as well known by its native title *Joyeux Noël*, this World War I drama was nominated for an Academy Award as Best Foreign Language Film.

in an exchange of Christmas wishes. They wonder why they are there—sent off to war—and what will happen when the truce is over. We witness incredible scenes of Christmas carols being sung by all, and a Christmas tree placed atop the trench.

Writer-director Christian Carion has made a deeply uplifting movie that has been criticized for being overly sentimental, but that contains a simple decency. Among the soldiers are British

> ## "TONIGHT, THESE MEN WERE DRAWN TO THAT ALTAR LIKE IT WAS A FIRE IN THE MIDDLE OF WINTER." PALMER

brothers Jonathan (Robertson) and William (Laing), who rush to enlist in the war and are accompanied by their local priest, Palmer (Lewis), who registers as a stretcher bearer. The French Lieutenant, Audebert, is an especially complex character who is under the command of his father, the general (Le Coq).

Merry Christmas is beautifully shot and acted. It is hard to deny the film's impact and its desire to locate humanity and hope in the face of the horrors of battle. It delivers a powerful message, and was nominated for Best Foreign Language Film at the 2006 Academy Awards. Another fact worth noting is that the MPAA initially gave it an R rating for its depictions of battlefield violence, but upon appeal the R was overturned and *Merry Christmas* was accorded a PG-13 rating instead. An all-too-rare showing of good sense by the MPAA, but a welcome victory nonetheless. **CP**

►

A peaceful moment of respite from the battlefield violence.

OFFICIËLE SELECTIE
FILMFESTIVAL VENETIË 2006

CARICE
VAN HOUTEN

SEBASTIAN
KOCH

THOM
HOFFMAN

HALINA
REIJN

PAUL VERHOEVEN
ZWARTBOEK

ALS JE NIETS MEER TE VERLIEZEN HEBT, BEN JE TOT ALLES BEREID.

BLACK BOOK 2006 (HOLLAND · GERMANY)

Director Paul Verhoeven **Producers** Jeroen Beker, Teun Hilte, San Fu Maltha, Jens Meurer, Jos van der Linden, Frans van Gestel **Screenplay** Paul Verhoeven, Gerard Soeteman **Cinematography** Karl Walter Lindenlaub **Music** Anne Dudley **Cast** Carice van Houten, Sebastian Koch, Thom Hoffman, Halina Reijn

Paul Verhoeven's *Black Book* (a.k.a. *Zwartboek*) merges the European and Hollywood traditions of war movies. It stresses moral ambiguities and the lack of distinction between good and bad. Yet it simultaneously highlights the heroics of individuals and the efforts of small bands of idealists.

The story is set in Holland at the end of World War II: after she narrowly escapes a massacre among refugees by the Germans, the Jewish Rachel Steinn (van Houten) joins the resistance. Under the false identity of Ellis she seduces Nazi officer Muntze (Koch), becomes a secretary at the German police headquarters, and relays information to the Resistance. After the resistance cell she is part of is lured into a trap, she is suspected to be a double-agent and tortured. Amid the euphoria of Holland's liberation, Ellis finally uncovers the truth about the betrayals, but by then she has suffered so much humiliation that it hardly seems to matter.

Black Book is Verhoeven's first European film in 20 years. It builds on his epic *Soldier of Orange* (1977), which also chronicled the Dutch resistance and addressed issues of moral responsibility. But the distinctions between good and bad in

◀

In showing not only the many shades of gray but also the brutal implications of rushed judgments, *Black Book* testifies to Verhoeven's enduring ability to upset accepted accounts of war.

Black Book are even more blurred than they were in *Soldier*. The struggle is less one of fighting for a cause, or even one of opportunism, than of survival at all costs. True to the in-your-face style that made *RoboCop* (1987) and *Starship Troopers* (1997) such powerful films, Verhoeven has given *Black Book* a most visceral outlook. Violent deaths, executions, and abuse are shown for maximum emotional impact. The many torture

"EVERY HUMAN IS CAPABLE OF UNIMAGINED COWARDICE."

NOTARY WIM SMAAL

scenes are particularly unsettling, and it is impossible not to be reminded of the torture stories surrounding the War on Terror (the word "terrorist" is busied too frequently to prevent such a connection). There is a strong sexual component too, and Ellis's seductions are shown in some detail. Yet the sex is not gratuitous. As a counterpoint to the graphic details of the tortures, the sex scenes even come across as tender—as some of the few moments Ellis is allowed to *feel* instead of having to calculate reality.

Upon release, *Black Book* caused a minor storm in the Netherlands. Concerns were raised about how it sacrificed accuracy for spectacle. Verhoeven and his actors insisted their version of the story was as truthful as any film can be. Movies about the ambiguities much of the civilian population of Europe must have felt during World War II are still rare. **EM**

► Carice van Houten gives a steely performance as the Dutch resistance agent Ellis.

KARL
MARKOVICS

AUGUST
DIEHL

57° Internationale
Filmfestspiele
Berlin
Wettbewerb

DEVID
STRIESOW

MARIE
BÄUMER

DIE FÄLSCHER

Ein Film von Stefan Ruzowitzky

www.diefaelscher.de

THE COUNTERFEITERS
2007 (GERMANY · AUSTRIA)

Director Stefan Ruzowitzky **Producers** Josef Aichholzer, Nina Bohlmann, Babette Schröder **Screenplay** Stefan Ruzowitzky (from the book *The Devil's Workshop* by Adolf Burger) **Cinematography** Benedict Neuenfeis **Music** Marius Ruhland **Cast** Karl Markovics, August Diehl, David Striesow, Martin Brambach, August Zirner

The Counterfeiters (a.k.a. *Die Fälscher*) was Austria's first entry into the Foreign Language Film category of the Oscars, and it won the coveted prize. Stefan Ruzowitzky had previously demonstrated that Austrians can make solid horror movies with his two *Anatomy* films (2000, 2003). *The Counterfeiters* challenges conventional Holocaust films by placing a truly unlikable character at the center of its narrative.

Salomon "Sally" Sorowitsch (Markovics) is the king of Berlin's counterfeiters. In the pre-war hysteria gripping Germany, Sally is making a killing for himself forging passports and certificates of Aryanization, as well as his own vanity project of trying to "crack the dollar," which is apparently very hard to do. He is caught by Friedrich Herzog (Striesow) of the Berlin police in an elaborate sting operation. As both a career criminal and a Jew, Sally is immediately shipped off to Mauthausen.

Sally is discovered to be a pretty good artist and is sequestered to act as the official camp portrait painter for the Commandant and his family. Toward the end of the war, however, Sally is transferred to Sachsenhausen, just north of

◀

A Holocaust story with a twist that seeks to explore the usual good Jew–bad Nazi treatment.

Berlin. Jewish prisoners from across the Reich are being transferred here under the orders of (now) Sturmbannführer Herzog for his Operation Bernhard, a scheme to counterfeit and use forged currencies to help fund the Nazi war effort. These transferees all have special skills that Operation Bernhard requires, and Herzog recalls Sally's reputation from before the war. Sally and his team are well-fed, sleep on proper beds, are

"I'M MYSELF. EVERYONE ELSE IS EVERYONE ELSE."

SALOMON "SALLY" SOROWITSCH

able to shower once a week, and are given clothes and cigarettes. While they are still (mostly) Jewish inmates of a concentration camp and subjected to random beatings and the occasional execution, they are spared the atrocities meted out on the other side of the impenetrable wall that surrounds their little compound in the middle of the camp.

► The story of Sally (Markovics) is told through another inmate's eyes (Adolf Burger's own story), so we never get into the antihero's mind first hand, and he remains enigmatic throughout.

What makes *The Counterfeiters* such a remarkable film is that Ruzowitzky refuses to ennoble Sally; he is only out for himself and his desire to survive in as much comfort as he can. He even takes pride in his work allowing Herzog to feed his ego and aspirations for "cracking" foreign currencies. Sally's nemesis in the team is the Socialist Adolf Burger (Diehl, upon whose autobiography the film is based), who keeps his idealism and tries to sabotage Sally's counterfeiting operation to further hinder the war for the Germans. **MK**